A Divine Life in a Divine Body

A Divine Life in a Divine Body

NAVAJATA

SRI AUROBINDO SOCIETY
Pondicherry - 605 002

First Published: 3rd January 1991
Reprinted: 1998

ISBN 81-7060-119-3

Published by Sri Aurobindo Society, Pondicherry - 605 002
Printed at Sri Aurobindo Ashram Press, Pondicherry - 605 002
PRINTED IN INDIA

Introduction

Sri Aurobindo and the Mother have shown the way towards a unique and luminous future, a way to build a new man, a new society and a new world – the Supramental World.

Navajata Bhaiji dedicated his life to the realisation of this vision. He was one of Their chosen instruments in spreading Their message. He travelled extensively in India and around the world, giving innumerable discourses on the sadhana of the Integral Yoga. It was one grand theme: how can we make our life more perfect; what is the highest an individual can do; how can the whole world be happy; how can yoga be practised in the midst of this world, while working, talking, eating or even sleeping – at each moment of one's life; can death be conquered; can destiny be changed; how can one attain a divine life in a divine body?

Bhaiji lived this vision. He was enamoured of it. He had the great gift of making others see the same vision and fall in love with it. Listening to him, the flame of aspiration for the Divine was lit.

Very few of his discourses, unfortunately, have been preserved. Even among these, the recording is often faulty and incomplete. We have, however, tried to bring together in this book all that could be transcribed from his recorded talks. Hence, some of the talks may appear to be incomplete or to begin or end a bit abruptly.

All these talks were given extempore. Some editing has, therefore, been necessary and, because of the nature of the subjects, there is at times some repetition. We have, however, endeavoured to keep the text as close as possible to the original recording so that the reader may get the tone and flavour of the talks.

We feel that this book could serve as a very simple guide to Integral Yoga and the way to practise it in everyday life.

This book is offered, as Bhaiji would like it to be, at the Feet of Sri Aurobindo and the Mother.

CONTENTS

Sri Aurobindo — 1950

A divine life in a divine body
is the formula of the ideal that we envisage.
— Sri Aurobindo

The Mother — 1950

To know is good, to live is better, to be, that is perfect.
— The Mother

The Mother – Some Reminiscences

I first heard of the Mother and Sri Aurobindo in 1929 when I was only seven years old. Even then something in me, in a childlike manner, spontaneously accepted Them as my masters. Physically, Sri Aurobindo was not accessible to us except on Darshan days or through correspondence, so it was usually to the Mother that we referred problems and experiences – spiritual and material – of ourselves and of others. Her guidance invariably brought a ray of Her Divine Consciousness in our everyday lives.

Let me share with you a few – very few – of these reminiscences as far as I can recollect them, spread as they are over a wide span of forty-four years. In this brief talk I will try to cover some aspects of Her multifaceted personality. It is enjoined on us not to narrate our spiritual experiences, so I shall confine myself to some of those events which can be spoken of and which occupy a permanent place in my heart.

Long before I joined the Ashram, I used to visit here very frequently and seek Her guidance on a wide range of apparently difficult matters. For example, one day I asked Her, "Mother, is everything predetermined? What freedom has man and to what extent? In my own life I do not see any freedom. It is as though some forces beyond us always govern our lives and yet it is not possible to believe that life is just mechanical." Quietly and slowly came the reply, "One has several destinies. The plane of consciousness in which you dwell determines the destiny which becomes applicable to you. When you unite with the Divine Consciousness you are free. Prayers also change destinies. It is like a fruit falling from a tree to the ground; if you put a hand in the way, you can stop its fall." I was satisfied but returned to this topic after some days and asked further, "Is the putting out of the hand itself predetermined?" She explained, "It depends upon the plane of consciousness from which you see it." Again, on another occasion She remarked, "I tell you things can change."

Her answers to our questions despite the incomplete information placed before Her were invariably correct. One day I was reading a letter while waiting for Her. She came and I prayed, "Mother, a relative of mine is ill. The doctors are unable to diagnose what is wrong." She remarked, "It is the medicine", and walked away. The family sent for another doctor. He found that, indeed, it was the medicine that was harming the patient. The medication was changed and the patient recovered completely. This took place in Calcutta. She would sometimes see the photographs of persons who were to be given responsible positions for work. At other times devotees sent photographs of couples proposed for marriage to enquire whether a particular match had Her approval and Her blessings. So I queried, "Mother, how do you judge a person by his photograph?" She replied, "There is no written rule about it. When I hold a person's photograph or his hand, the past, present and future of the person come to me."

I worried that I was taking too much of Her time by asking such questions. So I prayed to Her, "How do you always give the right answer? If I had this capacity I would not bother you with so many questions". and for the first time She taught me how to quieten the mind and seek guidance from deep within.

Her way of working was unique. Once, some work of the Ashram had to be attended to in Bombay. The Mother instructed me to tell a friend of mine to look after it. This friend was in Calcutta, while I was actually going to Delhi and had no plan to meet him. In those days the Delhi plane used to stop at Hyderabad. When I landed there, I learnt that my friend would also be landing at Hyderabad ten minutes later, though his plane had been scheduled to arrive much before ours. I was surprised. If his plane had been on schedule, he would have gone into town and I would have missed meeting him at the airport; if he had arrived later, my plane would already have left for Delhi. It was amazing how the Mother had arranged the meeting! We met and I conveyed to him the Mother's instructions. He already had plans to go to Bombay, so everything just fitted in. Experiences of this type were very common in our working with the Mother.

When the Auroville project was approved by Her, we had neither money nor manpower. In answer to questions like who was directing Auroville, who was financing it, She wrote: "The Supreme Divine"! One day in answer to a question on Auroville, She took a paper, drew a circular design and marked a spot on it. Everything was finished in two or three minutes. The architects however, designed the town on the pattern of a square. After one year and much research, they found that the circular design was more satisfactory. They were intrigued that the Mother should have given in two minutes this design to which they arrived at after

The Mother inaugurating the Ayurvedic Section of the Ashram. Shri Navajata, on the right, holding the tray — 1957

so many trials and errors. As a result they decided to learn to get inspiration from a deeper plane. Once when our chief architect took the design of a model village to the Mother, She remarked, "He got it exactly as I saw it."

At one time, many years back, in my sadhana I was not sure whether I should meditate on the Sākāra, the form of the Divine, or on the Nirākāra, the formless. So, as usual, I turned to Her for guidance. I asked Her, "Mother, on what should I meditate – your physical body or the Nirākāra, the formless Divine?" She answered, "What is the difference? If you think this body is the Mother, you are limiting my force to twenty-five percent. When people ask me questions, they get conveyed to the Supreme Consciousness and the answers come from there."

On another occasion I pleaded with Her, "Mother, please tell me my defects so that I may improve myself." "No, no, my child," came the Motherly reply, "I shall show you your qualities so that you may improve yourself." I wish all parents and teachers would apply this key to progress.

She sometimes assigned me duties which entailed travelling outside Pondicherry. So I enquired if I should return during the Darshan days. She replied, "It is better to come. But if you cannot, you have only to concentrate and you will see me there."

She knew all that was necessary to know about us. At an international photography competition, the judges requested the Mother to select the photographs for the first three prizes. They had already made a preliminary selection and the selected photographs were arranged in a room. The Mother was giving us Her blessings before going to this room. I was keen to be present, but was too shy to ask Her. She quietly came to me and without my having asked, whispered, "You can come." Later I enquired, "Mother, how did you know?" She replied, "I always know. But I keep quiet when it suits me."

Just before the Chinese attack, an Indian yogi conveyed to the Mother his apprehension that China would attack and overrun India. The Mother asked me to tell him, "India will not be overrun, because the Supermind has descended."

A few days before She retired, I told Her that it had come to me in meditation that we should have a world magazine in all languages. She nodded, and Champaklal gave Her a paper and She wrote down, the *Next Future*, and then asked for another paper and wrote in French, *Le Prochain Avenir*.

And now when She has left Her physical body, I feel that, as in a drama, She has only gone behind the curtain, so that the next scene, the next future may follow. What this next future is going to be depends on Her Grace.

The Supreme Mother personified Herself in the physical body as the Mother of Pondicherry and manifested the Divine Perfection possible on earth.

Blessed is the earth that Her Feet have touched.

A Divine Life in a Divine Body

The vision of Sri Aurobindo and the Mother is unique. They have said that we are here not merely to repeat what others have done. In another context, while narrating the story of Rishi Vishwamitra, Sri Aurobindo once mentioned that the deeds of the past were indeed great but would pale before the greater achievements of the future.

In Sri Aurobindo's yoga if we want to succeed – it is a very arduous and difficult yoga – we should make the divine body, the divine life, the centre and goal of all our efforts. Today we will try to understand this concept of Sri Aurobindo, what is the way to realise it and how to overcome the obstructions.

There is a significant example given in our epics and mythology. It is of Hanuman. He could fly or leap from Rameshwaram to Lanka. He could fly from Rameshwaram to bring back a part of the Himalayas, all in a night. The question is: are such feats possible or is it only imagination? Can these be performed? After reading Sri Aurobindo and Valmiki, I was convinced that Hanuman could have done all that he did.

I am giving you this example, because the divine body, as envisaged by Sri Aurobindo and the Mother will be able to achieve all that Hanuman could do.

Each god represents some attribute of the Supreme Divine. And Sri Aurobindo wants us to realise the Divine in all His attributes. It is really amazing that when you read Sri Aurobindo's works, it is almost like reading a fairy story. If we understand the various aspects of a divine body, we shall come to realise how this can be possible.

Sri Aurobindo and the Mother have said that the new body will have four aspects. First, it will be luminous. (I am talking here of the final stage; the intermediate stages we shall discuss later.) It will have no blood, skin, or bones. Many of the organs will even disappear for they will not be needed and the various centres will open to become centres of forces. For example, you will not have the need to speak; whatever has to be communicated, will get communicated through you. It will be a body of light which will not need food and water for its sustenance. Can you imagine a greater research of our times? We are spending millions in research – research in this disease, research in that malady. But Sri

Aurobindo goes far beyond all the researches we can ever think of and presents the culmination of all human endeavour. So, to come back, Sri Aurobindo says one of the attributes of the new body will be luminosity.

Another will be lightness. It will be able to fly. The Mother gave a very interesting example that sometimes you dream that your body is flying. You give a thrust from the right shoulder and you fly in that direction; you give a jerk from the left shoulder to take a turn and you fly in the left direction; you give a push with your feet and you go up very high. She said that all this you can accomplish with a divine body. All that the physical body cannot do, in a divine body it will be possible with the body.

The third attribute will be plasticity. It will not be vulnerable. Even if somebody shoots at it, there will be no damage because the body will allow the bullet to pass through.

And the fourth will be adaptability. You can put it in a small jar and it will nicely fit in it. Or like Hanuman, it will expand and become 500 feet tall. It will adapt itself to any size to suit any situation, any circumstance.

So, luminosity, lightness, plasticity and adaptability are the four main attributes of a divine body. Someone asked the Mother, "Mother, can this body be seen by any person or only the yogis will be able to see it?" She said that a man in the street will be able to see this body. Not only this, but more. She has stated that this will be a body which can be projected at twelve different places at the same time. You are projected in America doing some work; you are projected on the moon doing some other work and you are projected in India doing some third work – a body which can be projected simultaneously in a number of places. So you can understand what Sri Aurobindo and the Mother mean when They speak of a divine body. The bodies of the gods are luminous. So it will seem as if the gods were inhabiting the earth. Sri Aurobindo has said that Shiva has even committed himself to come down to earth in a supramental body, when the supramental transformation takes place. So you see, the vision of Sri Aurobindo is the highest fulfilment of all we have dreamt through the ages – all that we have dreamt spiritually and all that we have dreamt materially.

This substance, this supramental substance does not exist at present in the world; it will be a new creation. Once this substance is created, there will be two kinds of beings – the Superman and the Supramental Being. There is a distinction which Sri Aurobindo and the Mother have pointed out. The Superman would be that being who, out of the present physical body, evolves into a divine body. The Supramental Being would be that being who will take a divine body directly, without undergoing the process of a physical birth and hence will have no animality in it. The Supramental Beings leading a collective life would form a new community which Sri Aurobindo calls a *gnostic community*. Can you imagine people on earth having bodies of light, bodies which would not need food and water for their sustenance, able to fly about, project themselves in different places and return when necessary? And further, the bodies will not be prone to old age, disease, decay and death.

It is for this new divine creation that Sri Aurobindo holds out a hope which we can realise. And the Mother says that the time is *now* to realise it. She says that the Supramental Consciousness has already descended to the level of the subtle-physical plane. But the physical consciousness has to feel it and the material body has to realise it. After its realisation, man will not have to take birth, grow up, become old and die. He will straight away take a body, as I said, a supramental body, act in the world for either an hour or two or for a few hundred years and leave the body at will. It will be an absolutely new kind of creation. We are fortunate to have come to that point in evolution where we are aspiring for its full manifestation.

The Mother was asked, "How long will it be for such a creation to take shape?" and She said, "Three hundred years." People were very much surprised. How could one live for three hundred years! If one prolonged the life with a diseased body, an old and decaying body, it will not be very pleasant to continue to live. The Mother gave a beautiful answer which I would like to read out to you. She said: *Well, there is a change. It is no more the same body. You must know that even before the total change comes, a change will start in the body.* Those of you who have the slightest inner contact with the Supermind will feel the change in your life, in your vocation. If we do not feel it, there is something wrong with us. Somewhere we have closed the window to the Descent which the Mother has brought down for the benefit of all. She has brought this Ganges of Supermind and yet we stand on its bank without seeing, without drinking its water. That is the unfortunate situation. The important thing to know is that once the Supermind Consciousness touches our body, it will be able to remain in good health and we will also be able to prolong our life. How can life be prolonged? We will try to understand this when we come to the aspect of sadhana.

But now let me continue reading to you the Mother's remarks about the three hundred years: *When our little humanity says three hundred years with the same body, you say, 'Why! when I am fifty it already begins to decompose, so at three hundred years it will be a horrible thing!' But it is not like that, if it is three hundred years with a body that goes on perfecting itself....* So, we have to go on perfecting ourselves. How do we do this? That also we shall see when we come to the aspect of sadhana. From year to year, when the three hundreth year is reached, you will perhaps say: "Oh, I still need three or four hundred years more to be what I want to be." If you want to manifest the Divine in all His attributes, another three hundred years will not matter. You must not forget that if you leave the body now, you may be born again after some hundred years and under different circumstances. You will then find it more difficult because you have not made enough progress in this life.

The progress in this life, the Mother says, will not only help you but will enable you to realise it *now*. This is very important. If each year that passes represents a progress, a transformation, would you not want more and more years so that you can transform yourself more and more? So, you have to make sure you are progressing each year, being transformed every year. And in order to check every year, you have to check each day and in order to check each day, you have to check each moment. You have to plan your day very carefully. When something is not as perfect as you want it to be, for example, plasticity, lightness, elasticity or luminosity, will you not then need at least two hundred years more so that it can be accomplished to perfection? You must not be depressed and think it is going to require two hundred years more! You should, on the contrary, say that two hundred years more are the absolute minimum for the work to be truly done. When all is done, when all is perfect, it is then no longer a question of years, for you become immortal. So, for Sri Aurobindo and the Mother it is a matter of physical immortality. This is the highest ideal you can put before yourself and your children.

Now, there are a few points we should know before we come to the actual sadhana. First, this transformation will come about through a descent from above; it is not by human effort that it can be done. Human effort, I would say, is barely one percent; ninety-nine percent of the change is going to come through a descent. How are we going to have the descent? How are we going to put ourselves in contact with the supramental force? The second point is to make the cells of the body conscious and cohesive, cohesive around a centre. How? Here I would like to caution you. The will plays a very significant role in the supramental life. The human will and the human thought have to be transformed. If your will and thought are not transformed in the very initial stage, later there will be difficulties. You know the old story. A man came and sat under a tree. It was a special tree, it fulfilled all one's wishes. The man was hungry and he said, "Oh, I wish I had something to eat." Immediately, very delicious food appeared before him. After eating it, he became thirsty, so he said, "I wish there was something to drink", and some very nice drinks materialised. Then he said, "Oh, I wish I could have some dance and music", and his wish was granted. So he said, "What is all this? I hope it is not the play of the devil", and the devil appeared before him. He was afraid and exclaimed, "Oh, what will happen if the devil swallows me!" and the devil swallowed him. So, if the will and thought are not under control, a higher life is not possible.

The first step in attaining this new life is to want it – to want it solely, to want that above all. And to eliminate – the great art of rejection – to remove the impediments from your path. To eliminate all that contradicts, all that wastes your time when you move towards your goal. Once the decision is taken, the next step is aspiration. I have here a prayer of the Mother. It is in French – I will translate it for you in English. It has just three lines but is one of the most effective prayers for the transformation of the body.

The Mother says: *Lord Supreme, Take possession of this body, Manifest Thyself in it.*

What a beautiful prayer! You pray, you aspire to the Divine to take possession of your body, to manifest Himself. This is the easiest way. If He could descend and possess your body and manifest, nothing else would remain to be done.

Now, to start your sadhana you need four basic requisites. Three have been given to us by Sri Aurobindo and the Mother: the

Guru, the Shastra and the Kāla or the Time. Our Guru is Sri Aurobindo, who has already brought the Supermind into His body, is present amongst us and by meditating on Him, we can get in contact with the Supramental Consciousness. The Shastra – the books written by Him like *Savitri*, *The Life Divine*, *The Synthesis of Yoga* – is also with us. And about the Time, the Mother has said that now is the time for transformation; this is the *Hour of God*, as Sri Aurobindo puts it. Those who miss this present time, this moment, will miss it for many years to come. Such an opportunity will not come again for a long time.

The fourth requisite is 'utsāha'. Do you feel enthusiastic about the aim? Are you determined to realise the Divine? This is a question of great importance. If you decide you want to realise that, the Divine fiat will go in your favour; the Divine Force will descend in its fullness to help you, in spte of all your shortcomings and weaknesses. But you have to take the decision: "Lord, I pray for a divine body, a divine life. But with my present imperfections, my limited capacities, my fragmented personality, it is impossible for me to realise it – not in one life, not in three hundred years, not even in three hundred lives. My only hope is You. If You descend, You can take possession of my body. You can take possession of my mind and illumine it, You can take possession of my vital and remove the wrong impulses and transform it." This is the only hope for transformation. And through centuries He has given the promise – you will find it in the Gita, in the Bible, in Sri Aurobindo's writings – that whenever men have knocked at His door and called Him, He has always come. Relying on this supreme promise, having faith in it, you have to embark. The first step is to ask Him for it. That is the fist step.

But in Sri Aurobindo's yoga the steps are integral and many-sided and a psychological perfection is needed. The psychological perfection starts with our attitude towards life, things, events. If our attitude is wrong, our reaction is wrong. And ninety percent of our lives is all reactions. In our effort to have psychological perfection the one thing that could help us is to open ourselves to receive the Divine guidance. Most of our lives we insist on making God listen to us and do not try to hear His voice. We pray to Him all the time for this and that. We want Him to listen to us but we have no time or inclination to listen to Him. And that is the tragedy of the whole human life. You must learn to listen to Him.

You must try to seek His guidance from within you, again and again with the same attitude: "He is everywhere, He is in every cell of my body, He is in my mind, my vital and, if I invoke His guidance, He will make me ready to receive it." You do not have to say, I must first prepare myself, I must first do this, I must then do that, otherwise how will I receive His guidance. Sri Aurobindo was once asked if it was necessary to quieten the mind before having the Descent. He replied, "No, to me the quiet mind came after the Descent." So, on the one side, you have to invoke the Divine guidance and on the other, you have to build up a faith that the omnipresent, the omniscient, the omnipotent Divine, the all-compassionate Divine will answer your call. And if in all sincerity, you have called He will surely help. You will then find that half your work is done.

There are also other aspects of psychological perfection. I will go over them briefly. The Mother has called the champa flower, *Psychological Perfection*. Its five petals represent five qualities: Sincerity, Faith, Devotion, Aspiration and Surrender. But a full psychological perfection would require many more, maybe subsidiaries of these five fundamental qualities. The first one the Mother has stressed is sincerity. By sincerity, She means not to allow, not to admit in your consciousness, any influence other than the Divine influence. This is extremely important. Without this, it is like putting poison, it is like putting a point of contradiction in your consciousness against the Divine Presence and, although you aspire for a divine body, it will not permit you to progress much farther. Sincerity means to make yourself cohesive around the Divine Presence.

Now, sincerity, faith, and the other qualities can be cultivated by yoga. If you say: "I am in any case going to die, so why not keep faith in God, surrender to Him, pray for a divine life in a divine body? Then if I die, it does not matter. I would have put myself in the hands of the greatest guru, the greatest doctor, the Supreme Himself and, if anything goes wrong, why should I worry?" If this is your attitude, I can assure you that even if you do not have sufficient faith but can take this bold risk, which really is no risk at all, nothing will go wrong. The life we are leading at present is a life of confusion, ignorance – in a word, of stupidity. It is no solution whatsoever. We spend ninety-nine percent of our time in reading newspapers, in parliamentary debates, in so-called business – it is all a wastage, a wastage. We succumb to this kind of wastage because we do not take the trouble to make ourselves ready for a higher life. It has become a habit with us.

Now let us take surrender. Without surrender there is no gain, without surrender there is no unity with the Divine, without surrender you cannot listen to Him, without surrender you cannot follow the path, because the forces of the lower nature are so strong that they pull you down. In this programme you have to be relentless in your effort, if you want to succeed. Here I can give you a small practical suggestion. I had tried it many years ago and found it very useful. You make a daily list: sincerity, aspiration, constant remembrance of the Divine, all the qualities you want to cultivate, including working for the Divine, taking food in silence – I will come to every detail – all, all that you want to do. And everyday you give yourself grades, A, B, C, in order to know if you were able to achieve each quality: which quality was C, which was B, which was A. I tell you, if you keep a check on yourself – but you have to be very honest with yourself, that is part of being sincere – it will be a great progress indeed.

Now we come to the main plank of our theme: how to make the body conscious, how to make the cells of the body conscious. First we shall take meditation and mantra japa. If you accept to have as your goal a divine life in a divine body, you must try to do mantra japa with the body. Each cell of the body should vibrate 'OM, OM'. You should feel the vibrations in your bones, in your skin, in your blood. The sound of OM should permeate all around you. If you like you may chant any divine name like Sri Aurobindo, the Mother or any other. This kind of awakening, an awakening of the cells to the supreme sound will be a great help in making the body conscious.

Along with the mantra japa or separately, you should meditate on Sri Aurobindo and the Mother in their luminous forms – the same form, full of light but without any blood, skin and bones – throughout your body, in each cell of your body and all around you. And the third is to place yourself in Them. This is one of the traditional methods of meditation: to meditate that the disciple is in the heart of the Guru and the Guru is in the heart of the disciple. This twofold meditation, that you are in the heart of the luminous body of Sri Aurobindo and Sri Aurobindo is in your heart, will give you a double protection – protection from external forces and from internal conflicts – and will bring about unity with the Divine. Further, your meditation has to be dynamic and, if possible, collective. That is why in the centres and in the family you sit together and meditate collectively with friends who have a common ideal. The Mother once spoke of an old Chaldean belief that if twelve sincere people got together and aspired for the Divine, the Divine would manifest Himself. So, collective meditation has its importance, too.

Physical education also plays a significant part in our program. The aim of physical education, exercises, should be to make the cells conscious, whether by asanas and pranayama or by exercises. For example, while doing Tadasana, you could try to reach the Supreme, try to bring the Supreme Consciousness into your body, open the cells and make yourself receptive. But before you start on anything, first meditate; meditate to open your body to the force, so that the force can play through you, can work through you. I have found this to be very effective. I know of a young boy who used to play table tennis – an average player, rather a poor player, I would say. Whenever he first meditated on the Divine before playing, he would win. If by chance he forgot the Divine and did not open his body to the Divine Force, he lost. Many people engaged in physical education have told me this; they have also written on it. While in London I was watching a BBC programme on TV where they interviewed the best tennis and golf players. Amazingly, all of them said the same thing, that their best shots were those which they played without thinking but by opening to a higher Force, not trying to think that they should play in this or that manner. This is also the first principle in yoga. So, the important thing for you is to make your own programme, your own set of exercises. Before you start, step back and pray to Sri Aurobindo: "Sri Aurobindo, how can this exercise make my body conscious?" To those of you who dance, I tell you, dance is one of the best means of making the cells of the body conscious. To those who sing, I tell you, open the cells of the vocal cords while singing, so that they may become conscious. Every action of the day, whether you are lifting up a file, walking on the road or taking your meals, all, all action should be directed towards making the body conscious.

I will now take up Karma Yoga – the actual work aspect. As an example, when you meet a person, you say, "How are you? I am pleased to meet you"; a common enough greeting. Normally, when you meet a friend you are pleased, you are happy. These words are spoken spontaneously. But that is not yoga. You must hold yourself back for a moment, put yourself in the Divine Consciousness and feel, when you say "How are you?", that the words have come from that Consciousness. So, this kind of holding back before speaking, stepping back before doing anything, is very essential in the early stages. As you progress it will become spontaneous. So, for Karma Yoga, the important thing is that you make yourself conscious throughout the day, you plan your day. The Mother has said that the body works very well if the day is planned – time for work, time for meals, time for exercise, time for rest. If you want to follow the path of Integral Yoga, you should be very, very sincere. This is sincerity: anything that runs counter to your decision to move towards your goal, you must constantly and tirelessly put out of the way.

Another aspect which is of great relevance is food. If you take food in the right spirit, it will help you immensely in bringing about a change in your body. As to the right type of food to be taken, the Mother has said that you must choose as though you have a chemical knowledge of food. People generally get addicted to certain types of tastes; some are fond of sweet things, while others prefer hot and spicy food. I will show you one easy way out of this – and that is prayer. If you simply offer these habits to the Divine, He will remove them from your consciousness. There is a prayer the Mother has recommended before eating. It is Her own prayer: *O, my sweet Lord, Supreme Truth, I aspire that this food which I am assimilating infuses in all the cells of my body, Your omniscience, Your omnipotence.* As the Divine is all-knowing, each cell of the body becomes conscious and by this omnipotence, each cell becomes all powerful. Much before I joined the Ashram, I told the Mother one day, "Mother, I can remember the Divine very well during the day, even while I am working but I forget Him while taking food." She said, "You must be taking your meals with many people." And that was true. I understood Her immediately and, after returning to Bombay, for one year, I took all my meals alone in my own room, without meeting people, without inviting anybody, just eating in silence. And this helped me greatly. If you really want the cells of the body to become conscious, you should, in the early stages at least, concentrate and take all your meals at the appropriate time and not go on nibbling tidbits all the time. This effort has to be made till you have come to a stage where you no longer need to concentrate as you can spontaneously feel the Divine consciousness in everything and at all times, where the ordinary consciousness has been replaced by a higher consciousness which has become a part of your life. Concentrate on the light in the food, concentrate on the Divine Presence in your body, concentrate on the actual movement of eating and eat as if you are offering the Divine Presence in the food to the Divine Presence within you. And with this aspiration to the Mother that each cell may become conscious, quietly take the food. Try it for one day, just one day, and see the result.

From food we move to speech. As I said, the Integral Yoga and the integral transformation require an integral effort. It is an effort for twenty-four hours and not for twenty-three and a half hours. Every time you utter a falsehood, every time there is a distortion in what you say and do, you are delinking yourself from the Divine Consciousness. You are taking a step towards mortality and not moving forward to reach immortality. So, you have to take a very firm decision that you are not going to speak till the Divine wants to speak through you. If you remain in silence in unity with the Supreme, you will find that the right things happen to you by themselves. If you want to speak to somebody, he himself will ring you up; if you want to meet somebody, he himself will come. If you have come to this new law of being, to this new law of living, if you can achieve this, everything will change for you. The ordinary kind of talk will not then be necessary for you, either in a family life or in a collective life. So, a very firm decision has to be taken to be utterly truthful, not from the mental point of view but utterly truthful from the standpoint of being a vehicle of the Divine. You should remain absorbed in Him and whatever He wants to say will be spoken through you. If He has nothing to say through you, why do you want to chatter? Is it necessary? And do not read useless things if you really want that your consciousness should not be stuffed with worthless matter. The Mother once told me when I joined the Ashram more than thirty years ago, "I do not read newspapers. If I have to know something, it comes to me." I thought the Mother does not want me to read the newspapers, and this was Her way of guiding me. She would not say do this or do not do that. She would simply say that She would not do this, She would not do that. So, if you really want a transformation, control of speech is indispensable.

I would also like to say a few words on health and illness. People who are advanced in age, who already have some ailment settled in their bodies may say in despair: "Oh, how can we change in this life! We are already half way or a quarter of the way to the other side. It is now very difficult." The Mother has held out a hope for them. She has said that wherever there is illness, there is disharmony in the body. If we can put that afflicted part in contact with the Divine Consciousness, the harmony will be re-established. And what is amazing is that it is possible to do this in a moment. She does not say in hours or in days; the harmony that has been disturbed would return and the illness would go away immediately. If we had the patience, if we had the wisdom, if we knew the art of putting the ailing part in touch with the Divine, this would be the result.

There is another important thing I want to mention and that is Brahmacharya. The Mother and Sri Aurobindo have stressed that sexual indulgence is one of the greatest obstacles to the transformation of the body. It is not a question of legality. Even if you are legally married or if you have a night emission, it is bad as far as physical transformation is concerned. You must get this clear in your mind. Sri Aurobindo and the Mother have explained in great detail how to meditate, how to put light on sex organs and sex matters so that they may not respond to thoughts, emotions, impulses concerning sex. Their aim is elimination – not coercion – elimination from your consciousness. Their constant help is available, but you must be clear-headed, determined, strong, sincere in order to achieve this.

There are one or two other obstacles that come in the way of realisation. One is our traditional way of thinking about destiny. A horoscope shows that the life of a person is so many years. The Mother has said that destiny can be changed if you put yourself under the Divine Law. Not only sickness but destiny and even death can be changed. She has written a lot on how to conquer the fear of death. One of the interesting methods She has explained is to consciously take your subtle-physical – your astral body – out of the physical body, act in the world and return. Thus, you would have already experienced death without actually undergoing it physically and this would remove the fear of death.

I would here like to put before you a different aspect and that is occult knowledge. If each centre in our being has to develop into a centre reflecting its origin, of the force it represents – the Mother says the body is full of centres and each centre represents a force – then you must know which centre it is and what force it represents. The seven or eight traditionally known centres of the Kundalini are not all. Our body is full of thousands of centres. Occult knowledge, the knowledge of the inner worlds, is very much a part of the Integral Yoga and both, Sri Aurobindo and the Mother, have written a great deal on the subject.

There are one or two points about the sadhana I want to mention briefly. The first is that your consciousness has to be widened. If you cannot do this, you cannot progress in the sadhana of a divine life in a divine body. As you progress you will realise that in a divine body the consciousness will become universal, because in the Divine Consciousness all action is automatic. The second point is that there has to be sincere and constant aspiration for self-progress, self-perfection. Keeping this in mind, your visit here to the Asrham will be fruitful if you can make a strong determination: "With all my shortcomings, O Lord, with all the difficulties of my nature, of collective life, economic life, social life, political life, I offer myself to You, put myself in Your hands, for this supreme transformation – a divine life in a divine body." And I assure you, the Divine will respond.

So finally, friends, having come to the Feet of Sri Aurobindo and the Mother, having come to Pondicherry, the central point of radiation of the Integral Yoga, it would be most unfortunate if we satisfied ourselves with anything less than a divine life in a divine body. Let us all collectively work for this ideal for all mankind.

May the Blessings of Sri Aurobindo and the Mother be with you all.

The Sadhana of Sri Aurobindo's Yoga

The subject announced for today's meeting is: "The Sadhana of Sri Aurobindo's Yoga". It is such a vast subject, one could as well have announced the beginning, the present and the future of mankind. A subject as vast as that cannot be dealt with in depth at a meeting of this kind; it can only be touched upon briefly. I will make an attempt to speak on it in three parts – the concept, the practice (I would like to stress more on the practice so that you can benefit by your visit today to the Bhavan), and the result. What will be the result if you practised Sri Aurobindo's yoga?

Sri Aurobindo's vision, at least as far as I know, is the most integral ever dreamt of in the history of mankind. It is the most integral in its concept, the most integral in its practice and the most integral in its result. Sri Aurobindo takes the past, present and future, the inner and outer life of man, the individual and collective life and the whole life of mankind in His sweep and presents a solution to all the problems. When you read Sri Aurobindo you will be amazed to find that He has posed a thousand questions; some of us may have thought of ten or twenty, but Sri Aurobindo has posed a thousand questions. He also describes the basic aspirations of man – his aspiration for God, his aspiration for Immortality, his aspiration for Light and Freedom, for the Omniscient and the Omnipotent – and he shows a way to realise them all. It is the master key for all the problems which confront mankind today, whether psychological – the problems of ego, greed, hatred and jealousy – or the problems of economic, social or poltical nature.

But if He has posed a thousand questions, He gives just one answer. When we come to His master solution we automatically feel that it is the answer to all our problems, it is the way of fulfilment of all our aspirations. We realise that there are no more problems because there are no two solutions. If there were two possibilities you would ask yourself whether you should do this or that. But if there is only one solution then the path becomes easy and you can safely proceed. This is what we will try to understand.

First, Sri Aurobindo says that the world is in evolution – matter to plant, plant to animal, animal to man. However, man is not the last step, he is only the intermediate step in evolution. The evolution will go further from man to superman. In the supramental change there will be an anatomical change of even the human body. Before I read Sri Aurobindo, I had read the famous verse from the Upanishad: "Asato mā sad-gamaya / Tamaso mājyotir-gamaya / Mṛtyor-mā amṛtaṁ gamaya." The idea was that from a mortal consciousness one could go to the immortal consciousness. The best one could say was, now that I have realised the immortal Divine consciousness within me and am living in that consciousness, physical mortality does not matter. But one never thought that immortality of the physical body could be possible.

In Sri Aurobindo's yoga, this physical immortality is envisaged. This, we have read in mythological tales, but we never thought that in actuality a physical immortality for man could be possible. Sri Aurobindo's concept of physical immortality does not mean a body of blood, skin and bones, but a body of Light, a body of Light which will be free of diseases, which will not be subjected to old age, in which all the higher faculties would develop, in which the normal way of communication will not be necessary, food will not be necessary. And this is only the next step; it is not the final stage in evolution. Sri Aurobindo's vision is not a limited vision. If mankind can evolve on earth and manifest the Divine fully, it would also lead to its highest material fulfilment. The highest material perfection which a man can dream of, would be realised through the yoga of Sri Aurobindo.

Individually and collectively, the vision of Sri Aurobindo, the aim of His yoga, is physical transformation. To those of you who might feel old, to those of you who might have crossed an age where you think that time has passed you by and now you can only try again in the next life, I would like to tell you what the Mother once told me. One should never think of giving up one's body and never stop trying. She said, "Till the last breath there is a chance to realise the Divine and it should not be reduced by even one day."

The second thing She said was that life can be prolonged. Then She added, "My child, you are hypnotised by mythology. (I was interested a great deal in Hindu mythology.) You think things cannot be otherwise? I tell you things can be otherwise." So here comes a great message of hope for us that everything can be otherwise. How it can be otherwise we will try to understand when we come to the actual practice of yoga. But the first thing I want you to understand is that in Sri Aurobindo's yoga it is not a moral and pious life that is envisaged, not even a life in which you meditate on the Divine, live in the Divine consciousness and die one day. Sri Aurobindo's aim is to change human life into a divine life on earth of which one aspect is evolution from man to superman.

Another aspect of Sri Aurobindo's yoga is the advent of a spiritualised age, leading ultimately to a gnostic community. Now this is very interesting. Individually we are evolving, socially also we are evolving. Sri Aurobindo calls the present society an economic society – He calls it rather *economic barbarism*. Everyone is trying to make money at the expense of others, you know, and everything is governed by money. You need a house, you need medical treatment, you need education for your children, you need old age provision. So your whole life, all your energy is spent in earning some money for an ultimate need. This is all the value we place on human life. Sri Aurobindo has said that if the aim of life is to evolve, if the aim of life is to manifest God on earth through a new body which would be a better instrument of manifestation, then a social order has to evolve which will give man the conditions which are conducive to his growth. Then nobody will have to work for a living. Everybody will be free to choose the work which he likes and make it his free domain for manifesting the Divine. How can this be achieved? The community would pay for his food, for his clothing, for his entertainment, for his golf, for his music, for his painting – everything will be free. And in return he would give his service free to the community. In such an order a person would occupy the place for which he is best suited and would take according to his need, his true need (you know, as I said even music can be a need, painting can be a need), and give according to his capacity, his fullest capacity. This can only be possible if he is free to choose the work for which he has the greatest aptitude. This new socio-economic order will be much better than anything that could be placed before mankind by communism, socialism or democracy.

Here also I am reminded of an incident. When the Auroville project was launched, our chief architect invited a communist architect to participate. He was a leading architect of Russian origin. But he did not want to participate as he did not believe in all these ideas of spirituality and God. So our chief architect presented him with some books of Sri Aurobindo. After he read them he exclaimed: "I did not know that this was Indian spirituality. This is the highest that communism aims for." And he took official permission of his Party to work on the Auroville project. Not only this, but the Russian government, you will be glad to know, has taken the Ashram's permission to translate *The Synthesis of Yoga* into Russian and circulate it officially in their country. This is a big step forward for a communist country.

So the important thing to know is that yoga, and especially the Integral Yoga as envisaged and developed by Sri Aurobindo, is not a creed. It is something which fulfils the basic need of man. If you practise Sri Aurobindo's yoga it does not matter if you are a Hindu, a Christian, a Muslim or even an atheist. You see, nearly all the yogas start with the first assumption that God is Omnipresent. Sri Aurobindo is the only one who places an atheist's point of view before you and more strongly than any atheist can do. And He goes on to show that if we accept this viewpoint, some questions still remain unanswered. He then explains the Indian concept of Brahman and the manifestation and by the time you understand His vision in *The Life Divine* you see the great truth in His point of view, because it is the most integral and gives every other concept its right place.

When the Auroville Charter was drawn, the Russian representatives objected because there was a sentence which read: 'To live in Auroville one must be a willing servitor of the Divine Consciousness.' It was explained to them that the Divine Consciousness was not a part of any religion, but the Divine Consciousness was the Perfect Consciousness in man. So the Russians said that they had no quarrel with the Perfect Consciousness. (You see, beyond mind is Intuition, and much beyond Intuition is the Perfect Consciousness.) So for them the sentence was changed to read: 'To live in Auroville one must be willing to serve the Perfect Consciousness.' Now, it was for them to find out the meaning of Perfect Consciousness. For us, Perfect Consciousness – "Pūrṇaṁ idam" – and the Divine Consciousness are the same. Sri Aurobindo has placed before us His ideas so logically, so perfectly that if properly understood, nobody can have any quarrel with them.

Another interesting aspect of Sri Aurobindo's thought is that the world is in evolution, is a field of evolution, because there is already an involution which has taken place. The Divine is involved. This theory is not new. Our Vedas, Gita, Upanishads, all accept the theory of the "Ashwattha tree" whose roots are up and the branches are below. This is the process of involution. In Sri Aurobindo's yoga the Divine consciousness has two aspects – the static and the dynamic – the aspect which is unmanifest and the aspect which is manifesting. The Power that manifests the Divine, Sri Aurobindo calls the Supermind. Everything is derived from it. From Supermind comes the Overmind plane, the realm of gods. From the Overmind plane, come the planes of Intuitive Mind to Illumined Mind to Higher Mind and to Mind. Then comes the vital, the life energy, and then come the subtle-physical and the physical planes.

Sri Aurobindo who was a great poet Himself has quoted certain lines from Shelley, Shakespeare, Wordsworth and has pointed out that this line comes from the Higher Mind, these lines come from the Overmind or the Intuitive Mind, and you can see the difference between the lines Sri Aurobindo has quoted and the other lines. You will find no other poet dealing with the *source* of poetic inspiration in this manner.

Sri Aurobindo describes not only the inner planes, but also their colours. The Supermind colour is gold, the Overmind is sky-blue becoming more and more dark at the Higher Mind level. The Mind is yellow, the vital is red – pure vital – coming to the physical which is dark red. Then there are combinations of colours like violet, purple and others. All these colours Sri Aurobindo has described from His own experience. And the amazing part is that all these fully tally with the ancient concepts of the Tantras, the Vedas or the Upanishads. He independently comes to certain conclusions and when we look at the ancient systems, we find there is no contradiction. He accepts the Kundalini, He accepts the different chakras, with the same nomenclature, only His method of opening the Kundalini is different. But He does not decry the other methods. If another method is true for some individuals let them follow that method, it does not matter. The aim is the final result, the ultimate realisation. So each one can follow it in his own way.

Sri Aurobindo accepts the idea of evolution and involution and not only accepts the ancient scientific, botanical, biological concepts, but He gives us something which is missing in them. You see, all the scientists have described *how* things happen. Sri Aurobindo has also explained *why* things happen. And in such a scientific manner that it is amazing. He says that there is a Divine Consciousness in everything. This Omniscient Consciousness has a Self-Will – what He calls the *Real Idea* – and somewhere it wills: "Here in this tree I will become a mango tree", and because of His Will, the tree becomes a mango tree. And this applies to everything in creation. Somewhere it wills: "Here I will become copper", and the chemical reactions start. So ultimately, it is the Divine Consciousness which works out the creation and acts through the multiplicity of its creation. If once this theory is accepted then the missing links in science can be established. How? The recent researches in genetics have shown that when a woman conceives, certain atoms regroup and become a nose; certain others regroup and become an ear. So science says that there is some affinity in the atoms and there is a consciousness in them, and that is already a big step forward. Now, if science could accept as one of the hypothesis that there is a perfect consciousness pervading the universe in which knowledge, power, will are self-existent, then science will break new ground and progress very far. I personally feel that with the ongoing researches in psychology, psychiatry, in fact in every field, the gap between science and spirituality has very much narrowed.

This is one aspect of Sri Aurobindo's vision. Another aspect, as I told you, is of a spiritual community and of the future of humanity. Sri Aurobindo has said that the world is moving towards a larger and larger aggregate – man, his family, the society, the small city, the state, then the nation, and now the effort at world unity through the United Nations. He describes this process, the centrifugal and centripetal forces, people coming together and falling apart, nations coming together and breaking up, He says all this is because of two things. When the units are small, they have much cultural progress but there is instability and insecurity because there are conflicts. When the units are big there may not be any conflict but the life force gets centralised in the capital and the periphery starves. Nature thus brings about a situation where the whole thing falls apart. This is because Nature wants an ideal way. The ideal way, according to Sri Aurobindo, is world unity. World unity, but not with one government, one parliament, just a bigger copy of a nation. Then all the problems of all the nations would be magnified on an international scale and that would be a hundred times worse. The kind of human unity we want cannot come about merely by external means. Spiritual and external means have to go together.

In His book, *The Ideal of Human Unity*, Sri Aurobindo has described how human unity will ultimately be realised and create an outward material structure where every human being will find not only his spiritual but his highest material perfection. If this is not done, Sri Aurobindo says, then human unity has no value.

So, Sri Aurobindo places before us a great vision and in its realisation, He says, India will take the lead, because the base of the vision is spiritual. Unless there is a change in the consciousness of man, unless he unites his being with the Divine Presence within him, no external solution is possible. We have tried so many ways but all have failed.

I remember when the Auroville project was started, the Deputy Director-General of UNESCO gave a speech in which he said that the UNESCO programme had failed. As an example he said the Germans had bombed England very accurately in the War because they had been trained in England. So the student exchange programme which was meant to create unity had done just the opposite. He added that UNESCO, therefore, turned to Auroville for a solution because the stress here is on divinity in man. A very important question before us, is: does the Divine Consciousness exist? If it exists, is it realisable, can it become real in human life and can it direct human life?

Sri Aurobindo has affirmed that not only can this be done but that it is the only way. Do not think what I am telling you is difficult. When you come to practise it, you will find it is not even half as difficult as you imagined. India has to be rebuilt and the Mother's words are: *The future structure of the world depends on India.* India is a whole world in itself. So many people, so many varieties of thoughts. If India can evolve a political and socio-economic system where man would have freedom and unity – unity in diversity – where man would progress spiritually and materially, where all strife and conflicts would disappear, then the world will follow India. Communism has come, socialism has come, many political, economic, social theories have come, but all have failed, because the soul was not made a part of it. To others, man is an external personality only. But to us, man is a soul, with a body, mind and life. So keeping this in mind, we will try to understand the practice of Sri Aurobindo's yoga, individually and collectively.

Sri Aurobindo's yoga is one yoga which has a collective aspect. All yogas have an individual aspect. The aim of all yogas is to realise the Divine. Traditionally, you did it in your Vānaprastha and Sannyāsa, the last two āśramas. The Gita's yoga went a step further – realising the Divine was not the goal, realising the Divine was the beginning. You realise the Divine and you do what the Divine commands you to do. That is the whole teaching of the Gita. You do what the Divine commands. How to receive the command, is the yoga of the Gita.

Sri Aurobindo goes a step still further. He says that you may receive the Divine command but you may not be able to execute it. For this you must become a perfect instrument for carrying out the command, individually and collectively. That is why Sri Aurobindo and the Mother have said that an individual evolution is not enough; the Supermind consciousness must descend upon earth. Individual evolution may be a preliminary step, but the Supermind consciousness must descend on earth and become a guiding principle, like the mind is at present. And when this happens, the world would change. Another aspect of Sri Aurobindo's yoga is that the supramental consciousness would not be the monopoly of some few individuals. If some mahayogi could make his consciousness universal, then the world would dwell in his consciousness and he could invoke the descent so that the Supermind could come down and flood the physical consciousness and slowly change the whole of mankind. This, the Mother announced, had happened in 1956 which opened many great vistas of progress for us. We shall try to understand how it can influence our individual and collective life, how it can affect our national and international life.

Speaking in a very general way, the first thing you have to do in yoga is to observe yourself. Look at yourself – why did this thought come to me, why did I have this dream, why is this thing happening to me? Unless this *why* comes at the start of the journey, you will not understand many of the things when you read Sri Aurobindo. For example, He says there are vibrations which go round and there are vibrations which come straight; and unless you have felt the vibrations coming and touching a part of your body, the vibrations coming and entering your head and in your brain becoming a thought, unless you have observed this, you will have missed the whole thing.

So, one of the most important things is to become conscious of your inner life. Some children are very quiet, they try to think things over. But the elders think something has gone wrong with the child. "Yeh to baat hi nahi karta hai, kya hogaya hai?" ("He does not talk, what has happened to him?") and they run to the doctors and spoil everything. I have known of people who, when a descent takes place in them, lament: "Oh, muje 'headache' shuroo hogaya, yeh kya hogaya? 'Doctor' yeh bolta hai, 'doctor' woh bolta hai." ("Oh, I have got a headache! What has happened to me? The doctor says this, the doctor says that.") This is all foolishness. If you want to practise Sri Aurobindo's yoga, you have to take a fresh look at life, at your business, at your education, at your political, social, economic structure. You cannot look at it in the old ordinary way. You must remember what the Mother has said: *We are not here to do what the others do.* Because others have done it, it is precisely the reason why we should not do it. We are here to organise our life with a new consciousness in a new way. What that new way will be, we do not know today.

So, the first question is how to get in contact with this new consciousness. The contact with the new consciousness is not easy as Sri Aurobindo's yoga requires an individual change, a collective change, a world change, an inner change and an outer change. So the sadhana also has to be integral, because it has a psychological aspect, it has a meditational aspect, it has a karmayogic aspect, it has a hathayogic aspect – though not asanas and pranayamas as we normally understand them to be – and a bhaktiyogic aspect also. It is integral, covering all the aspects.

The first aspect, the psychological aspect, we will divide into five parts. The five psychological aspects are symbolised by the Mother in the champa flower which She has named *Psychological Perfection* – you know, the champa flower, it has five petals. The Mother has given significance to these five petals: Sincerity, Faith, Devotion, Aspiration and Surrender. If you can develop these five in you, your progress will be very fast, very fast. When you open a window the sun comes to you, you do not go to the sun. So once you make yourself ready in the psychological way, the Divine will reveal Himself to you. You do not have to search for Him. You have closed the door of your inner being and you are searching outside for Him. When you open the door, He will reveal Himself.

The psychological perfection will make the Divine reveal Himself to you.

Sincerity should be linked with transparency. You should become completely transparent. All this thinking, "Woh kya bolega?" (Sorry, Hindi comes very naturally to me.) "What will this person say, what will that man do? He wants to harm me." Nobody can harm you an inch. The only one you have to look to is God, the only one you have to please is God, the only one you have to listen to is God. Everything else is unimportant. It is imperfection. If you are loyal to the Divine, you are loyal to everyone. If you are open to Him, you are open to the Highest. Your only reason, your only purpose in life is to become conscious of His Presence and become His perfect instrument. You have no other purpose in life. Every other purpose is man-made and is a sign of weakness, and I must say, has nothing to do with our central aim.

I would here like to share two experiences with you. One day a friend of mine who is an IAS officer invited me to his house. His wife told me, "Bhaiji, we have two daughters. I asked my older daughter what she would like to become. And she said, 'Mummy, I would like to become a doctor.' Then I asked my younger one and she said, 'Mummy, you will laugh at me but I want to become God.' " Now, there is nothing to laugh about. There are people who have come to a stage where nothing appeals to them, nothing has any meaning. The only thing which gives meaning to life is to become God.

One lady came with her daughter to Pondicherry – this is the second incident – and I asked the young girl (she must have been fourteen or fifteen at that time): "Tell me, what is the best you can do?" For a few minutes she remained quiet, and then said, "To remember God." – "What best can you do in the next five minutes?" – "Remember God." – "What best can you do in your whole life?" – "To remember God." She had already found a great secret of life.

There are children who are at a stage where they have already come to this conclusion but unfortunately the parents, the teachers, the community laugh at them and do not encourage them. They do not know that these children are meant for a supramental life. They are born during this age so that they can try to live the supramental life. This is unfortunate and I hope it will disappear.

So the first thing is transparency. You should be absolutely transparent. God is within you. Let Him see through your eyes, let Him listen through your ears, let Him speak through your mouth, and you will see the result. Even without their knowing it, people who look at you will start thinking differently because it is He who is meeting them, not you. It will be He who will be talking to them, it will be He who will be seeing them, it will be He who will be listening to them, through you.

The question is how to abdicate your ego. You do not have to do it. You normally say: "I want to abdicate my ego, I want to get rid of my ego." That is a very wrong approach. First establish the Divine Presence in you and the ego will disappear. If you go on struggling with your ego, it is just another form of ego. So try to establish the Divine Presence in you. Those who are devoted to Sri Aurobindo may do it in Sri Aurobindo's name, those who feel God in any other form, let them feel Him in that form and establish Him in that form, it does not matter. But first feel this luminous presence in you, feel your whole body full of His light, your breath full of His light, because sincerity means to admit no other influence in your consciousness except the Divine's.

Now, sincerity, transparency, abdication of ego, to admit no other influence except the Divine's, all these are the same. And once you make a resolution, His help comes to you. If you tell Him: "O God, I really cannot do this, I cannot establish Your Presence, I cannot stop other thoughts, other emotions from coming in. Why can't You do something? Please help me," what will He do? Do you think He is going to say: "No, I won't help you. You struggle by yourself"? That is impossible. He has given His word in the Gita and Sri Aurobindo has also endorsed it, that once "you seek refuge in Me, once you turn to Me, I will take your responsibility." It is absolutely amazing that when you once turn to Him, all the curtains between you and the Divine are torn asunder. This has happened not once but has been the word of the Divine through centuries. You read Tulsidas' Ramayana where Vibhishan, brother of Ravana, comes to meet Rama and the monkeys say to Sugriva: "Oh, this man has something evil in his heart. He may cheat us. We must be careful. He may be a spy of Ravana." Besides other things, Rama says one very interesting thing: "Sanamukha hoi jiva mohi jabahi / Janma koti agha nasahi tabahi." 'When the Jiva comes to Me, the sins of a million lives vanish.' It as simple as that. Because people do not make a sincere effort, they go on struggling. Sincerity, transparency, abdication of ego, they go together. This is the first and the master step.

The second quality is faith. Sri Aurobindo has described it very clearly. You cannot say that I must first have an experience, let God first give me His help, then only will I have faith. I remember once a person jokingly prayed to God: "If You give me a million rupees, I will give You half. If You don't trust me, give me only half. You can keep the other half." Our whole approach to God is not that of faith but of distrust. It is not the Divine who distrusts you, but you who distrust the Divine. "Oh, if I rely on God, He may guide me wrong. I don't know, I might be in some trouble." Now, this is a wrong approach because you have not clarified in your own mind the concept of God. Which God are you worshipping? Are you worshipping a God who is Omniscient, who is Omnipotent, who is All-Compassion? Then what is the problem? How can you ever dream that He would misguide you? How can you ever dream that with His Omnipresence He will not give you protection? It is absolutely impossible.

I remember my younger brother had gone on a tour of Europe. While in Italy, he sent a telegram that a war was going on in Greece and to ask the Mother whether he should go there to attend a conference. When I asked the Mother, She said, "Remembering me a man can go into the mouth of death and come back. Ask him not to worry. Tell him to go ahead, attend his conference and come back." So the important thing to know is, once you are linked with the Divine, nothing can go wrong. Sri Aurobindo says that faith is something in your soul that believes and knows that God exists. He will give you protection, He will look after you. This is faith which you cannot really understand with the mind but which comes from your soul. So you must cultivate this faith. What is the best way of cultivating faith? I can tell you by sharing an experience.

I was once with a friend of mine, a prince, in his jeep who was driving at breakneck speed on a very bad road. I closed my eyes (this was many years before I joined the Ashram) and something told me: "You have entrusted your life to this fool and you hesitate to entrust it to God!" This is the story of every person. When you want to entrust your life to God, you cannot calculate the risks and the benefits. You must tell yourself: "Well, I am going to die one day, so the best thing for me is to die for God. If I am going to live, the best thing for me is to live for God. How can I die unsurrendered to Him? For whom should I die, for whom should I live? For a small family? for a little confusion? What is there to live for?" And the family is included in God; it is not excluded. The nation is included in God. And can the result of surrendering to Him be death, the result of surrendering to Him be misery, the result of surrendering to Him be confusion and trouble? It is impossible. If you have not come to the stage where you say: "I would rather have death than not surrender to Him, for otherwise life has no meaning", it means you are not yet ready for yoga. You have to continue with your normal life till you come to that stage. So faith can be cultivated.

When I was a young boy of nineteen, I remember the Ashram had some financial difficulties and I wanted to send some money. I knew that if I asked my family, they would refuse. So I went to my uncle who was in charge of the company's finances and told him, "Uncle, I have a small department under me. I want to send some money to the Ashram. I want to withdraw some money from the bank and send it." He started laughing. I told myself that it would be better if my department closes, it would be better if my family laughs at me and throws me out of the business, but the Ashram's need should be fulfilled. "I want to send the money, whether you agree or not," I insisted. He knew that I would do what I wanted to, so he said, "If it is from your department you may send it." So I withdrew the amount – it was a few lakhs, not much – and sent it to the Ashram. That year, my department earned so much money without my effort, so much money, that we could not even dream of – in millions. The money just came pouring in from all sides. I said to myself, here I was jumping out of the window, knowing fully well I would fall to the ground, and the Divine keeps me in His arms!

If you want to have faith, you cannot calculate. You should not think that faith means you take a parachute, you take all the precautions, like putting a kind of net as in the circus, and then you jump. That is not faith. Faith is: if He is there, I am doing it for Him, He will take care of me. When you find that this works in life, your faith also increases.

Once we had a big problem a few years ago, a very big problem. There seemed to be no way out but we had faith that Sri

Aurobindo exists and that this problem will be solved. And it happened exactly in that way, exactly, and the problem was solved. Without faith there is no progress, because the whole approach of yoga is a complete offering to the Divine. How can you offer without faith? You must have some kind of faith in order to give yourself up to Him.

Here I am reminded of a story of Tagore which brings out the point beautifully. In this story Tagore says a man went out begging and he saw God coming in His golden chariot. God looked at him, smiled and stopped His chariot and got down. So the begger thought that now his poverty will end; he will go and spread out his bowl before God. But before he could stretch out his hands, God Himself stretched out His hands. The begger thought that God was playing a cruel joke on him. The begger took out a grain of rice and put it in God's out-stretched hand and returned home very dejected. In the evening when the begger turned his bowl upside down, he found that one grain of rice had turned into gold. Then he cried out: "Why did I not give all that I had to God!"

Now this is a very true spiritual experience. It is not imagination. The whole secret of turning dust into gold is offering. When you offer your mind to the Divine, you get knowledge; when you offer your will to Him, you get power; when you offer your body to Him, you get health and beauty; when you offer your psychic being to Him, you get love. It is like a drop merging in the ocean. How can you merge if you are always hesitating? You cannot learn to swim if you are afraid of water. You have to take a plunge and this has to be without calculation. You have to jump because you cannot do without it. You must want to offer yourself to God and leave all the rest to Him. Either He saves you or He does not save you. But do you lose or does He lose? You lose nothing, because in any case you would die some twenty years later. But how can He leave you; He who through centuries has built up the tradition that "he who takes refuge in Me, I will protect him, I will look after him." He will do everything for you. What can you do? You can do nothing. So, all the traditions will continue to stand, as they have always stood throughout the centuries. Have faith and take the plunge. Without taking the plunge there is no progress in yoga.

The next aspect is devotion. Sri Aurobindo has said that however great a yogi may be, howsoever great askesis he may have practised, ultimately he has to depend upon the Divine. To rely upon Him completely is the path of Bhakti, the path of love. If you love a person you do not calculate all that you have sacrificed for that person. You are happy to do it; you do not even think you are sacrificing because you just cannot do without it. You have to love the Divine. Love Him. Love Him physically (that is, the ordinary puja, aarti and the rest), love Him mentally, vitally, psychically and see Him and love Him in His creation.

One aspect of yoga is to see Him in every being and when you see Him in every being with whom can you have quarrel? Why would you need a parliament and laws? All this is a waste of time, waste of the country's money and energy. You cannot begin a new life by just passing some resolution or some law in the parliament by a majority of votes. A new thinking has to come from Sri Aurobindo's yoga, a new movement has to start from Sri Aurobindo's yoga. I am telling you this to increase your responsibilities and your first responsibility is to open yourself to the Divine, to become His instrument and to work for a world change. Our yoga is not a yoga of retirement from life. The path of Bhakti is the path of sacrifice to the Divine. Bhakti is an attitude of love for the Divine and without it, there is no progress.

And now aspiration. Aspiration means God's constant remembrance. Constantly you remember the Divine and aspire that He may reveal Himself to you, that you may feel His Presence in you and around you, that every cell of your body may respond to His Presence, His Force, that everything in you may belong to Him and nothing belongs to yourself. If you reach this state, then that would be the fulfilment of your life. And aspiration is the master key which brings about the change.

The last comes surrender. There are two sides to surrender. You can offer the good as well as the bad. If you offer the bad to the Divine even that gets transformed. So your surrender has to be total. You do not say: "Ah, this is bad, how can I offer it to Him!" This is another kind of ego. If it is good, it is all right, because the good is not yours, you are only giving Him what is His. Similarly, the bad is not yours either, because it is also a part of God, a part of Nature. So you have to offer it too. It is like yajna – whatever goes into the sacrificial fire, gets purified. For this you have to have endurance because there is the universal nature which persists. Even if you have conquered certain defects in you, they persist because they always flow from the universal nature. So you must learn to endure and offer, endure and offer. This is another aspect of surrender.

I can assure you that all these five together are not difficult to cultivate, if you make a resolution. This, then, is the psychological approach. But what should we do in our daily life to move towards the Divine?

I will first take sleep and dreams, because one-third of your life you are sleeping. You must know how to cultivate your dreams in order to come nearer to the Divine during the eight hours of sleep. Now, the first thing, before going to sleep, is to meditate. Do not just retire to your bed and go to sleep. If you want to realise the Divine, you need some discipline in your life. Even a little sport, a little music, painting, all require a firm discipline. The realisation of the Divine needs a super-discipline, a divine discipline. So before going to bed, meditate. Take your food a little early. Once you have made your goal the supramental transformation, and nothing less than that, once you have made your goal a divine life on earth in a divine body, you have to apply yourself to it totally. You cannot say that half an hour is enough. That means you are not ready for the twenty-three and a half hours. Once you have chosen your goal all your activities should converge on it.

So you meditate, you take your food a little early, you retire half an hour before going to sleep, read a book of Sri Aurobindo or the Mother if you are aspiring for a supramental life and put a will that you want to be conscious of your night. You pray that the Divine may lead you in the experiences which He wants you to have. There should be complete collaboration between you and the Divine in your life. When you wake up in the morning, you should get up feeling refreshed, feeling His Presence more and more. You should also be conscious of your night and remember it.

When you get up in the morning do not jump out of bed. Remain still, keep a diary near your bed and write down your night life, write down even the feelings with which you get up and try to remember your dream backwards, what had happened last and what had happened before that. Interpretation of dreams, visions, symbols, all we will take up at a different meeting, but for today it is enough to make a resolution to be more conscious of your life and to link it with the Divine.

When you get up you should pray. One of the best prayers I have found is the 'Morning Prayer' of the Mother, which you perhaps know: *Mother Divine, grant that today may bring to us a completer consecration to Thy Will, a more integral gift of ourselves to Thy Work, a more total forgetfulness of self, a greater illumination, a purer love.* Read the 'Morning Prayer' of the Mother. Read it everyday, meditating on every sentence. You will see how this helps. It will take you only ten minutes, but you will see a big change in your life. It is the most remarkable prayer you could read. And meditate on it.

Now we come to the daily routine. If you have decided to dedicate your day to the Divine, it is a very crucial decision you have taken, a decision which will open a big gateway. For example, my friend here is a judge. Everyday he has to go at a particular time to the High Court. He has to be sure that he delivers the judgement in the morning. So his life is organised for this purpose and that is as it should be. It is always good to organise your physical life. When he returns in the evening, he has his cup of tea and follows his routine. Now, suppose he takes the decision to follow Sri Aurobindo's yoga. How will it affect his routine? What will be its karmayogic aspect?

You see, in Sri Aurobindo's yoga work is indispensable. But what kind of work and how is it to be executed? Here we must know that our present work is work in ignorance. When we say we are working for God, it is not really so. First, it is our attitude that is important. And the first step is taken when we do not work for the result. Then it is "niṣkāma karma", but it is still not Karma Yoga. When the Divine starts guiding you, when you are linked with His consciousness, when you act in unity with Him, then only it becomes Karma Yoga.

So once you have decided that the day belongs to Him, then He will have to decide whether He is going to do His work today through you or not, whether you will go to the court or not, whether you will have breakfast at eight, at ten or not at all, because both you and the day belong to Him. He will have to decide when He will have breakfast, through your body, He will have to decide what work He will do that day, through you. When you decide, naturally, you will remember Him, because you will say if I forget Him how will He guide me? Let me remember Him and keep open to Him, let me feel Him within me. When you feel Him within you, when you decide on this, you will be surprised to find that the breakfast would be ready for you every time you have to take it, when a telephone rings you will know whose call it is even before you lift up the receiver and you will know what to say. He will take you to the court, He will make you study the papers with less effort, He will make you give the right judgement, to take the right decision. This is not only my experience but the experience of so many others.

The other day I was talking to a judge who had retired from the Patna High Court. I asked him, "How has yoga helped you?" He replied, "When I read my case papers, my finger automatically goes to the correct point. I do not know how this happens. In a murder case while I was giving the judgement, I felt something was not quite right. So I called the advocate and told him I was sorry but I wanted to hear the case once again. I then reversed the judgement I was writing."

Our Ashram physiotherapist, K, pressed my back and asked me, "Bhaiji, do you feel any pain here?" I said, "Yes, but how did you know?" He said, "I do not know what the Mother has given me, but my fingers go to the place where they should." So it is with everyone. A judge will have his judicial intuition, a physiotherapist will have his physiotherapeutic intuition, a musician will have his musical intuition. So unity with God will lead you to a higher material life, to a greater efficiency, not less efficiency. This I come to know everyday from my own experience and the experience of others, also.

An income-tax officer – now he is an assistant commissioner – related to me an interesting experience of his which I would like to share with you. He said he had the Mother's calender in his office and one day he was sitting and meditating before the Mother's picture. It was February and by March they had to complete certain collections – he was in charge of this work. While he was thus meditating, it seemed his assistant commissioner entered his office and found him meditating. The assistant commissioner naturally reprimended him, "What is this you are doing? We have to finish the quota by March and you are sitting in your office with your eyes closed and meditating?" My friend replied, "Sir, because I am meditating the quota will be completed." And it happened exactly like that. Without troubling anybody, the quota was reached fully. There are many, many such experiences and if I related them to you, you would be amazed.

An incident happened just three days back in Calcutta. One

man, a very important man in our country was in difficulty. I was coming by plane from Delhi and he was also on the same flight. I do not know why, but he walked up to me and said, "Bhaiji, I am in difficulty." I asked, "What has happened?" He said, "I have made a mistake. I may get hauled up." Then he added, "I am going. Give me the Mother's Blessing." I gave him the Mother's Blessing packet. He did exactly as he was supposed to do and the whole thing went in his favour. When he came in the evening, he was beaming. I asked him, "What happened?" He said, "Only absolute truth and the Mother's Grace. And everything went in my favour."

So I will tell you the secret of attaining your highest in material life. If you have a material problem, look within yourself. There is something wrong with you. Do not blame the society, do not blame the community, although many things are wrong with the world. If you have solved the problem within you, at least for you the result will show as it did in the case I have just related. Another person in his position might have suffered, but this man did not suffer, because he opened himself to something within him. So everyday, everyday take the decision. Whenever you have a material problem do not ask yourself whether I should do this or that. Just ask yourself whether you are in the Mother's consciousness all the time. If not, then the mistake is already committed. If you remain in the Mother's consciousness, I can assure you, I can guarantee you, that nothing will go wrong. This is the supreme secret – to remain in the Divine consciousness throughout the day, during your work, in everything you do, even while you are walking.

One of the most effective meditations is to recite the Mother's name while walking, invoking the light in the legs and the body. I have found this to be very effective to remove the inertia of the physical body. When we come to meditation we will touch upon this, but the important thing to know is that Karma Yoga means that you give your actions to God and to act in unity with Him. This unity will lead you to the highest material fulfilment. The life of trial and error will end, and you will be able to do the right thing at all times. I know a number of men (by number I do not mean hundreds, but a few) who have taken to the path and who are achieving success in their careers, who are able to solve their problems better, because they have sincerely taken to the path. If you take up yoga in a half-hearted manner, half timidly, half afraid, that is not going to work. If you are with God, how can you be afraid, how can you be worried about anything? He takes care of everything. You cannot imagine how much care He takes of you.

I will tell you of another incident. Once I was in Washington. It was raining very heavily and no cabs were available. I had an appointment. I simply prayed: "Mother, can't you send me a cab?" Would you believe it, within two minutes a cab comes along and stops before me. I find it is full, there are two ladies sitting in the back seat. I do not know what occured to the black driver – he was a student – to stop the cab for an Indian stranded there. He dropped me at the place where I had to go and he did not even charge me the fare! What I want to tell you is that when you turn to the Divine, even your material problems get solved, because then He starts working. When you are busy thinking, doing things, you cannot benefit from His guidance. But when you are surrendered to Him, you are a part of His universal action and then there is no limit whatsoever.

I will tell you about one more experience in this connection so that you can know how the universal action takes place. In 1970, the Sri Aurobindo Centenary Celebration Committee was formed, with the Prime Minister as the Chairperson. When I returned from my tour, the Mother suddenly told me, "You have to go to UNESCO to propose a resolution on Sri Aurobindo." Then, She added, "But you don't like France, you don't speak French." I said, "Mother, I like France, I speak tolerably good French." She said, "Then why don't you go?" When I came home I found my passport had expired and I had no money. I said to myself, I am not a member of the Indian delegation, my passport has expired, how will I go? Besides, the UNESCO session had already started and the Indian delegation was formed and would be leaving in a day or two.

The next day there was the Centenary Committee meeting in Delhi which I had to attend. So I phoned up Madras for a ticket. They said there was no ticket available. When I asked for the Station Manager, a friend of mine, I was told he was on leave. So I thought that it is all finished, I cannot go. From my house I went to the Ashram – a few houses away – and on the way I prayed: "Sri Aurobindo, You are sending me to Paris and You don't even get me a ticket to Delhi. How is it going to work?" When I returned home, my secretary comes and tells me, "There is a letter in the mail from the passport office." (Now this is amazing. Why did the letter not come two days earlier? Why did the Mother not send me one week earlier? The Divine is testing our faith all the time and the Mother has said that there is a choice before us at every moment, all the time. There is not one moment when the choice is not there.) The passport officer had written that he had just joined his office, he wanted to have the Mother's darshan and his friends had told him to write to me. So I asked my secretary to ring him up and tell him that the darshan would be arranged, but to let them renew my passport immediately.

Suddenly, a trunk call came from a friend of mine in Delhi. He said, "Bhaiji, we have a very important meeting and we want you to come." I told him, "I want to come but there is no ticket." He said, "Within half an hour I will advise you about your ticket. You will be our guest, we will pay for all the expenses of your hotel stay and for everything else." So I said, "O.K." Now, you see, why the ticket was not available. If I would have got the ticket, my friend in Delhi would not have paid for it.

After the meeting in Delhi I told the Education Minister, "There is a resolution to be passed on Sri Aurobindo in UNESCO and you have not taken anybody from the Ashram?" He said, "Why don't you come along, we will go and ask the Prime Minister now." He asked her and she said, "Yes, surely he should go." So I became a member of the delegation in five minutes! I was given a letter to the Reserve Bank for foreign exchange. I went to their office at four-thirty in the afternoon. There, one officer told me that I would first have to get the permission from the Reserve Bank in Bombay. I was in a fix, because time was running out. But the Director said, "I know you, I have worked in the Reserve Bank at Madras. You don't worry. You don't waste your money on a trunk call. You will have the exchange by five." And sure enough, I had the exchange by five. The next day we left for Paris.

What happened at the UNESCO session is another story. When I moved the resolution on Sri Aurobindo I found that UNESCO had decided to take a vote. They do not normally take a vote and we had not, therefore, talked to the other delegations. I thought the resolution would be lost. So I prayed: "Sri Aurobindo now I can do nothing. The resolution is already moved." I had found that some people were voting for us but one entire bloc just sat still. On my right was the Hungarian leader who told me, "I have read Sri Aurobindo." On my left was the Indonesian delegate and he said, "I have been to Pondicherry." But these fellows were just not voting. So again I prayed. Suddenly, I saw that one by one the hands started going up and the resolution was passed. But what is amusing is that after the meeting the representative of one of the countries came over to me and said, "We have voted for you but we don't believe in what you say."

I had no money when I left, as I told you, but money just poured in, and by the time I was ready to return home, I had such a surplus I could have toured for another year without any difficulty. Even people who are fully engrossed in the material world must know that the solution to material problems is to turn to the Divine. And the way of perfect living is not to plan your day yourself but to let the Divine plan it. Let Him plan your life. He is wiser than you. He knows what to do and how best to do it. He can reach out to do things which we human beings with our limited power cannot do.

Now I will tell you in brief about speech. If you want to follow the path of Integral Yoga, never tell a lie. *Never*. If you do not want to speak the truth, keep quiet. No exaggeration, no deformation, do not even praise Sri Aurobindo to the skies, unless you yourself believe it to be true. In the path of yoga every lie you say puts a curtain between you and the Divine consciousness. So the first thing you have to do is not to tell a lie. The second is that before you speak, you must meditate on the Divine: "O Lord, You say what You want to say. I am not concerned about people's reactions. You speak." And you will find how effectively this works.

Meditation is of many types. In Sri Aurobindo's yoga, you have to practise all the types, because you come in contact with the Nirguṇa Nirākāra as well as with all the aspects of the Saguṇa Sākāra of the Divine. His yoga is integral. He wants healing power to develop in us, He wants this power and that power to develop in us, and also all the attributes of the Divine. If all the attributes of the Divine could manifest in us, what could be greater than that?

Each meditation has to be directed in a particular manner. You should spend at least fifteen minutes everyday in being united with the Divine. Think of nothing in these fifteen minutes but only the

Divine, one with Sri Aurobindo and the Mother. I tell you, there is no greater meditation than this. When you practise, you will know the result. You will come out of this meditation feeling healthier, more peaceful, more illumined. You will feel the difference in one day. But make a firm resolution that in those few minutes you will become that. You do not want to be anything less than that. You have to concentrate so much on Them that you become identified with Them. This is the goal. You can take the help of a mantra for this. But you must spend these fifteen minutes in the morning and again fifteen minutes in the evening in complete union with Them, when you think of nothing but Them, and you will see the result.

The other thing I want you to understand is that in Sri Aurobindo's yoga, work is very important. One day I asked the Mother, "Mother, what should our members do for their growth?" She said that they should do three things. They must read something from Sri Aurobindo and the Mother. The second is that they must ask themselves: 'Why am I here? What am I supposed to do? What is the highest I can do in my life?' And the third is to work for Sri Aurobindo Society for at least one hour everyday. And in a selfless manner. Note that She has said *selfless* and not 'unselfish'. Selflessness means you feel as if you are not doing anything, the Mother is working through you. You are not working. Unselfishness means that you work but without any desire for gain or reward. This distinction is very important.

Here I want to mention that we would like to start a big programme. There will be a large number of centres in the country for spiritual education and community service. People must know not only what spiritual education is – that is only one part – but, as one grows in consciousness one must know how to apply it to everyday life. There will be a section for home science, there will be a section for teachers' training, there will be a section for leadership training, for politics must also change. If ninety percent of our leaders govern the country in ignorance, and they have most of the power, they have most of the money, the country will never progress. It is a shame that in a great country like ours this kind of nonsense is tolerated. And the greatest fault lies with the people connected with Sri Aurobindo, because we are among those who can and must deliver the goods. We cannot blame anybody. We must have a constant aspiration for the supramental descent. Nothing but the supramental descent can change things. Fighting and winning wars is not going to bring about a change. It is a new consciousness that alone can bring about a lasting change. The decision to belong to the Supermind and to be guided by it, is the highest decision a man can take and the highest fulfilment of his life. Even if a few of us can open to the supramental light, we can do the work of millions. Other people do not even know this. And we are in touch with Sri Aurobindo. If we miss this opportunity, it is our misfortune, not theirs. So the highest we can do is to constantly aspire for the Supermind to guide us. You will see how the doors open.

If each one did a little, if each one got up in the morning and, instead of thinking of a hundred things, simply said: "Tell me, O Lord, what I can do for You today? You use me", you will see how this helps. You will see how the doors open and you will see that He will do ten times more for you, without your having to tell Him anything. You will discover that a new chapter has opened in your life, only if you decide to follow what I have told you today. If you can go a step further and pray: "I want to live every moment of my life for You. You have to guide me whether You put me in an office or anywhere", you will be surprised at the result. He will use you on every occasion. You are travelling in a train and you may find that next to you is a person who is interested in Sri Aurobindo. You are sitting in your office and He will send you the man who is destined to have some link with you. Once you take this decision His force will start working like the 'Sudarśana Cakra' moving and doing things for you and you will go, as Sri Aurobindo has said, from *marvel to marvel.* You will wonder at what is happening, why it is happening, but all this can only take place when the fundamental decision is taken by you.

As I said, Sri Aurobindo does not want you to work only for your personal salvation. It is not the yoga of Sri Aurobindo. It is not even the yoga of India. He wants you to work for a world change.

According to Sri Aurobindo a new light, a new and different generation in the world will come from India. And that India has to rise, has to guide, that India has to deliver the goods. How will India rise, how will she deliver the goods, I do not know. But the least India can do is to offer herself, as she is, with all her shortcomings, all her difficulties, all her problems. If you pray: "From today, we belong to You. Use us as You like", you will find that it will be the beginning of a new life.

Let us then work for it. Sri Aurobindo and the Mother are always ready to help us. Let us take Their help and work for a national change, a world change, as guided by Them, not as guided by our ignorant minds. And you will see how things develop.

May the Blessings of Sri Aurobindo and the Mother be with you all and may Their Blessings help us to build a new India and a new humanity.

Half an Hour with the Divine

One of the greatest problems of man in both, life and yoga, is to have communion with the Divine, to build a line of comunication by which he can receive the guidance and act accordingly. Man does not know that he does not have to build the line of communication, he does not have to do communion himself. The Divine builds the line of communication, the Divine reaches out to you. He puts your consciousness in order, He says what has to be said and does whatever has to be done. Only, you have to get plugged in to Him, you have to just switch on to Him. That is the only thing needed from your side. All the rest He does.

That is what Sri Aurobindo has said: *All would change if man could once consent to be spiritualised.* So the main thing is your consent. 'I want to change, I want to be perfect, I want to be divinised', and to put yourself in His hands in a very open and sincere manner. All your desires, all your preferences, the desire even to serve humanity, the desire even to do good, come in the way of your opening to the Divine, of your switching on to Him.

The best thing I can advise you from a very practical angle is, when you get up in the morning, spend half an hour with the Divine. Make it a rule of your life: 'I want to spend at least half an hour with Him, just with Him'. Whatever be your concept of Him, whatever be your shortcomings, your hesitations, doubts, lack of confidence as to how there could be any easy way to establish a communion or communication with Him, despite all these, make a resolution: I want to spend half an hour with the Divine everyday in the morning, I want to talk to Him, put my problems before Him, put my aspirations before Him, just as I would put them to somebody dearest and closest to me, with the faith that the Divine is Omniscient and Omnipotent and that He will hear. Try it for one day and see the result; for one day and you will know what happens to you and what *can* happen to you. Just half an hour one day. And if you do this properly for one day, you will want to do it the whole day, the whole night, and the next day and all your life.

For those of you who are ready, who really feel the need to be guided by Him, really feel the need to be perfect, this is the first and decisive step to take to establish unity with the Divine. You know, in our consciousness there are established from childhood, from birth and from even previous lives, a number of 'saṃskārāḥ' in the mental plane, which obstruct our communication with the Divine. But once we have established this rapport, He puts them right, He cleans them away and everything then becomes different for us. So, you must know that this is the simplest way to solve the difficulties; every other way is of great tapasya, of great effort. But this kind of communication with Him, communion with Him, will help you realise how He puts things right in your consciousness.

When you talk to Him, you will be surprised to find that even the imperfections in your thoughts disappear, the imperfections of your aspirations disappear, these will simply vanish. You will feel that what you are trying to talk to Him is imperfect, it has to take another shape.

So this is what I would like to tell you very briefly: learn to communicate with the Divine and be with Him at least for half an hour every day. And this is the best contact you can have during the twenty-four hours, the half an hour you spend with Him. So on this occasion, I invoke the special Blessings of the Mother and Sri Aurobindo for all of you that you may open to the Supramental Light and Force. May Sri Aurobindo's Consciousness awaken and settle in your mind, life and body, and manifest itself so that each one of you can become a radiating centre of His Presence and His Manifestation. May His Blessings be with you.

The Importance of Sri Aurobindo's Teaching and Work

Humanity is passing through a critical period in its history. The old values, ideas, philosophies, theories have been found wanting to meet the demands of the changing times. Science has placed in the hands of men inventions by which he can ensure the welfare and progress of the whole of mankind. On the other hand, by misusing them due to his egoistic consciousness, he may spell the doom of mankind.

A small atomic bomb can destroy people and objects within a radius of ten thousand square miles and can do great damage within a further radius of ten thousand square miles in the direction in which the wind is blowing. This is the potency of only a small nuclear weapon. Weapons of much more dangerous magnitude are stockpiled by rival nations.

There is an 'authority crisis'. Nobody wants to obey anybody. The leaders do not realise that it is not possible to subdue people by coercion and people do not know how to solve this problem of authority and discipline.

Leading statesmen all over the world are baffled. The problems have not only multiplied but have become global. Population problems, problems of unemployment, political problems, economic problems, all have become global. Some leading statesmen from different parts of the world, look to India for a solution. They themselves have stated that they do not know why, but they feel that the solution will come from India.

There is a reason, a deep, subtle reason for this intuitive faith in India. Ancient India was a leader not only in the cultural field but in several others also. It was like a number of suns radiating at the same time from this great nation, in the fields of literature, mathematics, astronomy, botany – a number of things. It is India that gave to the world the concept of 'zero'. And most important of all was India's contribution to the organisation of a collective life. We have seen the Ramarajya, we have seen the great kings who were also yogis, who ruled as guided by the Divine. The great Rishis created the Vedas and the Upanishads, again guided by the Divine Consciousness. People were happy then.

But a time came when the synthesis of spiritual and material life became imperfect. The spiritual meaning was lost and people clung to outward forms. That is how the country degenerated because most of these outward forms, rituals, rules and conventions were misunderstood, misinterpreted and wrongly practised. The ancient glory was possible because our forefathers could take a total view of life, in unity with the Divine consciousness. The Rishis could synthesise everything – politics, law, the economic aspect of life, labour and management relations, family relations, ethics, religion, the entire spectrum of life, in line with the basic law of evolution, in the fundamental knowledge that the Divine is in everyone and everywhere and the aim of life is to manifest Him.

All the writings of the ancient seers have two aspects: one permanent, another, temporal. As I said, the permanent aspect which should have changed humanity was unfortunately lost sight of and people continued to cling to the temporal and followed it blindly.

The time had come to restate the ancient Truths as suited to the present times and the need of the future. In an evolving world where society and men are both evolving, there has to be an evolution of thought, too. A new synthesis was needed which could harmonise all the divergent aspects of life. This great work was done by Sri Aurobindo. He wrote his experiences and His vision of the future in English, a language spoken in the largest number of countries in the world.

When Sri Aurobindo was fighting for India's independence, he felt the limitations of human capacity, He felt He could not fight the British because the Indians were not well organised nor did they have the proper means.

Sri Aurobindo thought that if our forefathers could work so many changes by their spiritual powers, why could He not also develop these powers through yoga and fight for India's independence by spiritual means. That is why He started practising yoga. But as He grew in consciousness, as He went to higher and higher planes, His vision became global and He could foresee India's independence as a certainty. To Him, the crucial question was, what would India do after gaining independence; what path would she show to mankind. He believed India had a leading role to play in the history of humanity.

When Sri Aurobindo was in the Alipore jail, Swami Vivekananda appeared to Him and revealed to Him the necessity of an individual and a social change through the descent of a higher consciousness. Sri Aurobindo perceived that it was not a small improvement which was required but a transcendence, a further accelerated evolution from man to the Supramental Being, so that life on earth could really be transformed and men would develop such powers that all the scientific inventions, all that the future had in store, could be utilised for the benefit of mankind.

Out of jail and acquitted of all charges, Sri Aurobindo dedicated His life to the evolution of the supramental consciousness in man and to the establishment of a divine life on earth. As people flocked to Him from different parts of the world, seeking a similar vision or a similar truth of existence, He guided them on the path. He placed before us a fourfold, interconnected and interdependent vision of a very great future for mankind, a future not yet realised, a future really worth striving for, a future that is inevitable.

The teaching of Sri Aurobindo starts from that of the ancient Rishis, that there is a Divine consciousness, a Brahman consciousness pervading the whole universe and, by a process of involution, this consciousness has become mind, life and physical-material creation.

Sri Aurobindo says that after this, the process of evolution started. This evolution was possible because there was an involution. The first step in evolution was from matter to life, that is, from stone to plant and plant to animal. Life, which was latent in matter, evolved, and Nature created a form to manifest it.

Then there was a further evolution from life to mind, that is, animal to man. Again, Nature created a new anatomy that could manifest mind, because an animal could not have manifested mind properly even if it had developed it. With its guttural organs, it could not have sung; with its paws, it could not have written. So Nature created a new anatomy. This is the big difference between Sri Aurobindo's view of evolution and the scientific theory. It is not only an evolution of form; it is simultaneously an evolution of consciousness and an evolution of form.

Sri Aurobindo believes that evolution will not stop with man, it will go further from man to the next stage, the Supramental Being. And the evolution, according to Him, could be expedited, accelerated, by certain practices which He calls Integral Yoga.

The second aspect of Sri Aurobindo's vision is that this evolution cannot be carried out in isolation. It has to be a collective effort, at least of small communities. So He envisaged a social transformation, a collective life in which every person would occupy the place for which he is best suited, and give his best to the collective life. In turn, the collectivity would look after his basic needs for his experience and progress. In this way every individual would have an opportunity to progress and to grow to his maximum, and thus the highest in the collective life would also be realised. Sri Aurobindo calls this a *spiritualised society*, where the aim of collective life would be to manifest the Divine, through education, music, painting, through all the activities of life.

His third vision is that of human unity in freedom and in an organised diversity. Sri Aurobindo takes an integral, a total view of world issues. He points out that the world is moving towards larger and larger aggregates, from an individual to a family; from families to clans; from clans to small kingdoms and city states; from small kingdoms and city states to empires and nations – and now to the United Nations. He also points out that when the units were small, they were bubbling with vitality and cultural activities but they were at constant warfare with each other and as such, were vulnerable. When the empires came, though the warfare stopped and there was more peace, all the cultural and other activities of life shifted to the capital, and the other parts lost their life force and vitality. But, since this was not the ideal solution, the empires also broke up.

Sri Aurobindo has said that if world unity has to come, we have to find a synthesis between individual and collective freedom, between individual and collective progress. He says that all the political systems of mankind – democracy, communism, socialism – are an effort to search for a way of life where everyone could be happy, where everyone could find his highest possibility. But all these have some lacunae. For example, let us look at the communist theory: it believes in giving everyone according to his need and taking from everyone according to his ability. This cannot be fulfilled by law alone; it can only come about when man grows in spiritual consciousness.

So also is the case with the democratic principle of liberty, equality and fraternity. Sri Aurobindo says that if you want to bring about equality, you have to take away some liberty; and if you want to have liberty, inequality is bound to come. Both could coexist only if these were based on fraternity. This again is a spiritual concept. So this is the fourth aspect of Sri Aurobindo's vision that the future of the world lies in the evolution of a spiritual consciousness in man. He says that the world has to pass through three stages: the infrarational stage, then the present age of rationalism and the future which will be an age of suprarationality.

Sri Aurobindo tells us that in the coming age, India has a key role to play, because India with her spiritual knowledge, her spiritual wisdom, her faith in spiritual values, is *the* country which can prepare on a mass scale a new life on earth. For this preparation, Sri Aurobindo sees again two simultaneous movements. One movement is the embodiment of a supramental consciousness in the elite who will be the leaders of the future. He feels that just like the evolution of mind, there will be an evolution of Supermind. As you know the Mother has declared that the Supramental Consciousness descended in the earth consciousness in 1956. If people could open themselves to it, it will guide them; if people could aspire for its help, it would lead them. There has to be a small group of realised people who can embody this intuitive consciousness, this consciousness which is more powerful than the mind so that they can be guided by it and can act in a more effective manner. And simultaneously, there has to be a larger collectivity as in the ancient times, that would be willing to follow them and organise its collective life in the light of the Divine guidance, like the Rishis.

In fact, if you think quietly you will realise that the future authority of the world has to come from within man, from an inner discipline, where every man has to make a choice either to belong to the old humanity or to work for a new transcendance.

It is with this ideal in mind that we, the disciples of Sri Aurobindo and the Mother, and as members of Sri Aurobindo Society, have to organise our activities.

With the growth of our Centres, we have also to add comprehensive community development services, including education, training and employment, leadership training, home science training, health training, architecture and area planning, industry and commerce, agriculture, all based on the Integral Yoga. People who want to build India could then get together as a cohesive group in every bloc, practising yoga and developing their own faculties. In this way they can receive the guidance from within and simultaneously, give something better to their fellowmen by working for a social transformation, where there would be no unemployment, where each one could attain his highest fulfilment.

We could begin by opening small Centres with a library, a meditation room, a lecture room and a few other facilities, as a first step where people will take a total view of life, where people will open themselves to the Divine Consciousness and thus improve in their health, mind and consciousness.

As people start getting ready, there would be teachers who would impart knowledge by a new method, doctors who would administer medical aid in a new manner, and so on. A new leadership would come, guided by the Divine and dedicated to the welfare of mankind. There could be a training programme in Pondicherry and other places so that people could come for training and go back and work in their areas. A fund could be set up for full-time dedicated workers, which could be financed partly by the Centre to work out the programme in each area.

We have already had International Conferences on Human Unity as a result of which the Auroville project was born. We could now work for a World Assembly for Human Unity to take further steps to draw up a charter for human unity and to work with dynamism towards the realisation of an effective human unity.

In India, we could form a National Assembly with two representatives from every district who would work for national development in accordance with Sri Aurobindo's teaching.

Sri Aurobindo Society could make a beginning in a modest way. We could divide our organisational pattern into a National Council, State Committees, District Committees, small commissions for education, agriculture and so on, grouping our members in these committees so that they could effectively help in their own area of activity. Let us invoke the Grace of Sri Aurobindo and the Mother and make a beginning.

How to Meditate

The subject of today's talk is: 'How to Meditate'. It is a very vast subject and in the short time at our disposal, I would like to divide it into two parts: First, why one should meditate, what is the scientific principle behind it, what are the benefits and second, the different kinds of meditations, and how exactly to meditate.

People have very wrong notions about meditation. Some ask me to tell them how to meditate. I ask them, why do you want to meditate? Nine out of ten who come, say they want to meditate for getting peace of mind. That is the only result they expect out of meditation. They think that if they closed their eyes they would have all the peace around them. And the one remaining, he too is confused as to what he wants out of meditation. Out of a thousand people, perhaps one or two are clear about what exactly is meditation and how to benefit from it.

Human life is imperfect, man himself is fragmented, his consciousness is dispersed. Meditation is the way by which he can remove this fragmentation and integrate his personality, concentrate his consciousness and direct it on what he wants to achieve. Divine realisation apart, the benefit accruing, say to a doctor, can be immense, if he really knows how to meditate, meditate with open eyes. He can then diagnose the disease by merely touching the patient or by looking at him he can give the correct prescription. I have known of such people. We had a physician in the Ashram, not a highly qualified doctor but people came from all over India to him. I asked him one day, "Vaidji, what do you do?" He said, "Main Bhagwan kā dhyān kerta hu. Jo dava dhyān main aati hai, woh detā hun, aur patient theek hojata hai. I do not know how it happens, but the patient 'theek hojata hai." ('I meditate on the Divine and whatever treatment or medicine comes to me in meditation I give to my patient and the patient gets well.')

There is a force to which we can open through meditation and channelise it and realise it. Meditation is not a way of retirement or running away from the world. Meditation is fulfilled when you get linked in your consciousness with the Divine within you and raise your lower consciousness and direct the force of the Divine consciousness in your life. How to direct the force, how to get linked, we will try to understand. In meditation I include meditation during work, meditation during sleep, meditation while taking food, meditation all the time.

It is only in this meditative consciousness that a human personality can be well integrated and can be linked to the Highest; otherwise it would lose the link. Your consciousness, your mind is normally involved in the ordinary nature of your personality. When you are involved in the ordinary nature, your thoughts are selfish, your actions are selfish and egoistic and the result is misery. If you do not want to lead a miserable life, one powerful way is meditation – meditation for twenty-four hours, but not with your eyes closed. With eyes closed, you can do it for half an hour, but for the whole day, with eyes open. You cannot isolate meditation from your general goal in life. You have first to establish your general goal in life and then for every meditation you have to fix a specific goal: today you may want to meditate for healing, tomorrow you may want to meditate for receiving the Divine guidance, the day after, you may want to meditate for developing intuition in you or you may like to be a poet.

When we come to the various kinds of meditations we will also consider the benefits of meditation; what kind of meditation we should do for a particular kind of result. When I read Sri Aurobindo for the first time, I was surprised. Sri Aurobindo has written: *If the French Revolution took place, it was because a soul on the Indian snows dreamed of God as freedom, brotherhood and equality*. And this yogi's consciousness must have transmitted the idea and it got communicated to some people in France.

The highest inspiration comes from the Divine. Men normally have the mental consciousness but if someone can receive ideas in his mental consciousness and relate these to other people, even those who are not in conscious link with the Divine but are themselves dynamic, can benefit from it. Sri Aurobindo has related two very interesting experiences. For the first one, He said that people would not believe it and it would look *ridiculous and also arrogant if I were to say that I worked for the success of the Russian Revolution for three years....* The second is that He found it much easier to sit inside a closed room and direct His consciousness to people who, had He guided them personally, would not have agreed with Him and would not have followed Him. He gave an example of the Spanish War and a few other examples where he linked His consciousness with that of certain generals and brought about the desired result. And His is a very scientific attitude. He describes where He succeeded and where He did not. He said that where the instrument was good He succeeded and where the instrument was not receptive, He did not succeed. The instruments did not know Sri Aurobindo, they might as well not have heard of Him. But Sri Aurobindo would concentrate on him – the instrument – and help bring about a certain result. Through meditation, you not only develop your inner capacities but you develop your effectiveness in everyday life to bring about certain events that normally you cannot. We shall take up a few aspects that would be helpful for a preliminary understanding and then go on to meditation proper.

The first thing to know about meditation is that everything is important – your environment, every thought you think. You cannot say that I had a bad thought, but it does not matter as I have not spoken it. A bad thought is a bad action at the mental level. So meditation requires a complete inner control and a helpful environment. Now, how to create a helpful environment, how to have the inner control, we will consider these when we come to them. We will also discuss all kinds of physical aids, including breathing exercises. A proper control of breath can help to keep wrong thoughts away. These small exercises to quieten the mind are very important. Over the years, the Indian yogis have developed a number of methods to quieten the mind. We will consider some of these methods that actually help to quieten the mind and develop intuition or some other faculty. When the mind is quiet, it helps.

You must create a helpful environment. You can try to meditate, as I said, for all the twenty-four hours, but within the twenty-four hours, you must also fix a specific time. If you establish regularity, it becomes automatic at the fixed time. You will find that after some time it becomes effortless.

Then, the meditation should be dynamic. Passive meditation is not very helpful. There should be a goal, there should be an intense aspiration for the goal and, depending upon your intensity and sincerity, the result will be quick or slow.

One more thing that can help in yoga and meditation is a guide, but a true guide, because he can communicate many things to you. He can communicate in various ways which normally we cannot even imagine, unless we have the experience of it. He puts you in touch with certain vibrations, certain ranges of consciousness and you change instantaneously. Instantaneously. I remember the

Mother once put some people in contact with an Indian yogi and when they returned, She told them, "Your faces have changed." All in a very short time – there was no talk, no conversation, just looking at one another.

Through meditation you can develop the capacity to communicate with the higher consciousness. You must also try to understand the principle behind this. The mind has the capacity to take the colour or the quality of the object or subject with which it identifies itself. Suppose you concentrate on a flower and identify yourself with it, you take the quality of that flower. If you concentrate on the power of a god you can open to that power. All the gods are powers of the Supreme. In yoga itself there is only one God – the Supreme, the Brahman. All the others are His aspects representing certain original powers in the Divine. Suppose you want to heal, you have to get in contact with a particular power of the Divine; if you want aesthetic sense, you get in contact with another power; if you want prosperity, you contact a third power.

Meditation in this respect explains how to get linked. The mind has the capacity to become quiet so that the higher power can act or the higher power can descend in the mind. Then it is no longer your old human mind but your mind and this power together which bring about a result in the inner consciousness as never before. That is why you must know something of Indian philosophy about the gods. The gods do not have a physical body; they have a physical form but not a physical body like a human being. All of them have a luminous body. Their bodies are in you. They can become universal and they can become very small. They can enter into you and work through you. When you are in meditation your thoughts get concentrated and things automatically happen. Because of this capacity to reflect the higher plane, the mind identifies itself with the object or subject to such an extent that it gets fully absorbed and it automatically knows everything about it. This faculty is the result of an exercise of meditation.

The practice consists of three parts. The first is restraint. Restrain your mind from running pell-mell. You see an object, you remember having seen it in Kashmir. A chain of thoughts starts in you and you spend the whole day in actions, reactions, repulsions, attachments and the consequent generation of thoughts in you which may be harmful. So you must learn to restrain the mind.

The second thing is to learn to concentrate your mind on the object of concentration. And the third is, if you can change the quality of the mind itself by a descent from the higher plane, the mind may become divine. Sri Aurobindo wants the mind to become a divine mind, not a human mind, but the Divine descending and guiding you directly through your mind. So this is the faculty of the mind. But you must know that meditation is not only mental – mind is a major factor, no doubt – but there is a whole inner range of consciousness.

In the human personality, besides the mind there is the psychic. The psychic is normally under the influence of mind, life and body. Through meditation you release it. You can also rise in consciousness. When you go to the Intuitive plane, you can act from that plane. When you go to the Overmind plane – it is the plane of the gods – you can act from there and when you go to the Supermind plane, you can act from that plane. What this means is that you achieve a higher level of consciousness during meditation and you can integrate your actions and personality around your psychic being or in a higher plane to obtain a particular result. It is this that gives a new meaning, a new force to your daily life.

We will now consider a few types of meditations. The first kind is normally for realising the Divine. That is the accepted principle or objective of all meditations. The second series that we will take up will be meditation during work, including occult knowledge.

According to Indian yoga, if we meditate on the human system we come to know all about the human anatomy. There is an old legend about the physician, Cyavana, who sent his disciples to the forest to find a herb which had no medicinal properties. They returned after a long time and said that they had found no herb which did not have medicinal property. If a yogi in a meditative attitude touches a herb, he can know its quality. The herb communicates to him. The herbs do not articulate; it is through an inner consciousness when sufficiently opened, that this knowledge is revealed.

The third thing we will talk about is a very preliminary exercise. Our inner consciousness is dormant. There is a very simple exercise – meditation on light – which opens the inner consciousness, which in turn can open up the faculties of clairvoyance, telepathy, clairaudience, a number of faculties in you even before your mind is quiet. Just by meditation on light. I will tell you later the principle behind the Gayatri Mantra, one of the greatest contributions of our forefathers to Indian spirituality.

We will also consider collective meditation. For the collective organisation, for the collective mind, collective meditation is very important. In Sri Aurobindo Ashram, there is collective concentration and collective meditation. How this is done, we shall come to later. We will see the link between occult knowledge and meditation.

I will narrate to you a small incident. The Mother has written that She had seen two beautiful little girls – twins – who reminded Her of a very famous painting of Reynold. She mentioned this to their mother who said that while she was expecting, she had hung above her bed a very good reproduction of Reynold's painting. Everyday, before going to sleep and as soon as she got up, she would look at that picture and pray that her children may be like those in the picture.

So you can imagine how this helps. In India some people are aware of this truth, that if a pregnant mother meditates on a particular image, she imparts a specific aspect of that image to the children. These are some of the benefits of meditation which we shall try to understand.

Let us then start from the beginning. First we take up Divine realisation. Which meditation should we practise? The first important thing to understand is that the Divine consciousness alone is self-luminous. All the planes, the lower planes, the Overmind plane, which is the realm of gods, the mind plane, they all get their luminosity from the Divine to a lesser and lesser degree. None of them is self-luminous. Self-luminosity belongs only to the Divine consciousness.

The second point to know is that the Divine consciousness alone is all-pervading. None of the other planes is all-pervading, howsoever large or big they may be – they have certain limitations. And because the Divine consciousness is all-pervading, omnipresent, it is also omnicient. All knowledge in the world, scientific, medical, botanical or whatever, has its source in the Divine. Only those who can intuitively go to the higher planes can carry out the best researches, compose the best poetry, write the best literature. It is the link with the Divine that gives the special quality and which they express in their everyday life. The Divine consciousness is omniscient, self-luminous, omnipresent and because it is omniscient and omnipresent, it is also omnipotent.

Now according to yogic experiences, the Divine has a thousand attributes – He is all-health, He is all-knowledge, He is all-aesthetic sense. When we meditate on a particular aspect of the Divine, that particular aspect awakens in us. This is a very great principle of meditation.

But the first question is how to get in contact with the Divine consciousness. As I told you, the initial step is to awaken your dormant consciousness and this is done by meditating on Light. You meditate as if you are sitting in the sun – this is a preliminary step, not a very high or an advanced stage – as if you are sitting in the sun or, if that is not yet possible, you may do 'tretak' on the tip of a candle. I tell you it is very effective. If a person concentrates on the tip of a lighted candle, he will go quite far. It is only a question of time and consciousness. Even better would be to meditate on the sun. Though the Divine consciousness is a million times more luminous than the sun, to begin with, it is easier to contemplate on a physical object and even if it is night, it does not matter, you should feel as if you are sitting inside the sun. You should try to become like an empty vessel; you see, an open pot has the sky inside and the sky all around. So you fill yourself with Light and surround yourself with this Light. Then, only the outer form remains and in this form you apply your will, you concentrate that this form will absorb the Light and will become luminous. Try, and you will see the result. The interesting aspect is the result of the meditation, if you do it right; even if you cannot do it completely right in the beginning, the result will come though it may be a little delayed. This is not a mere physical exercise, it is something much more deep. The important thing is to meditate on this Light, as if you are sitting in the sun and as though you give yourself entirely, you fill yourself with this Light and feel it around you and your entire body absorbs the Light.

After this, you offer your meditation to the Supreme, to the Supreme who is self-luminous and immobile. So it is always good to sit in a posture, a posture which is comfortable and in which you can be immobile. It does not matter if you have a support or are without support. Without support, the posture is best. You put your hands on your knees and make you body neither stiff nor too relaxed, but just right. This is the best position, but you need not bother too much if you cannot sit thus. Some people are accustomed to another posture and they can follow whichever suits them. But immobility of the physical body and immobility of the consciousness are very essential. Both are brought about by the action of the will. The will is very important in meditation.

You *will*: "I want my body to be immobile." You *will*: "I want my consciousness to be immobile". The will is the 'Agni'. In our Vedas, Agni is 'Chit-Shakti', it is not the physical Agni. The will is the Agni. This exercise is tapasya and the more you put your will in the direction of the Divine, the better is the result. So you meditate on the Light within and the Light around you. Saturate your body with the Light, sit still and offer the meditation to the Divine: "You, O Lord, meditate through me. I do not know. You are the Param Guru, you are the Supreme Guide." This is the first step.

The second step is to see this Light in everything. If you have a guru, meditate on the guru in a twofold manner: the guru in your heart and you in the guru's heart. In this way the guru's consciousness combines with yours. When the two combine, the benefits of the guru's consciousness automatically come to you. That is the principle behind the Indian idea of "diksha". A guru gave his disciple diksha, that is, he communicated his consciousness to the disciple. If, after a few years, the disciple progressed sufficiently, he too got the right to have disciples because by that time his unity with the guru's consciousness had become complete and he had gathered in himself spiritual strength.

In our Indian system, when a succession of gurus gave the diksha, the real diksha, it gave rise to the 'parampara'. You will find some parampara having 150 names. And you will be surprised to find there the names of some of the greatest men in India, because all of them have had diksha in some form or the other for their spiritual growth. Whatever the guru had achieved he passed on to his disciples. It did not become less, it increased and it was passed on.

So you offer yourself to the Divine that He should meditate through you. Then you widen yourself and feel that the Divine is in everything. You tell yourself that the Divine is in everything. Slowly your consciousness expands and widens and you feel that the Divine is in the room, in Delhi, in all the people in India, in the world, in the sun, moon, sky, the stars, as far and wide as you can spread, even beyond the universe. Sri Aurobindo says there is a consciousness which existed even before the universe was born. So there is no limit to your expansion. You go on expanding, expanding, expanding till you melt in the Divine, till you lose your identity in the Divine. This is the first step – to see the Divine *in* everything.

It is initially a kind of imagination, a visualisation, a will with which you start. This kind of imagination and visualisation gradually opens the door and it becomes a living fact which, in a sense, you actually start experiencing. Later, you do not have to meditate on this, you do not have to visualise that, you do not have to imagine things. They actually happen.

After you have carried on this meditation for a few days (how long this takes depends on each person), you have to get yourself settled in a wide consciousness. The second step in meditation is to see *everything* in the Divine. When you come to the second aspect of meditation, you will be surprised to know that while standing in your room, you feel as if the sun is moving in your consciousness, the cars are moving in your consciousness, the planes are flying in your consciousness. Once you are settled completely in this consciounsess everything becomes different. Then, when you want to direct it and Sri Aurobindo says it can be done – directing one's consciousness to some general in Spain or somebody in France or Russia – and if your consciousness is enlarged, it becomes easier to put it at the desired point. But if it is not widened, how will you direct it? So, when we come to the aspect of work, we will try to understand the advantages of this enlarging and widening of the consciousness.

To recapitulate: the first step is to see the Light, the Divine *in* everything, the second is to see *everything* in this Light, the Supreme Light, and the third is to see everything *as* the Divine.

That is the most important object of meditation. But here comes the crux. How do you see everything *as* the Divine? Now, one day you see a friend, say Mr. X. He is wearing a suit. The next day, he comes in a different suit but you know he is Mr. X; the third day he comes in yet another suit, but you know he is Mr. X. So, once you arrive at these two initial stages of meditation, you slowly start realising that in every human being the light is shining, that every human being is an embodied soul and that mind, vital and body – manomaya koṣa, pranamaya koṣa and annamaya koṣa – are like your shirt, your bunian and your suit. But you see the soul and when you see the soul you say he is Mr. X, he is the Divine.

Everything is the Divine – "Sarvaṁ khalvidaṁ brahma". Everything is the Divine. When you come to the third stage repeat to yourself, "Sarvaṁ khalvidaṁ brahma" – everything is Brahman. "I am Brahman", "I am Brahman". Then you start repeating the Mantra 'OM'. Though we are speaking of the third stage, you can do it even in the first stage, because OM removes obstacles. OM is the sound of the Supreme which removes obstacles on the path of realisation of the Supreme. But you must decide on one of the two ways, as if you are calling Him or as if He is reciting the mantra in you. You are not reciting it, it is as if the Divine sound is coming through your mouth and through your body. Then it is effective. In OM you abdicate your ego, in OM you abdicate the sense of 'I am doing'. In OM the more you feel that He is working through you, the greater is the result. So with these three meditations you start: "Sarvaṁ khalvidaṁ brahma", "Ahaṁ brahma asmi" and "OM".

As a result of this type of meditation, a kind of peace, a kind of luminosity, a kind of intuition, a number of benefits will follow. You will be absolutely surprised to find that things will start happening in your life. But in this consciousness, you cannot say that for half an hour I will do this and for the rest of the twenty-three and a half hours I will do what I like. What you achieve in meditation you have to keep expressing during the day, throughout the day, through concentration. Your daily activities, as the Mother has said, are like an anvil on which you are being tested – whether what you are trying to gain in meditation, you are trying to retain during the day and going to the next step the next day, or you fall off each time.

It is a true aspiration to want the Divine to be active in you, but you should be completely surrendered to Him. When you take this attitude, three things happen. In the first stage you feel something, some Presence, guiding you, helping you all the time. In the second stage you find your actions are becoming more effective but the feeling of 'I am doing', 'I am meditating', is present; that has not gone even at this stage. The feeling of 'I am doing' persists. I am doing it by the Divine Grace; but 'I am doing'. This "I-ness" still remains.

A third stage comes when all sense of separative ego disappears. You are one with the Divine and it is He who acts through you using you as an instrument. For instance, when a letter comes it is not you who read it but the Divine reads it through you. He communicates it to you. Your consciousness gets divided – one is a witness consciousness which sees, and the other which acts. You find that whatever has to happen the Divine is making it happen. If He wants something to be said through your mouth, He does so. You say, "O.K., you will be all right", and a sick person becomes all right. But it is the Divine who is speaking through you. Your consciousness only sees things happening. You do not have to do any kriyā. At that level, the feeling of 'I am doing', goes away completely.

This is also not the last stage; there is yet another. This fourth stage is Sri Aurobindo's unique contribution to spiritual endeavour. But Sri Aurobindo says that you cannot say that I will give up these three and go directly to the fourth stage. There is a short cut, but not such a short one that you can jump over all the intermediate stages. So the fourth stage is when the Divine actually descends in your body and transforms it. That stage has not yet come, but it is sure to come. According to Sri Aurobindo *that* future is bound to come. It has come a little closer, you may say five percent, but the day has yet to come when the human body becomes a body of light. And for that, meditation is again an important means, so that the Divine consciousness may dwell in the human body. According to Sri Aurobindo, it is the Divine consciousness that has solidified itself in the material body. Just as hydrogen and oxygen become vapour and water, ice, and so on, by a reverse process they can again become hydrogen and oxygen. So by certain practices, you can awaken this Divine consciousness even in the physical body, leading to a physical transformation. The aim of physical work is to make the body conscious, each cell of the body conscious, the aim of mental work is to make the mind conscious and luminous and the aim of vital work, the will, is to make the vital being luminous and conscious.

Even before you get the contact with the Divine, you may want to have the Divine guidance; at least guidance in your day-to-day life. In the present complex life of man there is only one right way of thinking and there are a million wrong ways. All your values, all your notions of right and wrong, based on either religion or social thought, all are imperfect, none is valid. The only valid thing is what the Divine wills. But how do you listen to the Divine's voice even before you get the contact, even before all these developments of consciousness take place? This is a very important question: how to get the realisation in your daily life, so that your personality, your daily activities get integrated. Getting this guidance is, what I would call, an 'inward journey'.

First, let us take the body. The physical body is connected with the physical world through the eyes, the ears, the nose, the hands; all these are connected with the physical world. Then we have the vital body. Some psychological systems group everything beyond the physical body – the vital body, the mental body, the psychic, the soul – under the astral body and they are all looked upon as parts of the astral body. You have a vital body which is just around your physical body and it has a current, it has a luminosity. All the emotions arise in the vital body. The vital body is linked with our physical body through the nerves. The vital nerves and the physical nerves are connected to each other. And it is the vital nerves which receive sensations, physical nerves are only the means. In the vital body you are connected with the vital world. In meditation, if you can withdraw to your vital body, you can get in contact with the vital beings. In the vital world, you can make friends there and be effective on the physical world.

You can then withdraw to the mental world (the mental world is yellow in colour, the vital world is red or purple), and in the mental world, you have the mental beings, as also the hostile forces, what we call the 'asuras' who give you wrong thoughts, wrong emotions. In the mental plane you see both types of beings, the good and the bad. So you must know how to withdraw from the mental world, how to visit it and what to do there. It is very simple.

The will which you exercise while you are in your physical consciousness, that same will, if you exercise when you are in a higher consciousness becomes many times more effective. Suppose you have a problem. Some people get angry all the time, some people have other problems, even physical problems. If you can rise to a higher level and will from that level, you will find the result is much quicker, even instantaneous. That is how a guru helps, because he wills from a higher level for a disciple, establishing a link between his consciousness and that of the disciple.

So, in the mental world you see the mental beings and then you go to the other worlds, the higher mental and beyond, right up to the Overmental, which is the world of gods. This is sky-blue in colour. All the gods, Shiva, Vishnu, you will see them there. And colours are there also, you know. Then comes the Supramental world, which is the world of the Divine. So it is possible for you to actually go to each plane. The inner plane from which you can get guidance and which is a part of the Divine, is the psychic plane. Its colour is pink.

To come back, through centuries people have meditated and they have seen the same form, they have seen the same colours. When Sri Aurobindo was in Chandanagar He saw some goddesses in His meditation. It was later, when He was in Pondicherry that He identified them as Ila, Bharati, Mahi and Saraswati, the Vedic goddesses, the goddesses of Intuition, Intuitive Power and Revelation. There have been not one but a number of cases like this. To give you another example of the inner world, one day the Mother told us that when She was in France She used to see many gods and goddesses. But She never saw Ganesh. So She wondered whether Ganesh had a trunk or it was pure imagination. She went into a trance and saw a golden red figure with a big trunk, floating through the air. She asked, "Who are you?" and he replied, "Mother, I am Ganesh." The Mother of course can do it. All of us also can do it, but we do not try. That is the whole trouble.

As you withdraw to higher and higher planes, you make contacts, contacts on each plane, and each contact – you see, the external life only expresses what is in your inner life – you utilise in everyday life. This inward journey is a very important part of meditation. You must learn how to withdraw. As you withdraw, as you go to the higher planes, a little of the higher planes descends into the lower, always improving your life.

The more you aspire the more will descend but it is never the full descent. A full descent makes people mad sometimes, because they cannot absorb it. It should be allowed to descend as far as possible. Also, you should not pull and try to bring down the Force before you are ready to receive It.

If you want to know how to make the inward journey, you just sit, as I said earlier, in a position which is comfortable. I feel this posture is best when your body is evenly balanced with hands on your knees. And apply your will. Always before starting, offer your meditation to the Divine, pray to Him: "You must teach me today." Also, before you go into meditation, always decide for what purpose and on what you want to meditate. Then, you *will* that your consciousness from your feet is being taken up and coming to your heart; you *will* that your consciousness from your head is being gathered and coming to your heart; then the consciousness from both your hands, you *will*, you really *will* – because the *will* acts on the inner plane – and put it in your heart. This is most interesting. You will not probably be able to move your body or even a finger. It will be impossible, because the consciousness has withdrawn and you will be able to move only when it returns.

After you have made yourself immobile, you then turn inward – what we call 'antermukhi' – you turn inward as if you are looking within or you go upward. You then gather up your consciousness and start willing that you want to go to the next plane. You can go to fourteen planes in this way, not seven but fourteen, and even twenty-one, if you also count the intermediate planes. And you withdraw (it is only a question of practice) and be quiet. Observe, but do not try to interpret. As soon as you try to interpret, everything gets spoilt because your mind becomes active. After sometime you put your consciousness into what is called rest or sleep – quiet, quiet, quiet – just immobile. Again you withdraw to the next plane, but do not forget to put the earlier consciousness into immobility and in this way, you can go to each of the fourteen or even twenty-one planes.

Each plane has its own form, each plane has its own colour, each plane has its own time-sense. It is different from others. You know the story about Brahma. Brahma had passed only one day and one night when the whole creation entered pralaya. This is not false, it is not imagination. At that level it *is* one day and one night, the whole creation lasts for one day and one night and then it is destroyed. That is pralaya. At our level it is twenty-four hours for a day and a night. So in each plane it changes.

In this inward journey you finally arrive to the psychic, the Divine Presence in your heart. When you reach there, you may be confronted with two possibilities: you can either enter or you face a wall and you cannot enter. Then you *will* that the wall should break. Your will must be developed in a very strong manner, in a concentrated manner, not willing ten different things at the same time. Suddenly you break into a hall full of light. Once you have this experience, there is no doubt left in your mind. So long as you have a doubt there is a ninety percent chance that the experience has not fully taken place but only a very little reflection of it has come. But when you really have the experience the doubt does not exist. This is the best way to get the inner guidance. That is also what the Gita says when Arjuna tells Sri Krishna: "Tvayā hṛṣkeśa hṛdi sthitena yathā niyukto'smi tathā karomi." ("According as I am appointed by Thee, O Hrishikesha! seated in my heart, So I act".)

But this is not sufficient. Now the second aspect of your life is meditation during work. Meditation during work gives meaning to life. You can meditate during work, especially in Sri Aurobindo's yoga. People asked Him: "If we meditate and remain in a very high peaceful consciousness and do not work, will we get transformed?" Sri Aurobindo replied, "Not at all." If you want the transformation of your mind, life and body, if you want the transformation of the collective life, work is necessary. Once you decide to work for the Divine, the Divine consciousness descends in you. You do not have to meditate. Meditation will automatically come.

I remember one day, about thirty-five years ago, I told the Mother, "Mother, I cannot meditate." She replied, "Meditation is not necessary for you." After a year or two, one day I was meditating in the corridor outside Her room and She came and stood before me. I did not know She was standing as I was in deep meditation. Then She stamped Her foot and made a sound. I opened my eyes. I said, "Oh, Mother, I did not see you!" She said, "You meditate very well." I said, "Mother, I do not know how this happened." You see it just happened on its own.

Once you take to spiritual life, work done with the right attitude is as good as meditation. It leads to meditation, it leads to the link with the Divine. Meditation is not the goal, it is the means. The goal is to make your life perfect, the goal is to increase your capacities and faculties and channelise them in the day-to-day life and ultimately get in contact with the highest in you – the Divine Himself. You have to decide that you want to dedicate your life to the Divine. This is the only wise thing to do, the rest is all without importance or meaning.

As I told you before, you cannot isolate meditation from your life. Meditation is a part of your life. If your attitude is correct, you have the right meditation, you do the right thing in life. If the attitude is wrong, everything will go wrong. The correct attitude is only this: all your being, all you are, all you have, all you are capable of doing, belong to the Divine. Once you do this, you will have a big advantage. This is a way which I found very effective. You see, normally when your mind thinks of this object, that object, sometimes even wrong objects, you try to restrain it. I once read in one of the books in Marathi of a great saint who said that when the mind is restless, we should try to see the Divine within. And I tell you this is the most effective way. Then the vibrations change, things change, as if the whole world has opened to you and everything changes for you. Instead of trying to restrain the mind all the time, you should try to see the Divine everywhere. Normally the mind is not quiet. Instead of trying to hold it back – you know it is like a wild horse – you allow it to go but you put the Divine everywhere as if the Divine is in front of you. You will find that the mind automatically falls silent.

Meditation in work has to start with dedication to the Divine. You must get into the practice of meditating with open eyes. The best way to meditate with open eyes is to concentrate on your psychic centre and meditate on 'OM' or Light; or on Sri Aurobindo, your guru, Sri Krishna or Rama – whoever is close to you – as if he is seated in your heart, really seated. What the Gita says is absolutely true. It is on a luminous form that you meditate – on Sri Krishna, on Sri Aurobindo or on your guru as the Divine. If you think that your guru is only a physical being, it will not help. Even if he is a physical being, he is the representative of the Divine.

Then your mind automatically remains concentrated. Abdicating your ego, you try to listen from that consciousness, try to speak from that consciousness, try to see from that consciousness. Once you start doing this, you will find that the guidance comes to you and that is how you get integrated in action. Once you get integrated, once your consciousness is concentrated, the actions become automatic. And this power is enhanced in a collectivity. That is what the Mother meant when She said that if twelve people of goodwill unite in their aspiration and call the Divine, the Divine would manifest upon earth – that is the charm of collective meditation – and the world would change. But they must be people with realised consciousness who have the Light and who would be acting together. These are the conditions and the world would change.

In meditation, in work, we have to do many things. But there is one important thing – meditation before and during sleep. You know, when you have a problem you sleep on it and when you wake up in the morning you find it is solved. Or sometimes you find you get up in the morning feeling very fatigued, you did not have proper sleep, all because you did not do the proper meditation before going to sleep, you did not prepare yourself before going to sleep. Meditation before sleep need not be done sitting, you can do it lying down. It is a very simple meditation, very simple. Lie down in bed; if you have an 'iṣṭa-deva(tā)', imagine you are lying down in His lap, because in meditation all your consciousness has to be concentrated only on the Divine.

Once you are in contact with the Divine then He will use you as He wants to, for His work in the world. You cannot say that you want Him to use you in this way or that. Then you are dictating terms to Him. If you want Him to come down in His full glory in your mind, vital and body and in your daily life, in your daily activities, then you have to surrender to Him. If you say that you want Him to direct you in this thing only or that you want Him to channelise your energy only through this way, you limit Him and you limit your life, you limit your action. If you really want to act without any limitations, you have to offer yourself completely to Him. If you have a problem, place it before Him after this meditation, offer it to Him and go to sleep; then see what happens. Suppose you want to be conscious in your sleep, you can do this and aspire that sleep brings you rest and relaxation. One-third of your life you are sleeping, say for seven to eight hours daily. If you meditate before sleeping, you will see that the results will follow.

One of the best things you can do before going to sleep is to pray for your health, because in yoga health is very important. You have to prolong your life for greater and greater progress, otherwise the progress will only start again in your next life. In the intermediate period between death and rebirth, there is no progress. If you really want to achieve the maximum or if you want to give your maximum to mankind – whichever way you want to put it, at a higher level, both are the same – or if you want to realise and serve the Divine, you must lead a healthy life and be able to prolong it for as long as it is necessary for the Divine work. Never think of cutting it short even by a day.

Every moment there is an opportunity for progress. Why do you want to retard your own progress? There is nothing wrong in asking the Divine for health, for a long life or for anything else. You need not hide things from the Divine. "No, no, why should I ask for material things from Him." This is another form of egoism. If you have it, it is foolish. He is the only one who is all-compassionate and He is the only one who is nearest and dearest to you. If you do not ask Him, whom are you going to ask? There are many people who want to hide things from the Divine; something in their ego says no, I do not want to ask anything from the Divine, as if they are going to give some help to the Divine! Whatever be your problem – suppose you have a friend who is sick – the best thing to do is to place the problem in all sincerity before the Divine. Then the Divine will either cure your friend or will change your perspective. Once your perspective changes the problem for you gets solved; for the other person, it may not get solved. The Divine may also tell you why the illness has come to him and why it was necessary. The whole perspective changes. Really, the whole problem is solved for you. This thing is sure.

Another aspect of sleep is, as I said, to make it conscious. In the morning when you get up (this is in the early stages), write down your experiences of the night. You should meditate at night before sleeping and after getting up and you should write what you dreamt during the night. And think of it backwards, what happened last, what happened before that, and so on, from the last sequence to the first, not from the first to the last. After a little practice you will be able to recall and you will become conscious in your sleep, conscious of your dreams. You can slowly change your personality by the aid of this exercise.

The next thing in your daily routine after you wake up, is your bath. In meditation, everything is included; try it for two days and you will see the result. You offer the bathwater to the Divine Presence in you, saying: "Let this water awaken the Divine consciousness in me, in every action." Every action has to be offered in a meditative effort and in every action you have to lead your life not in an ordinary way but by remaining in the highest consciousness, so that you receive the Divine Guidance all the time. Even the clothes you are going to put on in the morning, let the Divine decide which coat you are going to wear today. So, unless you go beyond the mind and channelise, unless you practise all the time to seek the inner guidance and make it a habit of your life at every moment, unless you make this effort constantly, your meditation will be of little use to you.

Then comes your daily physical exercise. People think that asanas and pranamaya are yoga. You know the two standard books on Hatha Yoga are *Hatha Yoga Pradipika* and *Gherand Sanhita*. *Hatha Yoga Pradipika* is very emphatic. It says that those who do not do meditation, that is, those who do not know Raja Yoga and only do Hatha Yoga, are wasting their time. So it is extremely important to know that one asana done in one way becomes an exercise and the same asana becomes yoga if you meditate while doing it. Without meditation it is not possible. This you have to do carefully. Whether you are taking gymnastic exercises or doing asanas or playing tennis, remain absorbed in the Light. If you remain in this meditative mood, in this meditative consciousness, you will play better, your muscles will develop better, everything will be different for you – all the time. You should feel it is not you who are opening your eyes, you are not blinking, you are not raising your hand, it is the Divine in you who is doing so, His Light is entering your body and the whole movement is becoming conscious. Further, you should see that in your everyday activities you retain it. You may do meditation for half an hour but try to keep this meditative attitude throughout the day and it will bring you much better results.

Now we come to food. People do not know that food has consciousness also; not only vitamins and nutrition, but consciousness. We absorb some consciousness from the food itself. The Mother has said that you get the consciousness of the food you eat. Some of this comes from the people who cook and some from the environment. In India we have the system of prasad. When you actually invoke the Divine Presence in the food and say to the Divine: "You take it", it is actually the consciousness part of it that gets purified and then if you eat the food, it brings you a new consciousness.

I would like to share one small experience with you. I once told the Mother, "Mother, I can remain concentrated on the Divine very well during work, during the day, but I forget Him when I am eating." The Mother said, "You must be eating with many people." I said, "That is true." After that, for a whole month (this is before I had joined the Ashram), I ate alone and without speaking, and I tell you the result was marvellous for my health. So if you are serious, really serious about wanting to progress, it is better to exercise some restraint during mealtimes. A day may come when it will make no difference but in the early stages, it does. You should eat as if the Light is entering your body, as if your whole body is becoming luminous and the food is bringing you closer to the Divine and awakening the Divine consciousness in you. If you do it in a concentrated manner, you will see the result even in a short time. You will also see the difference in your life, in your body, in your mind. You may not see it today, you will see it after some time, but one has to be serious and sincere.

Another aspect is speech. You must remain concentrated when you speak, so that only what the Divine wants to convey gets spoken, is spoken through your mouth and through your voice. If you really practise this, you will not have to think about what to speak, it will automatically come and what you say will happen because He would speak through you. It is said that there are siddhis where, if you meditate on the throat centre, you can conquer hunger. So there are a number of meditations, each having a different result. But the thing to do is to bring Light into your mouth, right down to the navel centre, and do not speak till you have saturated yourself with this Light. Just saturate yourself, saturate yourself more and more and then when you speak, let your mind be quiet. The less you speak, the more your mind will be quiet. So cultivate the habit of not speaking uselessly. Again, it is a habit to be cultivated and you must cultivate it with a lot of perseverance.

The Mother once said to me – and the Mother was already on that high level of consciousness – that when She used to go to Sri Aurobindo She would tell Herself that if there was nothing of importance She would do without telling Him. And She added that eight times out of ten She would come back without speaking. Even though She was at that level, She exercised so much restraint on Herself. We all have to exercise restraint on ourselves. A restraint on speech is a very big help in doing mantra-japa and also vice versa. The more you recite the mantra in your day-to-day activities, the greater is your contact with the higher consciousness.

I now come to actual work. Some of you may be engineers, some doctors, some architects, some in politics, some in business.

How can this meditation be put into practice in your business? With the work aspect we come also to occult knowledge. Once a person was ill and the Mother told me to take him to Mr. X. "If he just looks at him, he will improve," She said. I took him and the man got well. I asked myself what is the principle behind this? He looked at him, like any other person would, then how did this man improve? I thought what a useless life we lead and what great wisdom, power, happiness are in store for us which we are missing. So I asked the person – he was an orthodox Indian priest who recently died – and he explained his theory to me (he and I had become very, very close). He said that it was a question of vibration and, before putting his patient in contact with the vibration – this vibration was achieved over years of practice – he would meditate that the Divine is in everybody and the Divine is all-health. There is no disease in the Divine, so there cannot be any disease in man. He said that when he looked at a person he did not see any disease. All he saw was health as the Divine was in the man. So this concentration can improve health.

The Mother has said many thing about healing. She said She used to see Sri Aurobindo sitting and looking at a person when a person with some disease was brought to Him. And something would come out of Sri Aurobindo's body and, just as you take out a thorn, He would pluck out the disease from the other person. Healing has so many aspects. In each case you have to invoke the power of the Divine and you get the result.

If you are in business, the Divine wants you to be prosperous, but you should not consider money as belonging to you, or become its slave. If you have become a slave of money, it is rather dangerous. You must consider it as belonging to the Divine.

There is a force of prosperity, there is a force of healing, there are all kinds of forces. Saraswati is the goddess of organisation. She is traditionally a goddess of learning, which is generally known, but she is essentially the goddess of organisation and perfection in work. If the power of Saraswati descends in you (the Mother always used to tell us that it was the power of Saraswati that was frequently in the front, in Her working), and if this power develops in you, then when you see a person, you will come to know everything about him, what is his destiny, what are the things he should do and can do best. You will be able to put people in their proper places. Without this power you will be only creating confusion as we are doing everywhere. We look at things in a subjective manner – how this is going to help us or harm us – and we decide and act accordingly. This can never be correct. We are messing up our lives and messing up other people's lives. So, a correct kind of meditation is one of the powerful ways to lead a perfect life. By developing our faculties through meditation we make our own life fruitful, progressive, integrated and compact. It is also the best way of helping others.

Now I come to the aspect of death. One of the practices of meditation is to learn to separate your astral body from your physical body. The astral body is normally very fluid and it is the physical body that gives it a material centre for action in the world. The first thing is to make your astral body concrete enough to separate itself from the physical body and to keep it in that concrete form. That is what the Buddha said, when he had the realisation, that he could almost see an armour of light around his body. It actually becomes like that, it actually becomes compact. By exercising your will you can cultivate it; it is flexible, you can expand it and direct it as you will. That is how the gurus in India put their emanations around their disciples, something of their own emanated and they put it around the disciples.

It is important to learn how to take your astral body out of your physical body. It is taken out from either the side of the body or from the back; that is the usual way. The fear of death vanishes after this meditation. If you can take the astral body outside the physical body at will, and re-enter the physical body at will, the fear of death can be removed. This also helps if you want to help others, to communicate with them more effectively. Moreover, it can enable you to communicate with people who have left their bodies. That is another aspect.

Meditation helps you in all aspects. I do not know of a single aspect where it does not help. All the books written by the great yogis which form our Tantric literature – not the Tantric literature which you see in the shops everywhere today, which is, I would say, a great distortion of our knowledge, even the books you see on mathematics, the books on ayurveda – how did they get this knowledge? Our forefathers did not carry out any research in the laboratories. All this knowledge came to them by intuition. They held an object and as they meditated on it, the answer came. The Mother gave spiritual meanings to some eight hundred flowers and a number of them have the same significance as it was given by our forefathers about which the Mother did not know. *Tulsi* is devotion, *Dhatura* is tapasya. All these things She did not know before. How was this possible? If it is really intuition, knowledge cannot change. It will be the same answer to the same question on the same subject, even if it is found by different persons.

If you want to lead a fuller life, it is absolutely necessary to purify your consciousness through meditation, to get in contact with the Divine through meditation, to develop your inner capacities through meditation. As I told you, the mind is both universal and individual. There is the universal mind which is common to all but we are not aware of it, and there is the individualised mind. For example, one man knows French, one man knows English, one knows Hindi and one knows two languages. When a person speaks to you and even if you do not know his language, but because of your contact with the universal mind, his thoughts communicate to you and you can understand what he is saying. You may not be able to tell word for word, but the thought communicates. So, your life can become more useful through meditation.

Finally, we come to collective meditation. Collective meditation, as I told you, is for developing a collective soul, which can manifest in a collective manner. Now, in a collective meditation, if you invoke the Divine and if the Divine becomes the focal point of guidance and manifestation of the collective life, just think what would be the result. The answer is very simple. If the Divine becomes the focal point, He will put each person in the right place. And what better place can there be for a man than the one the Divine has created and for which he is most suited, which is his unique place here and which no one else can fulfil? Unless the social order changes and unless everyone is in his right place, social problems will never get solved. No law can solve them. Also, collective meditation should have a collective aspiration. If one person is thinking of one thing and another is thinking of something else, this will not help collective meditation. If there is a leader of the collective life who can open his consciousness to the Divine, and then project that consciousness in the collective group, the collective meditation will automatically be fruitful.

If you have any questions, I will answer them.

I did not quite understand how to offer everything to the Divine?

You see, each person offers according to the state of his consciousness at that time. You do not expect the same thing from everybody – from a child of two years, a child of six and a man of twenty. If a child of two, say your own son, comes to you and talks about things in his childish manner, you will tell him, "O.K., O.K." But if a man of twenty comes and says the same thing, you will tell him, "No, you are not right." So also with the Divine. He accepts the offering from each person according to his level of consciousness. If a person is at level A, He does not expect him to do things from level Z; and if a person is at level Z, He would not expect things from him from level Y.

I will show you the easiest way to offer, so that you can do what suits your nature. And the Divine will accept. This faith you must have. He will accept in His own way, because He would not expect you to do more than you are capable of doing. Let us start with a simple example.

Suppose you want to offer your food to God. What is the first step you will take? You know, in yoga you require a great sincerity. You cannot cook in any way you like, choose anything you like, and offer it to God. (I am talking at the lowest level, I am not talking at the highest level.) What is the first step? Sincerely you say: "Tu bata tuje āaj kya khanna hai? Tu nehi bataigya toh mera kesur nehi." ("You tell me what You want to eat today. If You don't, then it is not my fault.") When you reach out to Him, the Divine holds you by His hand and lets Himself be felt and guides you. It is for Him to decide what is good for you. So the first thing is to keep quiet and pray: "Please guide me. What should be cooked today, what is it that we can offer You today?" Now, naturally your attitude should be that you are cooking for Him, as if you are actually doing the cooking for Him – whoever cooks, it may be your servant. If the servant cooks, then there is a problem, for you cannot guide him too much. That is why, I must tell you, you must be very careful. One day the Mother told me, "You must not eat the food you are taking because the servants cook it. This is not good. I will give you". I was lucky, She started giving me food Herself.

You should avoid food which brings lethargy, laziness, heaviness and have food which gives you light and energy.

You have to see that you cook it yourself or that it is cooked under the best circumstances. Suppose the food is cooked. When it comes to you, you meditate on the Divine Presence in you, in the food in front of you, in any form – Rama, Krishna, Light, OM, Sri Aurobindo – it does not make any difference, the Divine is One. Invoke the Divine Presence in your own way, in whatever way: "You are in this food. You are in this body, You are all around me. I am nourishing this body for You. Awaken me to Your Presence. Let every cell of this body be conscious of You. Let this food bring to this body Your consciousness." And you surrender each part of your body.

This is the minimum which anybody can do. For the maximum, let us leave if for today, because that can be done only when you come to a higher level. Otherwise the whole discussion will be only theoretical.

What happens to the vital when it is suddenly cut off by accident?

By accident? You know, there are two possibilities. When the human life is cut off by accident, normally desires remain and the astral body hovers around, either at the place of the accident or around the members of the family whom the person loved. It hovers around. It does not easily leave because the person's life has not been completed. It has been cut short without having gone through its full span. Sometimes, it even enters the body of a person whom he loved, if that person allows it to enter. The Mother once told me that we may love a person very dearly but when he dies we start getting afraid of him. Life can be cut short unnaturally in two ways. One is by accident and the other by suicide. If it is by accident, the vital body remains and this creates a very bad situation. Something has to be done for the vital to become quiet and help it on its onward journey. It is not the same as when one has a natural death. It is a big shock to the vital.

You have told us that during meditation there is one stage when you have to surrender. What is the principle of surrendering to God?

Principle or method?

Method.

You see it is again like playing a game of tennis or doing anything else. Each one has to do it in his own way. But there is one general method which I may tell you. Let us again start from the bottom – not from the top. Three questions arise: What is it that has to be surrendered? Who is it who is going to surrender, and to whom is he going to surrender? What is our concept of God? Who is going to surrender to that god? There is a very old saying: "Kasmai devāya havisā vidhema". Which God should we worship? Then again in the Vedas it is said, "Atma hota". It is the Atma who is going to surrender. You are not going to surrender completely and truly with your mind. Your soul, your Central Being, your true Self is going to surrender. But a beginning can be made at any level. Let us go step by step. The easiest surrender is material. You sit quietly and pray: "My body, my spectacles, my clothes, whatever money I have, my furniture, my house, all, all belong to You, O God, and I will look after them as belonging to You."

What will happen when you take this first attitude? You will waste nothing as it all belongs to Him. You will waste nothing. You will keep everything as nice and beautiful as you can, because it all belongs to Him. So materially, this is your highest. By this attitude of surrender, you will find that when you say, "I offer it", something will happen to you. He reaches out to you. Your clothes will begin to have a consciousness. I had said earlier that the talk on meditation is incomplete – we did not talk about how to meditate so that your clothes may awaken to the Divine consciousness. This is one of the important meditations in daily life. It acts as a protection. By surrender many things automatically awaken in you. God has given one eternal promise to the world: "Whatever you offer to Me, I will accept." If you offer 'halal' (poison) to Shiva, he accepts even that.

I now come to the second offering – the offering of your vital. What are you ultimately going to offer? The vital is a mixture. Materially, it is easy; vitally, it is difficult. The vital, the emotional side of every man today is a mixture – a mixture of generosity and greed, of anger and peace. This is because of the evolution from the lowest to the present half-animal, half-man state. When you offer your vital to the Supreme Light, to the Supramental Omniscient Consciousness, it is done by offering your will. The vital offering is done by offering your will. You pray: "I want to do what You, O Lord, want me to do. I do not want to be generous even." How are you going to be generous at the Divine's expense? Once you offer everything to Him, you have no right to be generous even. You have to be strict and disciplined. You will be surprised to find that you will feel as if He has accepted you, accepted you overnight. Things will start happening in your life.

The vital offering is the offering of the will; and the physical aspect of this is by meditating on the light in the vital and offering. What we actually do while offering is that we lie flat on the ground and offer our pranam – "sashatanga". This is your physical-vital offering. You meditate on the Divine in whatever form in which you have faith, and offer your entire body – offer your palms, offer your wrists, offer everything (it may take some time), right upto the tips of your fingers. That is sashatanga, the eight parts of your body touching the ground. And you get up feeling a different man.

When you put things into fire, they get purified. Similarly, when you put things into Light, the Supreme Light, the darkness is dissolved. You meditate on the Divine Presence in you and you offer yourself to that Presence or you meditate on the Divine Presence outside you and offer. Offering to the Divine Presence outside you is not as effective as offering to the Divine Presence within you. And it has to be done at every point. As you offer, you will find that your offering is like the sprouting of a seed – something has emerged and your whole being has opened to the Light – something like that. You feel it – it cannot be hidden. Quietly you go on offering. This is the physical-vital offering because it is both, vital and physical – vital on one side, and on the other, physical-material – like the physical-vital offering of your body by lying down on the ground – sashatanga – and offering to the Divine. You do it for two days, you do not have to do it for a longer time, to see the result. If you really offer, as I told you, you will see the change in you when you get up.

Offering of the physical is easy, offering of the vital is easy, but offering of the mind is most difficult. You pray: "No thoughts should come to me except from You, O Lord. I offer my mind." So long as you have desires, so long as you have forgetfulness and not constant remembrance, so long as you cannot invoke the descent in you, your mental offering will never be complete. Mental offering is made complete by a descent. Descent is a sign that He has accepted your offering – 'śaktipāta', as we say in Sanskrit. This comes again by a great sincerity, and it comes maximum in the meditation before sleep. This is one of the best meditations of the day, the meditation before sleep, when you offer yourself completely. So the offering of the mind will consist of stopping the thinking process, of eliminating all formations in the memory. Memory creates saṁskārāḥ – you like something, you want to buy it. That has to be eliminated. Offer. You say: "I want to live every moment in Your consciousness. I do not want the past and the future to be linked to the present. Everything should be linked only to You, so that the future belongs to You."

Now, with these offerings, comes the most important result. Suppose you make an offering, let us say, at seven. What will you do at five minutes past seven? Will you go back to your old routine? I have offered, now let me go and have my game of cards, do a bit of chit-chatting or watch television. If you really want to progress you have to do the offering continuously. Once you have done the offering, is the next move going to come from His side or from your side? He has to guide you. Then, at every moment, whether you are eating, taking a bath or attending to a telephone call, something will awaken in your life to such an extent that you cannot have any doubt that He has really accepted you.

The Divine accepts us. But from our side, even after this so-called surrender, we continue with the old routine, as if we have not surrendered. That is the biggest mistake in our lives and it is the biggest hindrance in our progress on the spiritual path. Surrender is surrender. It is final. You cannot do anything unless it is His command. So He has got to give you the command. Otherwise, there will be chaos and it will not be your fault. He would have allowed the mess to happen. But from your side you have to take this stand: "Unless You guide me, O Lord, I am not going to do anything. In order to receive Your guidance I will remain concentrated, I will keep my inner surrender." And you will be surprised at the result.

Last time I related a small incident. I will repeat it to you now because it is a true incident. There is a big hotel in Calcutta. Someone had bought it from an Englishman, but there was some problem about inheritance, so the money was deposited into the court. It came to many lakhs. The heir to the old Englishman was his granddaughter. She came to Pondicherry and met me. She said, "I had never heard of your institution a month ago and now I am here." So I asked, "Well, what's the point?" She said, "Something is happening to me. I want to park my car but I see no place. Then suddenly I hear a voice saying, 'Look behind!' and I see somebody taking out his car. I go to a departmental store to purchase something. I may go over the whole store but ultimately, I come to the same place. Something seems to be guiding me all the time." I said, "How did it start?" (I am telling you about people who have not been long in yoga. That is why I say, have faith; once you truly surrender, He accepts.) She said, "You know, I am divorced from my husband and I loved him very dearly. I thought if I get another husband he may be worse. But I loved him so much, now my life has no meaning. Now what do I have to live for? I have money, but no love, no husband, no father. What is there to live for? And if God can do this to me, who will not do it to me? I cried and cried and after two days I said to myself, 'People say God is Omniscient. People say He can listen. I do not know if He listens. I feel no contact. But if You exist, I offer my life to You.' " And her life began to change. So this is how it is.

If our attitude is truly of surrender, He reaches out to us. When we open the window the sun comes to us; we do not go to it. So surrender opens our inner window and He is there – only we have closed Him out by our wrong surrender, by our ego. On the other hand, ego does not leave us till He comes. This you must always remember. Ego can become thin, it can become weak, but it will never leave you till the Divine comes. There is no intermediate period of the ego going and the Divine coming. The Divine comes and the ego goes. There is not a time-lag of even a split-second. Surrender is really a great step for opening to the Divine and removing the ego. So you surrender and then insist upon maintaining it. When you sit in your office – I do not know what work you do – you say: "I offer this work to You." You have to take your stand and then insist upon God to take His stand. Then you will see how things change. Before you even open a letter, you will know its contents and the reply you have to give. Actually everything will change for you.

There is one more aspect of surrender which you should understand. Human personality has many parts. All the parts do not get surrendered simultaneously. One part may surrender but other parts may not. But do not think that your surrender has receded. This is another part that has come forward and you offer it. Offer it. It may come in the form of a thought, it may come in the form of an attachment, it may come even in the form of sorrow. If you have really surrendered then there can be no joy, no sorrow. So, as other things arise in you, do not get disturbed. Go on offering. Offer it all. If the first decisive step is taken, all others will follow. It is only the initial step that is difficult to take.

How to do Japa

"Srīaravindaḥ śaraṇaṃ mama, OM, OM, OM."
"Śrīaravindaḥ śaraṇaṃ mama, OM, OM, OM."
"Glory to Thee, O Lord, who triumphest over every obstacle."
"Gloire à Toi, Seigneur, triomphateur de tous les obstacles."

In many spiritual disciplines there is a great stress laid on the importance of japa for spiritual progress. Japa means repeating a name or certain alphabets or certain mantras in a particular state of consciousness so that you get in contact with the power or force of the deity representing that mantra. If you get a contact early it means you have made quick progress in your japa. If you do not get a contact it means that the japa has not been successful. So the question is, how to do japa in order to make contact with a particular consciousness represented by a sound?

We will take a few examples. The first example is of OM. Now OM is the original sound, the vibration in the Divine Himself. The Divine is full of vibrations. One side of the Divine is static, the other side is dynamic, full of vibrations. When the original vibration *opens* it produces the sound 'AU'. when it *closes*, it produces the sound 'M'; that is how it becomes 'AUM' – open, close – open, close, 'AUM'.

One should make an effort to contact this vibration and bring the sound of OM to the physical plane. That means you become the vehicle of the descent of the highest consciousness on the material plane. In order to do this, you should first meditate on a golden or white light which is static and saturate your body with it. Then you saturate your breath, as if you are breathing in and breathing out that light.

For doing japa properly, you should start with an intense dynamic meditation. When you invoke this light in all the cells of your body and make yourself into a luminous block, you feel as if you are not reciting OM but your whole body is creating the sound of OM and that the Divine, through your body, is spreading the vibrations of OM and removing the darkness all around. It is in this spirit that OM should be recited and repeated.

The other method would be to call, as you call a person. I call G-O-V-I-N-D, like that; A-U-M, like that. The more sincere, the more concentrated the way you call, the better it will come. Both are effective in their own way.

The second is namajapa. You repeat Sri Aurobindo's name, you repeat Sri Krishna's name, Christ's name, any name according to your affinity – God is One. The importance here is not so much on the sound as on concentration. Sound is also important, but more important is concentration. When you say 'Śrīaravindaḥ śaraṇaṃ mama', you must meditate as if you are inside Sri Aurobindo's consciousness and when you say 'śaraṇaṃ', you should feel as if your whole being – mind, vital, physical – you are surrendering to Him and merging in Sri Aurobindo, so that His force can act through you. Otherwise, 'śaraṇaṃ mama' has no importance. If He is outside you and you are sitting separate from Him, and you say 'Aham śaraṇaṃ, Aham śaraṇaṃ', that is O.K., but that has a very limited force and benefit. But if you are inside Sri Aurobindo's consciousness and are reciting 'Śrīaravindaḥ śaraṇaṃ mama' then you are uniting with His consciousness. If more and more people unite, they will become radiating centres of this light. So whichever consciousness you want to invoke, "śaraṇaṃ mama" is a very powerful mantra.

The second japa would be when you take a particular name. OM is the sound of the 'Nirākāra'. But the Divine is also 'Sākāra' and 'Saguṇa'. When you remember Sri Aurobindo, Sri Krishna or Sri Rama, meditation should be in unity with them and when you say 'śaraṇaṃ mama', you should feel them, because the mantra gets its power by manana (thinking); 'manana mantra', as it is called. And the repetition invokes their consciousness in you. So this is another kind of mantra for which you do japa. Here the individual consciousness unites with a higher consciousness and when you are united with Him, Sri Aurobindo's powers, His capacities, come into you.

There is one more powerful mantra: "OM Namo bhagavate Sri Aravindāya." It is a very powerful mantra, but I will take it up separately, as I have not done it today.

The third is a mantra like the Gayatri Mantra, which has been recited in India through the centuries, and I think it is the most popular mantra in India. More than half the mantras that are recited are only Gayatri; all the other mantras put together will be less than half. Now the Gayatri Mantra is predominantly a mantra of meditation. If we do not meditate on light, how is the mantra going to be effective? Mantra adds to the meditation. So the third is a mantra like the Gayatri Mantra.

Then there are many other mantras – mantras for health, for

power, for knowledge, even mantras for recovering stolen things. All the mantras are meditative mantras. You have to be in an intense meditation and then repeat the mantra.

Another kind of mantra is the 'sound' mantra, where the sound itself has the power. Now the sound acquires a power if the guru gives it to you. If you merely take it from a book and do it, well, it may work but not as effectively as when the guru gives you a mantra because he puts you in contact with the power behind it. Among the most powerful sound mantras are: "Om, Hrim, Klim, Srim, Krām, Krim". Then there are sub-divisions of this. Every alphabet in Sanskrit is a mantra: 'Kum, Khum, Gum, Ghum, Chum, Chhum, Jum, Jhum.' I tell you they are very effective and very powerful.

By practising one mantra well, it is easier to practise the other mantras. If you get 'siddhi' in one mantra and if you do the japa properly, the other mantras will become effective for you very quickly. So the important thing in mantra japa is, to first select your mantra, select your meditation and then do it in the way shown to you by the person who gives you the mantra.

For the traditional mantras they used to say that if the mind wanders somewhere, repeat the mantra; repeat it three hundred times. And if again your mind goes somewhere, sit down again and repeat it. That was such a strict discipline that you yourself decided: "Oh, God, let not my mind wander, otherwise I will have to sit for eight hours in all. I won't be able to do it."

There are various ways of doing japa. Upto now, I have talked about the japa which has to be done with the spoken mantra. Japa could be done purely by mental repetition or visualisation of the mantra mentally. You write down the mantra as if in light and visualise it, you feel that the mantra itself is a deity or you repeat it in the mind or do both. The third is 'listening' to the sound without repeating as if the mantra is vibrating all around you, it is vibrating in every cell of your body 'OM, OM'.

Even if you start by repeating the mantra, this has to be done sometime or the other, when you have to listen to it, as if it is vibrating in you and around you. You will be surprised to find that after sometime, it actually starts vibrating. So, if you want to awaken the cells of your body one of the best ways is to let them pronounce the sound 'OM, OM, OM', and you will see what happens.

Who is a Real Guru

The guru-disciple relationship is one of the most important, a crucial part of spiritual life. A real guru is one who has had certain higher realisations – if possible the realisation of the Divine – and who is either egoless or whose ego is so subdued, that the Divine force and the higher powers can act through him. When a person comes to him for guidance, a guru should feel that the Divine is receiving the disciple through his mind, life and body, or rather that the Divine is receiving Himself through the guru and the disciple, both at the same time.

It is the Divine who uses the guru, a real guru, for the mantra to be given to the disciple, for the sadhana to be done and for the guidance to be given to him from time to time. This means that a guru should be a person who has a constant link with the Divine Consciousness. He should also have the capacity to take the disciple into his own consciousness and guide him by communicating in silence his consciousness to him. This is a real guru.

To choose a guru is very difficult but some external guidelines can be given which may help a sincere seeker. The first thing you must try to perceive is that when you speak to the person or when you are near him, do you feel an affinity, do you feel some communication, do you feel that conversing with him removes your limitations, your ignorance, and brings in some light and a higher contact?

You should also see whether he helps you to formulate clearly the goal of your spiritual life and whether he is the one who you feel can take you to that goal. This is another aspect which is important. Most people who come to spiritual life are not clear about their goal. They enter the path because they find that the material life, the life they were leading was not congenial and they are in search of so-called peace.

To turn to spiritual life in search of peace because you were unable to get it in material life, is not the best way. Spiritual life is much more difficult than the material life. If we cannot withstand the blows and onslaughts of our material life and successfully conquer them, we are much less equipped to face the difficulties that come to us in spiritual life, in the form of greed, hatred, jealousy, anger with a vehemence that is multiplied manifold. We would be less equipped to conquer these, if we have already found our will weak while facing the less difficult problems of the material life.

So the first thing is to become clear as to why you want to lead a spiritual life and to ask yourself whether you are ready for it. Really speaking, it is your guru who will decide. But you cannot always know right from the beginning whether a particular person is competent to reveal to you your goal and lead you to it. Let me put it more clearly. The goal of some people in spiritual life is to realise the Divine; the goal of others is not only to realise but to carry out the command of the Divine in the world; and the goal of some – very, very few – is to become Divine, so that the Divine could act directly through them on earth.

Now in between these three, there are several limited goals or partial goals which all come under the category of spiritual life. So you have to know and decide whether your guru, the person who is to guide you is practising the sadhana in which he is supposed to lead you and whether he himself is capable of leading you and helping you. Only if he fulfils these two conditions, you may go to him. Then, there are other factors also. So you may watch, you may see, there is no hurry about these matters.

Another important thing is whether the guru is willing to accept you. If he is willing to accept you, how does he accept you? This is all from your angle. From a deeper and truer angle, if the guru is a realised guru, the acceptance is usually given even before you come to him, even before you have known him. He would know that you belong to him, that he is supposed to lead you to the goal and that someday you will come to him. He knows that the Divine will fulfil His task through his instrumentality to the extent it is necessary to do so.

You see, the guru has achieved enlightenment; he has got the Divine contact; he is like a lamp that is lit and you are like a lamp that has to be lit. And once the lamp is lit, you do not need much of his guidance, because then the Supreme Himself will start guiding you directly. Whatever it be, when the guru accepts you, he takes you into his consciousness and builds up a physical contact with you, maybe by giving you a mantra, by giving you his photograph, by inviting you to partake of the food with him, because even through food he communicates his consciousness to you.

How a guru communicates his consciousness is a very important part of the traditional yogas. He may give you some work to do for him so that the physical link remains, but the real link is spiritual. I have seen gurus who seem to talk of unimportant things from a spiritual angle but all the time they are communicating to you a higher and higher consciousness so that when you get up, you are a different person. By ordinary things I mean he may be talking to you about something very common like 'subji' (vegetables), but the real purpose is that you are in his 'sānnidhya', in his physical presence, and he is communicating certain things to your consciousness.

Now, there are various ways by which a guru can communicate an inner consciousness; by touch, that is, by 'sparśa', when he puts his hand on your head, it is again the higher consciousness which is communicated to you. He communicates to you through a mantra, through food, and the least through words, because in spiritual life, words have only a limited power to remove the inner darkness; but even then, they are effective. They are efffective because they come from a person who has some realisation. So the important thing to know is that when a guru accepts you, he accepts your total personality and makes it a part of his own, makes your problems his own and makes you an heir to his spiritual development, so that it gets communicated to you. This is how a guru accepts a disciple.

Now, a guru accepts many disciples but all do not progress in the same manner or at the same pace. One of the most well-known examples of how a disciple can benefit from a guru is that of Ekalavya. In the Mahabharata there is a story that the king of the hunters had a son by the name of Ekalavya. Ekalavya had heard that Dronacharya was the greatest teacher of archery in those times. So he approached Dronacharya to teach him archery, to accept him as a disciple. But Dronacharya refused. Ekalavya did not go back to his father's palace because he felt very much hurt, and instead went to a forest, made an idol of Dronacharya and said to it: "Now, you are my Guru", and started practising archery.

One day, Arjuna and other disciples of Dronacharya went to the forest to hunt and one of the hunting dogs strayed to the place where Ekalavya was practising and started to bark. He shot some arrows in the mouth of the dog which stopped its barking. The arrows were shot in such a manner that they did not hurt the dog but just stuck in its mouth without even touching the inner throat organs. But this stopped the dog's barking. The dog returned to the hunters. When Arjuna saw this he was surprised, for he himself could not have performed this extraordinary feat.

Arjuna went in search of the archer and came upon Ekalavya. He praised him and asked him who his guru was. Ekalavya said that his guru was Dronacharya. Arjuna was very annoyed because Dronacharya had promised him that he would be his (Dronacharya's) greatest disciple in archery. Arjuna returned to the palace and spoke to his guru in a very dejected tone. Dronacharya himself was surprised because he had never accepted Ekalavya or anybody else as his disciple. So he accompanied the princes and went to Ekalavya to enquire. Ekalavya told the master, "Yes, you did not accept me as your disciple, but I accepted you as my guru and through this idol of yours I linked my consciousness with yours, so that even without your knowing it your consciousness was guiding me." Now, mostly it is the other way around. When a guru accepts, he links his consciousness and guides without the disciple even knowing it.

I know of this personally and will give you an example. On the Mother's instructions, I was undergoing training with an Indian guru. One day I had a dream and I mentioned it to the Mother. She said, "This guru has given you the dream." Indian yoga is such that a guru can take you into his consciousness and only those thoughts can come to you which he gives you. If he wants to screen any thoughts he can screen them away also. But it is also possible for the disciple to link his consciousness with the guru's. So even while the guru links with the disciple's consciousness, a good disciple also makes the effort to link himself with the guru's consciousness. And to remain linked for twenty-four hours, because only then will a higher consciousness and force flow from the Divine through the guru to the disciple. That is why in the shastras it is said: 'Meditate so that you feel yourself to be inside the heart of the Guru and also meditate on the Guru's presence inside your heart.'

The best way to link with the guru is a double meditation. Meditate, remember your guru because the guru has already individualised the states of consciousness higher than the mind. So linking with him makes those states yours also. Meditate, as if you are inside the heart of the guru and the guru is inside your heart. In this double meditation you are externally protected and internally open. And this is one of the best meditations you can do: linked with his consciousness, with the help of the mantra he gives you, to concentrate on the Divine. This is the best way for a disciple to benefit from his guru.

A disciple's attitude to the guru is also very important. Traditional yogas have praised the guru in a manner which may seem to us a bit exaggerated, when they say: "Gurūḥ Brahma, gurūḥ Viṣnuḥ, gurūḥ devo Maheśvaraḥ." ('Guru is Brahma, guru is Vishnu, guru is devo Maheshwar'.) Now, you could interpret this sloka in two ways. One, that the guru is a representative of the gods. Or that you try to see Brahma, Vishnu, Mahesh in your guru and when you see them in your guru, they will get manifested in him, at least for you as a disciple. He may have twenty other disciples. For them the powers of the gods may not manifest in the guru, but for you they will manifest and come to you.

So, it is extremely important to know that in a guru-disciple relationship much depends on the disciple also, not only on the guru. It means that even if the guru has limitations, still, a certain kind of disciple can progress through him and can even help his guru. I know a lady who had a great inner development and an inner contact with a higher being. Once this higher being explained to her the role of the guru: "Your guru acts as a link. There is a tank which is higher and another tank below it. Your guru is the pipe through which the water has to flow from the higher tank to the lower, that is, from the Divine to you." So you have to know that your guru is the chosen instrument through whom you are going to benefit spiritually. It does not matter if you have more realisation than he has or less than him. That is not the point. The important thing is that in this life, he is meant to help you. That is how the whole relationship starts.

A disciple should build a relationship with his guru in such a manner that it gives him the maximum benefit. So that this may happen, you should be very frank with your guru. You should never hide your defects because when you speak to a real guru, the guru makes your shortcomings his own. When you place your difficulties before the guru and if he is united with the Divine, the Divine listens to your difficulties through him; your difficulties are communicated to the Divine. This is very true. Because of his link with the Divine, the answer to your problems also comes from the Divine. You should learn to see not only the physical personality of your guru, but the force behind it. And the more you get accustomed to this, the better will you receive his guidance and through him, the Divine Guidance.

You should try to be linked with the guru's consciousness and constantly maintain this link integrally – psychically, mentally, vitally, physically. As I explained, a physical contact with the guru – through letters, through words, through a mantra or by working for him – helps. Whatever you want, try to see the Divine Presence in that aspect in your guru and try to open to it. You may want to learn music, you may want to do painting, you may want literary capacity or faith or courage. You can get anything, because everything is latent in the Divine. By our concentration the capacities are awakened; by our aspiration we call them down; by our receptivity we receive them; by our surrender we assimilate them. That is how the process works.

There is something more. I have so far spoken of the *do's*, now I must tell you of the *don't's*. If you want a rapid progress do not choose the path yourself but let the guru choose it for you. Because of his union with the Divine, the guru has the capacity to see your past and your future, to see where you are at present, to know what is needed to take you to your goal, whether you should go by the steep path, which is really the speedier path but a difficult one, or whether you should go by the gradually sloping path which is an easier path but a longer one. Leave it to your guru to decide but never hesitate to put your problems before him. If you feel an urge or an aspiration for anything, tell him.

I remember one day I told the Mother, "Mother, I get a very strong urge to come to you at very odd hours. And I have to control myself because these are not the hours I should come and disturb you." The Mother smiled and replied, "You may come whenever you feel like coming. Don't hold yourself back, because that creates a wall. If I am free, I will ask you what you need and give you the answer; if I am busy, I will give you a flower. But do come." So the most important thing is to be always very frank with your guru about all your problems. Never try to be a good disciple in his eyes. Just be what you are, and you will see how the maximum benefit comes to you from him.

Whatever be the nature of your problem, material or spiritual, it will be solved. I will give you the example of Vivekananda. He had material problems. Ramakrishna sent him to Mother Kali. He did not tell Vivekananda: "No, don't ask for material things. Spirituality is everything." Ramakrishna asked Vivekananda to go and ask Mother Kali for whatever he wanted.

There are people who have other problems in their lives, like political problems. Let them put these before the guru; it is for him to decide what should be done. The guru will know how to guide you and will take you to the goal. So this, in a nutshell, is how a disciple may benefit by his contact with a guru. We have just touched upon a few points. The other aspects we will take up again some other time.

Planes and Parts of the Being

The greatest single contribution of Indian culture to the world is Yoga. All our botany, chemistry, medicine, that is, Rasayana Shastra, Ayurveda, all owe their magnificence, their development to the Rishis who practised yoga. It came to them by intuition. In the book *Charaka-Saṃhita* we find that the Rishis started getting diseases and they went to Bhāradwāja for advice and Bhāradwāja sought the guidance of Indra, the Lord of Intuition. And what was revealed to him then, is being practised even today. In almost all the ancient books, like *Shiv Parvati Samvad*, you will find Parvati asking questions and Shiva replying to them. It shows how all this knowledge had been revealed from a higher level of consciousness. Our forefathers not only attained this high level of consciousness but described in a very scientific manner the inner planes and how each plane was connected with the human personality. Modern psychology and psychiatry with all their achievements have not touched upon even ten percent of the ancient Indian psychology which is Yoga.

We will try to understand very briefly the ancient system of psychology and Sri Aurobindo's system of psychology which also includes cosmology. The Divine Consciousness, by a process of involution, created several successive planes and thus creation came into being.

The human personality is a mixture of several planes. An important aim of Sri Aurobindo's yoga is to individualise those planes which are not yet individualised in the world today, so that a new human being is created. By the individualisation of the Intuitive plane, you can be constantly guided by Intuition and faculties beyond Intuition, instead of being guided by the mind and its reasoning. And far more important is the individualisation of the Supermind plane which, according to Sri Aurobindo and the Mother, would lead to a physical transmutation. This means that instead of a body of blood, skin and bones, it will become a body of light, it will be flexible, it will not be vulnerable; if somebody even shoots at it, it will not get hurt. So the creation of this new body is an important aspect of the vision of Sri Aurobindo and the Mother.

The planes exist in their totality. But they apply only to this Brahmāṇḍa, that is, our universe. There are many Brahmāṇḍas, but what is the process of development in other universes we do not know. This process of involution and evolution exists only in our universe. So, this naturally takes us to the very important question of how to individualise the planes which are not individualised at present since the future of our collective life depends on this. There is a similarity upto a certain level in the description of the planes given by Sri Aurobindo and the Mother, and by many other Indian yogis.

Time and space are different in different planes. That is why they say Brahma's one day is like this, Brahma's one night is like that. Our forefathers were not wrong. Maybe the figures are exaggerated or maybe they are not; we have nothing to measure this by, today. Personally, I believe they are not exaggerated because our forefathers had the truth consciousness in them. But there can be a difference in interpretation and understanding.

The ancient Indian system describes 36 Tatwas – elements – or sometimes it lists 24 elements. There is very little difference in these 24 and 36 Tatwas because most of them are common – 5 Jñānendriyas, 5 Karmeindriyas and 5 Tanmātras. In the 24 elements are included four which are Manas, Buddhi, Ahankāra, Citta and others. The 36 Tatwas include the 12 inner planes. There is a difference between the nomenclature used by Sri Aurobindo and that given by the ancient Rishis. But in the basic concept that everything originates from the Divine, and by a process of involution the creation has come into being, there is a great similarity. Regarding the description of the Kundalini and the Chakras and the planes in general, there is very little difference. There you have 12 or maybe 14 Bhuvanas, because then you put Manas and Buddhi, Citta and Ahankāra with them or you take Sri Aurobindo's nomenclature which is: Higher Mind, Illumined Mind, Intuitive Mind, Overmind and Supermind – five planes. We will use Sri Aurobindo's nomenclature as He has gone into far greater details. Besides, it is not easy to correlate these with the traditional terminology.

These inner planes have the same basic colours as our physical plane. The three basic colours in the physical plane are: red, blue and yellow. Broadly, the three basic colours in the inner planes are also red, yellow and blue. (I would rather put it in that order, because yellow comes in between.)

There are also intermediate planes; for example, an intermediate plane between the vital and the mental. Their colours are also intermediate. The colour of the mind is yellow and when yellow and red mix, that is the vital-mental plane; when red and dark-red mix, that is the vital-physical plane. Each plane has its sub-planes and all these sub-planes and parts of the personality have to be developed in the right manner.

There is a gradation of the mind: Higher Mind, Illumined Mind, Intuitive Mind and Overmind; and the colour associated with them is blue. The colour of the Higher Mind is dark blue becoming lighter and lighter in the higher planes. The colour of the Overmind is whitish-blue – Krishna's colour. Krishna is an incarnation of the Divine, manifesting the Overmind plane upon earth. So when you see Rama and Krishna painted whitish-blue and if you know about the inner planes, you know also that it was not their bodies which were blue, but their aura which the great artists have brought out. So also with Sita and Radha. When they are painted white, it is their divine aura that the artists have brought out.

We will start with the body. Instead of starting with the Divine, we will start with the body and go the Divine. According to the Mother and Sri Aurobindo, every point in the body represents some part of the inner plane. If you can open that point not only in the Kundalini, but even in the other parts of the body, you will make contact with that inner plane. So according to Them, the microcosm represents the macrocosm; the human being represents in a finite manner all the aspects of the Infinite. The soul, the psychic, the mind, the vital, the physical are the windows to the planes and individualise these planes. As I said, we will start with the human being and as we go from the known to the unknown, it will become easier to understand the ancient system.

The first thing to know is that the body is the base. All the inner planes can be concentrated at one point because of the physical body. Along with the physical body we have an astral body which is more subtle; it can even pass through a wall. In the physical plane, most of the centres are not normally open. Opening of all the centres would require a new kind of body where all the centres are open, even every cell of the body.

So, between the physical and the vital planes, there is the subtle-physical plane. Everything which gets translated in the physical plane, first takes form in the subtle-physical plane. The colour of the physical and the subtle-physical is dark red.

The vital plane is red in colour – pure red, if one has a pure vital. The vital plane has its own time, its own space and its own form. In the vital plane we see Durga with eight hands, we see Kali as Sahasra Bhuja Kali. According to Sri Aurobindo and the Mother, the goddesses do not take these forms in the Overmind or the Supermind planes. These forms belong mostly to the vital plane. Kali at the Overmind plane has only two hands. There she is golden-red, she is not red only and not black at all. She is golden-red. There are also beings in the vital plane which do not have a head and fire comes out of them. We speak of Yakshas, Kinnaras, Bhutas, Pishachas, Pretas, or a number of such beings. Sri Aurobindo, as I said, has not always used the same nomenclature but we can try to find some similarities for our understanding.

The vital plane has several aspects – outer vital and inner vital; lower vital and higher vital. The vital has a puruṣa – prāṇamaya puruṣa – a part of your individualised personality. The vital puruṣa of each individual will be different. At the soul level, all are the same but at the psychic level, the mental level, the vital level and the physical level, the differences exist. So the vital puruṣa – prāṇamaya puruṣa – of all the people is not the same.

The vital plane is the seat of impulses, emotions and instincts. When a mother sees her child, she is very happy. The physical body only expresses the happiness; the happiness is actually felt, the joy is actually felt, in the vital body. In the mental body it takes the form of a thought: Should I give a present to my child? Why not give him something to eat? But that is a mental thought that follows this emotion. The thought may come first and the emotion may follow or the emotion may come first and the thought afterwards. There is no hard-and-fast rule.

The vital also has good emotions, great impulses for changing the world, for great sacrifices. All these are in the vital plane and the Mother has said that without the vital force nothing great can be achieved in the world.

All the emotions, instincts, or most of them, come through vibrations that exist in the general atmosphere. Vibrations are of two kinds – some are straight, others are circular. I was amazed to read in some books on traditional yoga that they were described in this manner. But when I read Sri Aurobindo I found that He too had described the vibrations in the same manner. They also touch your vital and your astral bodies at specific points. By following a particular vibration back to its source, one can find out from where it has come and what exactly is its nature.

These vibrations, or most of them (I do not refer here to thought vibrations), enter the vital plane, touch you and in you they become emotions. When a man who has hatred for you thinks of you, you get a vibration of a reaction of hatred. Similarly, if you think of somebody with hatred and if he catches the vibration of hatred, you say: "Oh, this man hates me." It is not that he hates you; it is you who hate him, that is the real truth. So once you know about the inner planes, it helps you to purify your consciousness.

The knowledge of the different planes is important. When some children misbehave their mothers often scold them: "I will not give you food today", or spank them for being mischievous. The Mother has said that this is strange. The fault is of the vital and you are punishing the physical body of the child! This is not the correct solution. What you must know is how to control the vital of a child without punishing him physically and also, how to control the extra energy in him without giving him a physical punishment. We will come to this later, when we come to child care and child education. Today we are trying to understand only the inner planes.

This knowledge of the inner worlds may become one of the more important aspects of education of the future. Sri Aurobindo has said that this knowledge will become a part of education. In ancient India this deeper knowledge was given only to a few, but now after the supramental descent, more and more people will acquire it, maybe in a hundred years, maybe in fifty years from now. I am not talking of tomorrow. Their consciousness will become so pure that occult knowledge will be given to many and most of it will come from within.

Now we come to the method of having this knowledge. According to the Mother and Sri Aurobindo you can never have this knowledge by the method of reasoning or deduction. True knowledge comes by identification. For example, in child psychology, you have to identify yourself with a child in order to know what he knows, in order to understand what he understands, in order to think what he thinks and then only can you help him to grow. How do you identify with a child? Of course you cannot do so physically. Then what is the method? You may remember the story of

Arjuna. Dronacharya, the preceptor of the Pandavas, had arranged a competition to see who was the best marksman in archery. The target was the eye of a bird on a tree. When all were ready to take aim, Drona asked them: "Do you see the bird?" – "Yes" – "Do you see the tree?" – "Yes" He told them: "You are not fit to shoot the arrow." Then he called Arjuna and asked him: "Do you see the tree?" – "No" – "Do you see the bird?" – "No" – "Can you see the eye of the bird?" – "Yes" – "Then you can shoot," Drona said.

So, when you want to identify yourself with something or somebody you have to concentrate on that object, that person, that idea or that problem, in such a manner that your entire consciousness is concentrated on it, your whole attention is focused on it. With this kind of aspiration and concentration, the Mother has said that you feel as if a door has opened and you have gone into another level of consciousness. Then you can get identified with a person and come to know all about him. Now this reversal of consciousness can take place on the mental, vital or psychic level. In our normal life we do not make use of these processes, we do not use them in our education, in our business, in our political life or in our social life. That is why there is so much misunderstanding, confusion, trouble, quarrels and so on. The understanding of the inner planes is the beginning of the development and utilisation of our latent faculties.

There are two more things which will help you understand the inner planes. One is the phenomenon of dreams and the other is the phenomenon of death. In dreams we are released from our physical consciousness and we go to different inner planes where our thoughts can take different forms or we see the forms that exist. If you know about the inner planes, the interpretation of dreams becomes easier, even the control of dreams becomes easier. How? I will give you an example of an ancient tribal custom. But first, let me tell you that we should not imagine that all the knowledge has been found by our psychologists in the modern times. Of course it is systematically classified, they have done much useful work, but it does not mean that it did not exist in ancient times.

Amongst a tribe in Malaysia, when they get up in the morning they gather around a fire. They are aborigines, but not in the sense that they are not civilised; they are perhaps more civilised than the modern man. The children come and bow to their grandparents and their parents and the first question the grandpapa asks, is: "What dream did you see?" (In our modern times, the father most probably would be reading a newspaper and would say: "Accha, ashirwad", or would tell the child not to disturb him. But not with this tribe. What dream did you see, is the standard question, for they believe it is a part of the child's education, his psychological education.) Let us say the child tells him, "I saw a tiger." The grandpapa will ask, "What happened?" The child replies, "I got frightened." The grandpapa will say, "Well, next time you see a tiger don't get frightened, after all that tiger has no physical body, it is only a dream tiger. You jump on it and see what happens." Surprisingly, these things are recorded.) I am not telling you of imaginery things, but of things that are recorded). After two or three days, the child will come and say: "Papa, today I again saw a tiger." – "What did you do?" – "I faced it." – "What happened?" – "The tiger became smaller and smaller and ran away." This is most amazing. The Mother has written the same thing in Her books. If you see a tiger in a dream and you face it, you will find it becomes smaller and smaller and disappears. How is it that a tribe in Malaysia that has never heard of the Mother is practising the same thing and having the same result. So, the inner planes which exist and with which you can build the contacts can not only influence your life over which you now feel you have no control, but once you practise yoga you can contact the inner planes and govern your external life in a better manner.

I will give you another example. Sri Aurobindo has written that during the War, He carried out certain experiments by joining His consciousness with the consciousness of some generals. He said that had He told them to do this, to do that, they would not have listened to Him. Besides, Sri Aurobindo had no technical knowledge of warfare. But just by combining His consciousness with the consciousness of the generals, they received the right inspiration and achieved victory which otherwise they perhaps would not have had. Sri Aurobindo also gave another example of a particular general in Spain who He had found very receptive but another general He did not find receptive at all. It is not only the power of communication, but also the receptivity of the other person that can bring about the needed result. If you know this process then you can make the life of every child you meet, each person you come across, better and that will be the real change in the world.

The Mother has said that there is a very old tradition that if twelve people of good will unite their aspiration and call the Divine, the Divine would manifest upon earth. So I think we should at least aspire to be one of the twelve instead of reading the same books, talking about the same things, having the same meditation day after day and progressing very little.

So, the first step is to know about the working of these inner planes, and this is mostly done by self-observation. What I am telling you here is only an indication; each one should spend sometime in self-observation. Why did this thought come to me, why did I have that emotion, why am I having a pain here, why am I feeling a pressure there, and try to analyse. Every time a person speaks to you, whether he is praising you or abusing you or telling you some story on politics, art or literature, look behind him, do not give too much importance to his words, try to see the force behind his words, the origin of things and this will give you a great understanding. You will find that every person, even a person who is trying to harm you, will ultimately do you some good, because the Divine is working through him. It is because we do not understand that the problems multiply. Just like in jujitsu or judo you take the force of your opponent and use it to your advantage, here also, you could take even the wrong attitude of the other man and use it for the Divine's work. I will not say to your advantage because your advantage and the Divine's work are the same in yoga, they are not two different things. Anything that is not a part of the Divine's work is not to your advantage. This, one realises at some point in life.

So the next plane we go to is the mental plane. Now, the mental plane is the seat of thought, memory, analysis, logic and intuition from above. If you can purify it – and Gayatri Mantra is a help here – if you can meditate on the sun and put all its light around you, the planes will get purified, the individual planes – or rather I should say the parts of the planes individualised in you, not the total plane. Only a mahayogi like Sri Aurobindo could purify an entire plane, could bring down a higher force and put the Light on the plane itself. This is what is meant by the Supramental Descent.

Psychologists have now found that we do not utilise even ten percent of our brain. Ninety percent of the brain remains unutilised. This is mentioned in a report of UNESCO. According to yoga we are not utilising even 0.0001% of our mental personality. The vital personality, as I told you, could pass through a wall; mental is yet more subtle. Most people do not have an organised mental personality. If you could organise your mental personality you would not easily get influenced by others. You would know what to do and how to do it.

How to build an individualised mental personality? We will come to the details later; but for the present, three things may help you. The Mother has said that you must choose a central idea and organise your mental thinking (I am not using the words mental personality, I am saying mental thinking), in creating a mental synthesis around a central idea. Say, you have created a central idea to want the supramental transformation. Now whatever helps the supramental transformation you accept, whatever does not help, you reject. Another person may not be interested in the supramental transformation; he may like to help humanity. We may disagree with him for we believe that the only way to work for the upliftment of India and help humanity is to supramentalise ourselves. There is really no other way. The person may not see it in this manner, but he may have a mental vision to work for India's national reconstruction. Once he has thought of that, all his life he has to plan around that central idea. So you must first find that idea around which you can synthesise other ideas.

The second thing to know is that most of the thoughts which come to you are not your own thoughts. They come either from others or by association. When I think of A, I immediately remember the Centre in Baroda and the talk we had in Pondicherry, simply because I thought of him. Or he leaves a book on my table. I see that book and start thinking of him. So most of the thoughts come by association, inner association or through a physical object which reminds you of a person. It may be an idea, it may be something in the book. Mind works by association or by a process like telepathy, without knowing that the thoughts come from others.

Here again, I would like to give you two interesting examples. One is the Mother's. When She used to meditate in Japan, She found that people with whom She meditated at that time got the same thought; I would not say the same impulses, I would say the same thought and the same idea. I read in a book on psychic phenomena in Russia that a man went to a psychic person and said, "Show me something." So the psychic person wrote down something on a piece of paper, folded it up and gave it in his hand. In the meanwhile, this man started scratching his ear. After some time he was told to open the paper. When he opened it he saw what was written there – "Scratch your ear"! Without this man knowing it, the psychic person had communicated the thought to him and the man had started scratching his ear. So this is how things happen on the mental plane.

Then there is also a collective mental plane. When President K wanted to get elected in his party he put many of his volunteers in the party headquarters, shouting, "We want K! We want K!" You know, it is this projection of collective thought that is behind processional shouting, people getting emotional as in the India-Pakistan affairs. It is a collective mind and a collective vital at work. Both the individual and the collective minds can be channelised.

Sri Aurobindo has described the nature of the higher planes and has given some beautiful examples from the poems of Shelley, Wordsworth, Shakespeare, where they had received inspiration from the higher planes. He has pointed out that this line has come from the Overmind plane and that second line has come from the Higher mental plane. Such examples of correctly identifying the source, are very rare. You will not find in other books such a scientific approach to the inner planes. Also, in His letters to His disciples, to each one Sri Aurobindo has said that his inspiration came from this level, that his problem came from that level, that one must do this thing to solve it, that these are the parts of the being coming into play.

The soul and the psychic are in Sri Aurobindo's yoga parts of the Central Being. The colour of the psychic plane is pink. The psychic is the soul in evolution. The part which is evolving is the psychic and not the soul. People do not usually make this distinction.

This psychic being is the permanent personality in evolution. The soul is beyond evolution. The soul presides but is not involved in creation, not involved in life and birth and as such, has no evolution. The soul of a Robert or the soul of Sri Rama or Sri Krishna is the same. The difference between an avatar and an ordinary man is that in the avatar it is a direct descent of the Divine Consciousness taking up an individual personality. This is not an evolution of the psychic being from birth to birth, while the psychic being of a human being evolves. That is why Sri Ramakrishna spoke of 'iśvarakoṭi' and 'jivakoṭi'. This distinction has been explained at great length by Sri Aurobindo when He speaks of a surface soul – the desire soul – and an inner soul. So, in man there is an outer personality which is under the influence of his desires. When you speak about a man's personality do not club everything together. In Sri Aurobindo's parlance Citta has its significance, Manas has its significance. He does not put them together. It is a great treat to read and understand Him.

When a person leaves his physical body, his astral body remains in the astral plane, normally between six months to three years. When the person is born again, he may carry the memory of his previous life by taking back a part of his astral body. But if the astral and the mental bodies have disintegrated and if the psychic takes birth after that, then in order to get the memory of the previous life, a person has to get in contact with his psychic. Even though he can make contact with his psychic, he would not have a total memory because the psychic carries only the essence of the previous lives. It only carries the memory of those events which have influenced its growth.

The Gita tells us that when a person dies his Jiva takes the experiences of his life just as the wind takes the fragrance of a flower. Similarly, the Jiva takes the essence of life. In fact, your next life is decided just before your death. It is not decided when your psychic being is resting in the psychic plane. Just before death, the psychic being takes the sum total of your life, as we do in the cash book – you know 'bāki', a kind of balance – it takes out the balance of life. Here also the Mother has given a beautiful example. In one life, say you are a king and you find you are fettered and tied down and you cannot do what you want to. In the next life you want to be more free and to lead an average life. So you are born in an average family and you have an average development. Such important decisions are taken at the time of death and not after death.

So you must know that all the work you do for your progress is done in the physical life on earth. There is no work or progress after the physical life ends, unless a guru helps you. A guru can help a person even after death. He can give him support; he can wipe out his old 'saṁskārāḥ' and give him a new birth. When a person I knew, died, the Mother called me and said, "You know, I have advanced his realisation by a few lives. He would normally have had the realisation in his fifth or sixth life. What I have done is that that part of his psychic being which had aspiration for the Divine I have separated and the other parts I have dissolved. So now in the next life this man will have realisation."

Now this kind of help only gurus like the Mother and Sri Aurobindo can give. But we also can try to reach the stage which They have reached by making our surrender to Them complete. Since yoga is the path of surrender, we also should be able to reach that stage. But with one difference – the line of manifestation of each one will be different. It will not be Sri Aurobindo, it will be Sri Aurobindo as Mr. A; it will be Sri Aurobindo as Mr. M. This means that the consciousness of Sri Aurobindo and the Mother will unite with everybody's consciousness and will manifest according to his aspiration and need, as water and sun support every tree to grow according to its seed. The differences will exist, but if our surrender is complete, Their power, Their knowledge will manifest in us; otherwise, our surrender is not complete. We are not sufficiently open to Them. As we surrender, the path to the Divine will open. That is the only way.

One day a child was taken to the Mother. When She saw the child, She said to Herself, his face is familiar. And then in the afternoon when She was in Her meditation, She had a vision. She saw a huge Egyptian palace and in that palace there was a courtyard. It was a king's palace, and in that courtyard there was, you know, a water drainage, an open drainage for the water to flow out of the palace. In that drainage the Mother saw a child playing who had the same face as the child's whom the Mother had met earlier in the day. She saw a tutor coming, and asked him, "How can you let the child play in there?" And he answered, "Amenhotep likes it." Then the Mother knew that the child She had met earlier in the day was Amenhotep. So this is how the psychic memories of the previous lives can come.

I remember I once took my friend's family to the Mother. When the Mother came to the wife of the man – there were three generations, the mother, the son and his children – She said to the lady, "I know you. When I was in Egypt, you were also present." All such things the psychic knows. So when you make contact with the psychic you know about your previous lives.

It is a very interesting experience to spend sometime in self-observation and putting your inner being in order. It is also very important and necessary for all those who seriously want to learn and practise yoga in a scientific manner. I do not know of any person more scientific than Sri Aurobindo or our forefathers for whom nothing was imagination and everything was experience.

It is also very surprising that when the inner planes open, you hear sounds, you see forms, you see colours, that are more concrete, more clear than the sounds you hear on the physical plane and the colours more brilliant than the colours you see on the physical plane. There the things are so concrete that you can actually see, hear and feel them. Most people see them in their dreams; in yoga you see them not only in dreams, not only in meditation, but even with open eyes. As you learn to go to different planes with your eyes open, you start seeing things in those planes and once you know how to withdraw, you can see them more concretely; more concretely than you see your neighbour sitting next to you. There is no doubt left in your mind about how things work in the inner planes. If you do not know about the inner planes how are you going to individualise your personality.

The Mother has said that the aim of the Integral Yoga is a divine perfection, not a human perfection. In human perfection there have been many people more perfect than us throughout the centuries, not only now. We cannot dream of being a Leonardo da Vinci now. His perfection we cannot even think of today. There are many people, engineers, architects, musicians, who have dedicated their lives to achieving perfection in their field, some even from a spiritual angle. So if you want to aspire for a divine perfection on earth, a divine knowledge within a divine perfection, then a divine integration of your consciousness is indispensable. And for this a knowledge of the inner planes and parts of the being is still more indispensable.

All these are but a few glimpses of the vast knowledge Sri Aurobindo has left us. For the rest, you must read Him in depth. To read Him in detail on the planes and parts of the being, would take a long time; it cannot be done in a few days. Without this knowledge, we would continue to lead the life of ignorance.

Sri Aurobindo and the Mother have opened the way for us, not only the mental way, but the psychic way to the planes and parts of the being. What should we do to become conscious of them? First, it is to make our mind silent, then to observe. You do not have to struggle in order to make your mind silent. Some people asked Sri Aurobindo: "How can we have experiences if we are not purified." Sri Aurobindo told them that his experience had been different, that He had always had realisation by meditation first and the purification started afterwards as a result. Also, that most of it – purification or whatever else you may call it – came by a descent of the higher planes. When He meditated, the descent came and the descent purified.

We belong to a Guru who has not only opened for us great vistas which have never been opened before, but who is here with us even now. Sri Aurobindo, after leaving His physical body, has come closer to us. Each one of us can now identify himself better with Him. And when we identify with Him, the knowledge we get from Him no books can give. Once you identify yourself with Him, and then when you read His books, you will say: "Oh, yes, I have already had this experience. This, I know, but He has described it more clearly."

So you must try to practise silence. Silence also comes by self-observation. If you tell yourself, let me observe and see from where the thoughts come, you will be surprised to find that your mind has become quiet immediately. You may be sitting for fifteen minutes and you will observe that not a single thought has come. This is because the very fact of observing has taken you out of the stream of thoughts. Thoughts are like cars and pedestrians on the road. If you are walking in the middle of the road you will obviously dash against the cars. But if you are in your house you are outside their reach. Similarly with the inner consciousness. Once you start observing yourself, you are out of the range of mental thoughts.

Similiar also is the process of finding the psychic. You must gather, you must everyday gather up your consciousness and direct it from the head to your heart, from the feet to your heart and from the hands to your heart, and go inward. You must *will* that you want to find your psychic being. Will is the instrument, will is the Agni, will is the tapasya. Most people do not know how to use the human will. I have found that most people, even those who have taken up yoga, do not realise the importance of the will. If you do not apply your will for twenty-three and a half hours and for only half an hour you exercise it, it will not work. The will should be under your control all the time. So also the consciousness. Buddha has said: "I have made my consciousness like steel around me."

We must first have a mental understanding, then have a spiritual experience, then have an opening to the inner planes and finally channelise them to the physical plane. An artist can channelise the higher planes in his art, and a housewife, in her household work. Sri Aurobindo makes no distinction between the two. It is extremely interesting to know that in the future evolution, this knowledge of the planes and parts of the being would manifest in our daily life, in our day-to-day work. How? In future instead of saying, "Yeh woh rāga gāh raha hai" (he is singing that rāga), you will say that his inspiration comes from the Illumined Mind plane or from the Overmind. "Rāga to sabhi gā jate hai. Ek hi rāga do admi do plane se gāte hai." (Everybody can sing a rāga. Two persons can sing the same rāga but from two different planes.) When you sing from the highest plane, you create rāga.

I remember a great Indian yogi, a very great yogi, who one day told me, "I accept you and will help you like an elder brother guiding a younger brother in his life." Now, is it possible to accept and guide another? When you are really united with the Divine and if a person comes to you, you will know what to tell him, because then the Divine dwells in you. When you are not united, it is all mental. If you are really united, He will guide you and tell you which mantra to recite. If you are really united with Him, your touch will be His touch, the Divine's touch. It is this which is our goal. Our goal is not to always remain what we are today.

On the one side you should open yourself to the higher consciousness, the Divine consciousness, and on the other, in the beginning, you should close yourself to the horizontal influences. Later, if you want to help others, then you will have to take their vibrations into yourself. You will have to open yourself and take things into yourself. You can send out vibrations which each one will receive according to his preparation and will benefit from it. If you cannot do this, you cannot help people. But could there be a greater service to mankind than to firmly establish the Divine Consciousness in you and around you and become a centre of His radiating vibrations at the mental, vital, physical planes and the lower planes? Could there be a greater service to mankind? I cannot dream of a greater service. If you can radiate His vibrations to all the planes, you can deal with the problems there. Though I am using the word *you,* it is not you who are taking on the problems, because then the Divine has taken over the problems through you. When you are united with the Divine, every person you meet, it is He who is meeting, every person you talk to, it is He who is talking, every problem of others that you take on, it is He who is taking and He will find a solution. It can even be that you take somebody's illness into yourself for it is He who is taking it and He will cure it.

Unless you are surrendered, how will you have the joy of swimming in an ocean of Consciousness, how will you know what it's like to be in an ocean of Light? When you are united with Him, things happen by themselves. You neither accept nor reject them. It is He who accepts, it is He who rejects, using you for His purpose. Till this happens, it is you who are rejecting, you who are accepting. This choice can be good, it can be sadhana, but it is not realisation. This process gets accelerated as you become more and more conscious of the inner planes. The rise in consciousness accelerates the process, and the acceleration makes you more conscious of the inner planes. Both movements go on side by side.

How is the link with the Divine consciousness to be established? And here comes another very important aspect. The Divine is both, Nirguṇa and Saguṇa. He is both, Nirākāra and Sākāra. How can He be both, Nirākāra and Sākāra? There is only one Divine, and the Divine is all-pervading. The Sākāra is a superimposition on the Nirākāra. The Divine Consciousness can be reached by several gates. We may enter by concentrating on Sri Aurobindo's physical form, another person may enter by concentrating on Shri Krishna's physical form, a third may enter by another gate by concentrating on the physical form of a person who has realised the Divine. The physical form is a superimposition on the Nirākāra, but the consciousness of a realised person is completely united with the Divine. So this distinction between Sākāra and Nirākāra need not create an opposition in our consciousness. The Mother told me that there is no essential difference. One day I asked Her, "Mother, should I meditate on your Sākāra aspect or your Nirākāra aspect?" The Mother replied, "What is the difference? If you think this body alone is the Divine, you are limiting my force to twenty-five percent. When people speak to me the thing goes up There. When I have to give an answer, the answer comes." This should happen to all of us. We have not met here just to talk but to understand and practise. Unless we practise we will not even understand how this works.

Now we come to the difference between Nirguṇa and Saguṇa. We speak of a thousand aspects of the Divine, of His infinite aspects. According to Sri Aurobindo and the Mother, we have to manifest the Divine in all His aspects – His power of healing, His power of knowledge, all His aspects. Now, how can this be done – the Saguṇa in His infinite aspects revealing itself. For this you will have to realise the Nirguṇa also, and manifest Him in the Saguṇa in all His aspects. You see, in Sri Aurobindo's yoga there is such a synthesis that nothing is left out. There is an integration which will go on even beyond supramentalisation. You will never be able to complete it. Nobody can ever complete it. The Divine is infinite, so His manifestation will always be infinite. Besides, in this participation in a Lila, in a game that is infinite, where is the limit to its joys? It is unlimited joy. One day you can manifest Him in one aspect, tomorrow you can manifest Him in music, the third day in something else. His attributes, His Saguṇa aspects are infinite, His manifestation is infinite. In order to manifest perfectly His every aspect, new instruments will have to be created. In microbiology we have now perhaps started to see new and great possibilities. One day microbiology and spirituality may combine. You see, materialisation and dematerialisation are not new things in spirituality.

Much before I joined the Ashram, some people came from the Ashram and stayed with us in Bombay. One of them was a devotee of Sri Krishna and he said that they would like to offer prasad, but it should not be cooked by the servant. So my wife cooked it. We meditated and found that a little of the halwa – the prasad – had disappeared and there were finger-marks left on it. The next day we were again meditating and one of the disciples said, "Bhai, bhai, take it", and there was some halwa, with a bit of kum-kum on it. Now at that time this phenomenon had no importance for me. What I want to tell you is that it is not correct to simply dismiss such things because they have no importance for us. We must know how they happen, how far we can control them. For such phenomena we cannot say, oh! it is all magic or some such thing. This is a wrong approach. If you want your life to be complete you must go to the root of everything. Everything can be approached in a scientific manner. But there should be a sense of proportion.

If you are going to London you are not going to walk all the way, halting at each house – you will never reach London. Our aim is supramental transformation. We should not give too much importance to such occurances, yet on the path nothing should be excluded. It is a path of perfection. Sri Aurobindo's yoga is a yoga of integral perfection.

I was with these same people in Madras (this is another experience) and I remember it was 8th April. (As I said before, I was the secretary of our Centre in Bombay at that time.) One of them told me, "You know, I was meditating and I saw in my vision Bertrand Russell's daughter-in-law, Susan, reading aloud from a book to him. And Bertrand Russell is telling his daughter-in-law: 'I remember the author as a truth-seeker and if he says these things about Sri Aurobindo, we must make an enquiry.' " After relating her vision, the lady tells me that Susan Russell will write me a letter dated 14th April – remember, we were talking on 8th April – and the words of the letter will be so-and-so and the word *often* will be underlined. So I told her, 'I am in business, accustomed to planning, cost of production, sales, marketing. If you tell me our actions are predetermined to this extent that on 8th April it is decided that a letter dated 14th April will come to me with the word *often* underlined, well, I will have to revise my entire attitude to life, because then the life I am leading is useless, it has no meaning, struggling from morning to night without this knowledge." And would you believe it, the letter dated 14th April came with the word *often* underlined, the same word, the same thing. I replied to the letter – they wanted some books on Sri Aurobindo and I sent them.

This was an amazing experience for me; so much so, that I almost lost interest in my business. I thought it is more worthwhile to have this knowledge than to waste one's life in this confusion and struggle. I asked the lady, "How did you get this knowledge?" (You know, we people in business are always practical.) She looked at me and said, "These paths are open to all."

When I was having all these experiences, I told the Mother, "Mother, I am not interested in my present life. I am interested in occult knowledge." In her typical way, She said, "I cannot teach you in between two trains." I asked, "What do you mean?" She replied, "You are always coming and going, always coming and going. When you settle down here, we will look into it." Much later She asked me, "Did you read my article?" (She had written that She would teach occult knowledge to those who are selfless, who are fearless and who have some faculties.) So I replied, "Yes Mother, I read your article. I understand what is meant by selflessness and fearlessness but I do not understand about faculties, because these are given by God." Do you know what She said? She said, "If you are surrendered to me I will give you the faculties." We have the great good fortune of having gurus like Sri Aurobindo and the Mother, so our entire life has a different meaning. It is wrong to complain about things. The only thing we should complain about is our own insincerity. If we are surrendered, the Divine's touch *can turn difficulties into opportunities, failure into success and weakness into unfaltering strength,* as Sri Aurobindo has said.

All this knowledge has a goal. It is not just a scientific research in psychology, para-psychology or psychiatry. This knowledge can be acquired to perfect one's personality. The goal here is to perfect one's personality. Sri Aurobindo has said that the aim of life is to manifest the Divine perfectly in time and space, and in order to manifest the Divine perfectly in time and space, the human personality has to be perfected. And divinely perfected. This is the labour for which we are all called here by Sri Aurobindo. We are not called for some trivial purposes, they are not the goals at all, they can be the means. Whatever work we do is only the means of perfecting our personality, individualising the parts which are not individualised. The Mother has made it very clear. She has said three things about the aim of Their work: to achieve a progressive universal harmony, to individualise the parts which are not individualised at present and in a propitious place to manifest a new race, the race of the Sons of God. So some great good Grace has brought us in contact with the source where this transformation is taking place. It is for us to make the best use of this opportunity in all sincerity.

When Auroville was being planned, the Mother wrote in her own hand: *We would like to make Auroville the cradle of the Superman*. What does it mean? It means that Auroville will be the place where people will not only become aware of the inner planes and parts and try to individualise them, will not only live a new life of Divine perfection, but it will be a place from where a new inner Light hitherto unmanifested, will radiate. If people would really practise yoga collectively in a place which the Mother has created for them and where She has poured Her Consciousness and Grace, a new consciousness would radiate through them, changing the world. Books, films and all such external aids will be of lesser importance though we will continue to make them and use them. But these are small aids acting only on the physical plane, the real work will be done from the supraphysical plane.

When Sri Aurobindo's biography was written, He had stated that nobody could write about His life for *it has not been on the surface for men to see*. Ninety-nine percent of His life was lived inwardly. Who can write about the life of a man who – to take a very small example – could unite His consciousness with that of some generals far away to achieve a particular result in the War? Who can write about such a life? Once you take up yoga, your actions will become a millionfold more dynamic and potent – not a hundredfold, not a thousandfold, but a millionfold! Where is the limit? The yoga which beckons us to Sri Aurobindo's Feet is not a yoga of meditation, it is not a yoga of equanimity, not even identical to the yoga of the Gita. Sri Aurobindo has written this very clearly. Though He lays a great emphasis on the Gita (He Himself has written a commentary on it), in answer to one question He has said that if He were to merely repeat what the Gita has said where was the need for Him to propound the Integral Yoga. And He has then pointed out the various differences in a letter to a disciple.

As I just told you if you want to go from here to England you will not go by a bullock-cart or on foot. You will take a plane, unless of course you have a desire to see places on the way. Similarly, if your aim is to practise Integral Yoga, knowledge and mastery of the inner planes are essential.

There is one more thing you must remember. In the book, *The Mother*, Sri Aurobindo has written about a *constant and unfailing aspiration*. Now, these words are very important. By 'constant', He does not mean 23 hours and 59 minutes. Constant is *constant*. We should know how to make our aspiration constant even in sleep, while taking food or while speaking. You should keep these words before you, these four words – *constant and unfailing aspiration* – aspiration for realising the Divine, for becoming conscious of the inner planes, aspiration for developing occult knowledge in the service of the Divine. Then there will be no limit to your aspiration.

So you must read about the planes and parts of the being and practise what Sri Aurobindo has written. You must do it in that spirit. If you pray to Sri Aurobindo, He will give you the understanding. I remember one day my sister came to me and said, "Bhaiji, don't you think there seems a contradiction between this line of Sri Aurobindo and that?" I was very busy, so I replied, "I will tell you tomorrow. I shall ask Sri Aurobindo and tell you tomorrow." I did not even read it properly. The next day she enquired, "Did you ask Sri Aurobindo?" "I have not asked Him, I have not prayed to Him, I shall ask Him now. Bring me the book," I said. (The book was *The Life Divine*.) Before I read it, I prayed to Sri Aurobindo: "You guide me, You explain." And the understanding came. He is your guide, your constant guide. If you read His books praying to Him, asking His help, He will unite His consciousness with yours and give you the understanding. When He can unite His consciousness with that of a general who does not even know Him, will He not unite His consciousness with you – you, who are aspiring to become a general of His yoga?

Many people say Sri Aurobindo's yoga is difficult. I say it is easy. Easy, because ninety-nine percent of the work is done by Sri Aurobindo Himself. Otherwise it would be not only difficult but impossible. But that one percent of sincerity that is required on our part, is most essential – sincerity in becoming conscious of the Divine in all the parts of the being and integrating them. You should be completely selfless if you want to progress. If you develop some power but if the Divine does not want you to use it, you should be very happy to let it go. Those who are not surrendered do not progress. They remain where they are. All this knowledge will dawn on you as you practise the sadhana of the Integral Yoga. It is only through practice that we progress.

Sleep and Dreams

Dreams can serve many purposes. Today we will try to understand how we can use them. They can be used for avoiding a disaster, for instance. We will take up dreams of past and future happenings and see how they come; also, dreams which can help one to solve problems. Let us first take dreams of premonition. One of the most well-known dreams is that of President Lincoln. He himself had stated at a dinner party that he had a dream in which he had heard sounds of mourning. He followed those sounds and came to a big hall in his own presidential house. He found a coffin lying there and soldiers keeping guard. He asked one of them, "What is the matter?" And the soldier replied, "Sir, the President has been shot dead."

Dreams are after all dreams, one might say. But then, within two months Lincoln was assassinated. So this is a dream of premonition which came true. Naturally, a question arises whether he could have avoided his assassination.

Here is another dream the Mother one day narrated in Her class. A person had gone on tour and was staying at a hotel. He had a dream in which he saw a boy dressed as a bell-boy, showing him a coffin and asking him to get into it. He got up in the morning very much disturbed. He was staying in a big hotel on the sixth or the seventh floor. When he left his room in the morning to go for his work, he came to the lift and found the lift boy looking exactly like the one he had seen in his dream, showing him the lift and asking him to get in. He remembered his dream and said no, thank you. And he went down all those floors by the stairs. In the meantime, the lift actually broke down, crashed and all the people in it died. Here was one person who had avoided his death. The Mother was asked who had guided him, how did he come to know, how did it happen? She said it was an entity, a good being, who had forewarned him.

But before we continue, I would like to explain one thing. You see, there are several planes – there is a physical plane, there is a vital plane and there are other planes also, and in all of them, there are beings, good and bad. There are good beings who guide you if by some chance you can get in contact with them. In yoga you can come in contact with them consciously. Even if you do not practise yoga, you can come in contact with them because of some experiences of your previous life or for any number of reasons. But in yoga, you can consciously make contact with these beings. The Mother said that an inner being, an entity had guided the person in the anecdote and he took the hint. If he had not taken the hint, he too would have gone down with the others and died in the lift.

President Lincoln, unfortunately, did not heed the warning. From a spiritual angle, Lincoln was a great man, a very great man. He was spiritually a great man though he was not a yogi. He perhaps knew that the time had come for him to go and that is why he did not pay any attention to the dream. Maybe America evolved more by his death than by his living. Who can tell? We never know how the Divine plan works.

In yoga you can become conscious of your dreams. You can go to a level of consciousness from where you can see the future and the past. Modern science is carrying out many researches. One of the dreams about the researches of the past is very interesting. There is a case of a professor of the Pennsylvania University in America. He was a professor of the Babylonian language, the language of Babylonia. A museum had received some rings with an inscription which they had sent to the professor to decipher. He tried but could not succeed and, with this problem on his mind he went to sleep. He had a dream in which an Egyptian priest came and took him to a temple. As he was a professor of Babylonian culture, he could place the priest at a period of several centuries B.C. The priest took him to an underground cellar where they found lots of jewellery, some vases and a number of other things. The priest told the professor (in the dream) that what he was seeing were not rings but earrings. A king had certain jewellery made for the deity. He wanted earrings also to be made for the idol. But he did not have enough jewellery. There was a small vase with some writing on it. He had the throat of the vase cut and had these two earrings made from it. Because the throat was cut in the middle the writing could not be made out. But if the pieces were put together, then it was possible to read the inscription because the letters were cut right through the middle.

The professor woke up from this dream in the night, went to his study and put both the rings together. He could then read the inscription. This intrigued him. So the next day he wrote to the Egyptian Government asking them where the relics of that period from the temple were kept, in which museum were they kept. He was told that they were in Istanbul. He took leave – in America the universities are liberal in granting study-leave – and he went to this museum in Istanbul. And there to his surprise, he found the same jewellery which he had seen in his dream. He saw the vase broken in three parts, in three places, and when the pieces were put together the rings fitted in the neck of the vase.

So there is a certain level of consciousness – some people go to it, as I said, by chance and some by yoga – from which you can know about the past, present and future, all together. How does this happen? It is like this: suppose in a building you go to the top floor, say to the fortieth floor. When you stand there you see a car coming from far away. You know that in five minutes it will be in front of your building and after five minutes it will be at the other end. So that car for you is the present; for a man standing on the ground floor, the car is still in the future because it will come to him after five minutes. At that level of consciousness you can see the past, present and future all together. Some people withdraw to that level, as I said, by some Grace but in yoga you actually practise how to withdraw to this deeper level. That is how these dreams come and that is how you vividly see them and relive them in your consciousness, because during sleep you enter that level of consciousness.

There are some other types of dreams which we will try to understand. There are two cases on record where two persons were awarded prizes and they got the clues in their dreams. One was a professor of chemistry. He was tackling some problem and one day he saw certain formulations in his dream which gave him a clue to his work. Dreams and sleep are not useless things – you get tired, you go to sleep and when you get up in the morning, you are fresh and the problem is solved. There is something more to this which can be cultivated to a great advantage, not only in the spiritual life but also in the material life.

Then there are dreams over which you have no control but they are partially symbolic. I remember one day a very dear friend of mine told me of a dream which I narrated to the Mother. He had a very big and beautiful house near the sea and in front of his house there was a tomb of a fakir. His daughter-in-law had just become pregnant. She had a dream in which the fakir had entered her home. So when I told this to the Mother, She said that it was true and explained that the soul of this fakir had entered the womb of this woman and the child to be born would naturally have a spiritual leaning, because it would bring the background of its past life as a fakir. Several dreams of this kind, for example, that of the Buddha's mother, are well known. We will not go into detail but they show that dream is a state of consciousness which we should not neglect. Dreams can be an education.

In Malaysia there is a tribe and in this tribe when the children get up in the morning they come and sit with their grandfather. The first question the grandfather will ask is: "What did you see last night?" The child may say, "I saw a tiger." – "What happened?" – "I got very much frightened." So the grandfather will say, "Don't get frightened. When you see a tiger next time face it courageously." So after a few days the boy would again say that he saw an elephant or a tiger. "What did you do?" – "I faced it." – "Then what happened?" – "It shrank, shrank, shrank and disappeared." The Mother has said the same thing that when you have such dreams you should not get frightened. You will find that they shrink, shrink, shrink and go away. In this way you can cultivate courage, patience and other good qualities by getting to know your own character through dreams. Dreams help you to know your own potential and character a good deal.

There is another very interesting dream which the Mother one day narrated to us. She told us that there was a writer who was trying to write but when he came halfway in his draft he found that somehow things were not working right, he could not arrange his ideas in a proper order. He quietly went to sleep and in his dream he saw a room in which there was an armchair and he was trying to arrange the furniture. But he was not succeeding. He sat down quietly and an idea came to him to put that armchair in the centre and then arrange the other furniture around it. So when he got up he had the idea that he must first put his main thought in the centre and then arrange the other ideas around it.

So it is like this. You sleep on a problem but the mind somehow remains active. The physical body goes to sleep but the mind and the vital are actually active during sleep, the psychic is active, and if you know how to control your sleep, you can benefit very much from it. The Mother has also stated that even dreams can be controlled. While you are dreaming you can control the dream sequence; also, you can start dreaming the next night from where you left off. It is a habit to be cultivated. She has also explained how to remember your dreams.

But before we come to that, I will take up the subject of nightmares. Nightmares are a problem, especially to children. I know of a person, a friend of mine who is a great poet. He wrote to Sri Aurobindo that in his sleep he went out of his body and entered a world where some beings took hold of him and beat him up. When he returned, though his physical body was lying down he felt a strain and a pain throughout his body. Sri Aurobindo told him that he had gone to the vital world where the vital beings exist and that he must know how to get the protection of Sri Aurobindo and the Mother so that even if he went to the vital world the beings there would not be able to harm him.

Nightmares have two aspects. One solution is not to go to the vital world; but then one would never learn, one would never know how to conquer, how to face problems. The second is to go to the vital world and not be affected by the vital beings but rather to influence and even master them. Most of the nightmares pertain to the subtle-physical and the vital worlds, but not beyond. Beyond the mind there are no nightmares at all. Beyond the mind are the worlds of delight. Really speaking, when you go beyond the mind your sleep becomes refreshing. So long as you remain in the mental and the vital planes, your sleep is not refreshing.

The Mother and Sri Aurobindo have also made a distinction between visions and dreams. There is on record a number of visions and experiences of Sri Aurobindo and the Mother. I would like to narrate two today. When the Mother was thirteen years old and living in Paris, every night when She went to bed She would go out of Her body. She would be clad in a golden robe and would rise straight up over the city. She would find Her robe enveloping and spreading all over the town. She would see old people, young people, children, all coming out of their houses and touching the robe – people full of sorrow touching the robe – and going back feeling happy. So this was a foreknowledge of Her role in the world to bring down a consciousness with which people would come in contact and go back happy.

Another vision She narrated while explaining how to interpret dreams, was of a man who saw in his dream that he was going up a hill in a carriage. The horses were finding it very difficult to climb. So the man got down from the carriage and started pushing it to help the horses to go up. Someone told him not to be foolish but to get back into the carriage and let the horses draw it up howsoever slowly. The Mother said that instead of invoking the Divine Grace and allowing it to take them up, men want to exercise their will and push things up on their own.

So it is like this. You have to learn to distinguish between visions and dreams and also to interpret them. Visions usually have a luminosity and, from the colour of the light – red, blue, light-blue, golden or white – you can judge in which plane you are seeing the vision. Visions and dreams both can be symbolic. You see the sun, you see a door – these are symbolic. You see as if you are entering inside a white dove or inside a white swan. Each of these things would mean something different. It would be even different from person to person. The interpretation is very much personal, but in order to do it, we must first be able to remember our visions and dreams.

The Mother has said that for more than a year She used to note down Her dreams regularly and it was only after a year that She was able to really come to a proper interpretation and control. She used to call it Her *night diary*. We also should begin by keeping a 'night diary'.

Sri Aurobindo's yoga is a very practical one. The Mother has said that if you want to have a good sleep, you should not eat too much but before going to bed you should have a cup of milk or juice or eat some fruit. That would give you better sleep. If you are tired or if you have had a very active day mentally, you should first try to calm down. When you lie in bed you should become limp like a rag. She has stated that if you become limp in this way a kind of transparency would come. In that state you can recite a mantra if you like.

The Mother and Sri Aurobindo have said that most of Their work was done at night. I would say ninety percent of Their work, and only ten percent was done during the day.

To come back, not only should you recite a mantra before going to sleep, but you should put a will that you should be conscious in your sleep. The old saying that one hour before midnight is equal to two after midnight, is true. The Mother gives a reason for this that the sun is setting till midnight and it starts rising from midnight. That is the period when it is the calmest. So you benefit greatly if you go to sleep early and you benefit the most from the energy which starts coming after midnight, if you get up early. This habit of going to sleep early and getting up early should be cultivated if you are really aspiring for self-perfection. If that is your goal, then you have to put a certain discipline in your life.

The Mother has said that you must divide your sleep into three parts – three hours, three hours and one hour – and you must sleep for at least seven hours daily. Once you have developed your will, you should wake up after every three hours, meditate a little, then go to sleep and wake up after one hour. I tell you your sleep becomes most beneficial if you can cultivate this habit. It is not only beneficial for your inner growth but also for refreshing the body.

She has also said that when you get up in the morning, you should not jump out of bed but lie there without moving, without even shaking your head. You should keep a diary near your bed and the first thing you do is to recall your dreams. If you continue doing this, after sometime you will be able to remember them. And you should remember the dreams backwards, what happened last, what happened before that, what was the first dream you had. If you persevere you will find that after you have finished one dream, you feel as if you have gone to another plane, and another dream which you had forgotten will also come back to you, will reveal itself to you and in this way, you will be able to recall two or three dreams in a single night. So you recall all of them going backwards.

I remember once the Mother had given me some work outside Pondicherry and I was keen to complete it soon and return. For three or four nights, I had almost no time to sleep. I finished my work and returned. And I felt as fresh as if I had just got up after twelve hours of sleep. When the Mother saw me She said, "You had better go to sleep." I protested, "But Mother, I am feeling quite fresh, I don't feel the need to sleep." She said, "I know, but still you go and sleep." (Now, this is another interesting thing. This is how a guru can take upon himself a disciple's need for sleep.) So I went to my room in the Ashram and slept. And to my surprise, to my utter surprise, when I got up, it was the next day. I must have gone to sleep at ten or ten-thirty in the morning and woke up the next day at lunchtime, say about one. It was such a beautiful sleep. I do not think I have ever had that kind of sleep in my whole life. It was an experience.

So the important thing to know is that you can control your sleep and if you have offered yourself to the Divine, He starts controlling your sleep, your waking hours, takes the responsibility of everyday of your life, which in itself is a great progress and a fulfilment for those who offer themselves to God.

About the hours of sleep and the afternoon nap, the Mother has said that it is a matter of an individual's need. She has not made any distinction between sleep at night and a nap in the afternoon. If the afternoon nap is necessary for you, you nap. What is more important is the nature of your sleep. The Mother has said that in sleep if you can go to the highest plane through meditation you can recover in twenty minutes all your energies. Then for the rest of the night you can do your occult work during sleep. Occult work during sleep is the most important work. If people knew how to do it, they would lead a fuller life.

There are two more things you should know about sleep and dreams. Some people have dreams about sex. Now, how can they control them? The Mother has said that if you practise yoga, even one such dream in a dozen could ruin months of hard work of your progress. In yoga the aim is elimination, transformation, not only control or curbing of the sex impulse, although that is very important, too. For this, the Mother has given a very practical suggestion. She has recommended a cold water bath before going to sleep. Then you put a will and meditate on Light and you will be surprised to find how this helps in eliminating wrong dreams. This is extremely important for those who practise Sri Aurobindo's yoga and are aspiring for the transformation of the physical body, because indulgence takes one closer to death. I repeat, it is not the curbing or controlling of impulse but the transformation which is needed.

Another point to consider is talking in sleep. Some people talk in their sleep. Why do they talk? The Mother has explained that in some people their mind goes out during sleep. Then they do not talk. But when the mind remains attached to the body they talk of their experiences or when they are seeing a nightmare or whatever. The mind thinks, the body expresses.

The Mother has also explained the phenomenon of people walking in their sleep. She has said that they walk on a kind of a precipice or on a side wall in a way which they would find impossible to do in their waking state. She has explained that sometimes during sleep the subtle-physical consciousness goes out but the physical is so attached to it, that the physical body also goes along with it. That is why people walk in their sleep. She has said that if one wants to stop this, one has to exercise one's will, for will is the main instrument. You meditate and you put your will that this should not happen. If you have progressed far in yoga you can even put your will on others, you can meditate and concentrate on them and join your will with theirs so that their will becomes stronger. These are phenomena which the Mother and Sri Aurobindo have explained in very great detail and about which I am telling you only very briefly.

Once Sri Aurobindo was asked: "When we see a person trying to attack us in our dream, do we surmise from this that the man is an enemy and that he wants to harm us?" Sri Aurobindo said that no, it could be that you have been thinking that he is an enemy and that is why he has come in such a form in your dream. It does not mean that he is necessarily an enemy. It is your thought, your imagination which has created this form.

So we see that there are dreams which are the result of our imaginations; there are dreams which are true experiences and not imaginations and there are visions which are different from dreams. Some people, after getting up from sleep, say: "Oh, I had a very good sleep, I had no dreams." Now, most of them are wrong. You have no dreams if you go to the subconscient. You are too tired, you go to sleep, you go to the subconscient and you have no dreams. But if you go to the conscient planes you are bound to have dreams, only you do not remember them and that is why you say you had no dreams. How does it happen? And why is it that sometimes dreams are mixed up? You cannot make head or tail of them. You see, when you go to sleep, your physical body is asleep. Normally, the subtle-physical and the vital also go to sleep, but the mental is awake. It may be creating, it may be thinking of some problem and the physical control which is imposed on it during the day when you are working, when you are thinking of something else, has gone and so it is free to think, to imagine what it likes, to move in the mental world. After sometime the mental gets tired and goes to sleep, it tries to rest, and the vital wakes up. The vital is full of emotions, impulses and it creates its own images or has its own experiences. So these are mixed images created in your dream. We sometimes meet people in dreams. Sri Aurobindo and the Mother were asked whether we actually meet them, what really happens. They said that there are many possibilities and one of them is that our astral bodies have met, though on the physical level we might not have met. It could even be imagination. So each case you have to study according to the circumstances, then you can come to know what actually takes place in your dreams.

The subject of dreams is very vast. We must cultivate our nights as much as we cultivate our days. If we cultivate the nights properly it will help us in many respects to progress to our next stage.

I would like to mention here how some children are taught by God – not by us. I remember I once went to meet a friend of mine. He had a granddaughter – a child of nine. He asked for coffee for me and she brought it. As she was coming I could see a beautiful light around her. I asked her, "Child, do you see any dreams?" – "Yes, I do." – "What do you do?" She said, "I lie down in my bed and I tell God to come and sleep here." (A child of nine and yet what could have made her think and act in this manner?) I asked her, "What happens?" "I sometimes see images in my dreams," she said. (Now this is very important. I know of a lady who told me – this was years ago – that an old man used to guide her in her dreams and whatever he said always came true. So there are beings and entities with whom, for some reason, a relationship exists or develops and those beings guide you. Sometimes we see in our dreams our departed father or grandfather and we say he guided us. This is a different phenomenon.) So I asked the child, "How does it help you?" She said, "When I go out shopping with my mummy, something guides me 'you buy this', and I always buy it." I was very much interested in the child. She felt an inner contact with the Divine which few grownups feel, unless they are spiritually developed.

The important thing is that you can receive guidance not only for the problems you have but in all aspects of your life. If you really open to a higher consciousness it can guide you quietly in your dreams to such an extent that you cannot ever imagine.

Now we come to the posture during sleep. The Mother and Sri Aurobindo have said that the posture taken during sleep has an effect. It was very interesting to observe the Mother's posture. Her back was like this (gesture of inclined plane), it was not flat. So the whole night She was like this (gesture) – reclining with Her feet stretched out, rather than sleeping. She used to have very many pillows – a pillow here, a pillow there. And I must tell you that a few more pillows make your whole sleep much more comfortable. I do not know why people do not think of these small things – some small pillows, some big ones – to make you ten times more comfortable. You must try to sleep in as reclined a manner as possible, and as limp as a rag, as the Mother used to say. This makes your sleep much more comfortable, gives you better scope for meditation and you get up feeling much more fresh in the morning. You must know how to prepare for your sleep, how to sleep properly and how to wake up.

What is the best way to sleep, the best way to be conscious in the morning, the best way to get up? The answer the Mother has given is that the best way for the day is also the best way for the night. It is to meditate in complete union with the Mother and Sri Aurobindo's consciousness, invoking Their Light in every cell of your body, in unity with Them and lie down in bed. Do not try to think of sleep; it will come by itself. And you should remain in this state and wake up in this state. If you do this, all the wrong dreams, unnecessary dreams will automatically get eliminated. It acts like a screen and whatever is necessary not only for your spiritual growth, but also for your material progress, will automatically be added to it. The interpretation of your dreams and visions will come to you intuitively. You will not have to work logically or tax your brain or make mistakes. You will find that when you get up in the morning it will be with a new strength, a new illumination, a new hope. If you practise it for a few days you will understand what I am saying.

In our shastras they speak of avastās – 'Jāgrat avastā', 'Svapna avastā' and 'Suṣupti avastā'. Suṣupti is the state when you go to the planes and levels of consciousness beyond mind and experience them and come back. So sleep and dreams are states in which your spirit, in which your spiritual and material progress can reach new heights. You can even individualise your inner planes of consciousness much better during sleep than during the day. We must therefore try to become conscious and the master of our sleep.

Death and Immortality

As you all know, today is the day when Sri Aurobindo left His physical body thirty years ago. I remember I was in Bombay when a telegram came from the Mother. It is very significant; the simple wording was: "Sri Aurobindo has passed away. Inform all." A few friends and I chartered a plane, flew to Madras and motored down to Pondicherry. The Mother was not seeing anybody but since the plane was waiting, She called me to Her room. To my surprise, I saw that Her body was white – not like ours, not fair but *white* – bright white. She asked me whether I had seen the Light around Sri Aurobindo. Then She told me that Sri Aurobindo would not be given Samadhi as long as the Light was around His body. The Light remained for four days. There was no decomposition. So we consecrate 5th and 9th December as the days of His passing and His Mahasamadhi.

The Mother was once asked what we should do during this period. She said that we should think of death and immortality. Today we will spend a few minutes in trying to understand the phenomena of death and immortality, as explained by Sri Aurobindo. When we read Sri Aurobindo and the Mother we learn that there are many things not in keeping with our traditional thoughts. But one of the things in Sri Aurobindo's yoga which is partly in keeping with our traditional thoughts is that death can be avoided, life can be prolonged, death can be delayed. The Mother has said that there is a race – a race between man and death – whether death takes hold of him first and he decays and dies, or he conquers death first. In Sri Aurobindo's yoga one can speed up one's progress and evolution. By some good fortune we have come in contact with Sri Aurobindo and so we have a chance if we follow the path shown by Him. Many others do not have a chance, they do not even know that death can be conquered physically. We will very briefly try to understand this path.

The Mother has said that it is possible to concretise the astral body in such a manner that one can go out at will and return at will to one's physical body. So when death comes, it holds no fear because one is already accustomed to separating the astral body from the physical body, having practised the process over a long period. This is another aspect of Sri Aurobindo's yoga in which occult knowledge is not ignored, but is developed for the service of the Divine, not for the satisfaction of one's ego. So, you can consciously go out of your body and return.

The third thing which the Mother has said and which I found very interesting is that when the representative of the Lord of Death comes – he has been ordered to bring so many souls each day – and if you have the spiritual power you can tell him not to take this person but to take some one else. It is quite possible to save one person from death and tell him to go elsewhere to fulfil his quota. I found this very amazing when I read it, because I did not know that such a thing could be possible.

I have given you only two or three aspects but someday we will take up in detail the subject of the phenomenon of death.

Sri Aurobindo and the Mother have described in very great detail what happens to the soul, the psychic being and the astral personality after death. The mind continues to exist, the vital continues to exist, even after death. Some people out of ignorance may say this man has become a snake, that man has become a cat, after his death. Now, that is not correct. A part of the personality of the person, the lower part, may join with a snake, a cat or a deer. This does not mean that his *entire* personality, including his soul, has joined with that animal. The Mother has given us two or three examples of this phenomenon. She said that a man She knew, a young man, died in the First World War. She was at that time living in Paris. She was sitting in Her room when suddenly a cat came and started pulling at her dress. She saw in the cat's eyes the eyes of that man and could feel his presence. She immediately knew that the young man had been killed. Later She found that he had indeed died on the battlefront exactly at the time the cat had come to the Mother. So the astral body hardly took any time to travel from a battlefield in Germany right upto Paris and get in touch with the Mother. That is the speed with which the astral body can travel; it can even go through a wall and keep its personality.

Once the Mother told us that there was a musician who had trained his hands to play the piano over years of practice. After his death his subtle hands got concretised – they got the skill – and so even after the man died, his hands, only the hands, remained in the subtle-physical. This is very amazing that not the total personality but the hands alone could combine with the hands of another person who was trying to become a good musician. But this second musician must be in an attitude of invoking – and this is very important – invoking some force to help him and for that moment he may play very beautifully, which normally he may be incapable of doing. This means it is quite possible to build a connection; to build a contact with the subtle-physical forces, and combine with even a part of the personality of another person who has died and thus improve one's life.

I am also reminded of another incident. A lady came to Pondicherry and I took her to the Mother. The Mother looked at her and when she left after pranam, the Mother told me that there was a man inside her. So I asked the lady, "When did your husband die?" She said that he had died some six months ago. I said, "Do you feel his presence?" She replied, "Constantly. I knew nothing about business before he died. But because my child was very young, I started looking after the business and I find my husband is constantly guiding me." This is quite possible. By a certain affinity it is possible to keep the astral body in a happy atmosphere or in an atmosphere where it can find its fulfilment. In the case of this lady, her husband must have felt that he had left his business unattended and must have been worried as to who would look after it. Since the man had a developed personality he did not disperse it but combined it with his wife's, after his death.

So death depends a lot on the kind of life we lead. One thing we should know is that no progress at all is possible after death. Whatever progress we make during life, our psychic being carries it to the next life and then waits for the next life to make a new progress.

Now I come very briefly to the phenomenon of rebirth, a subject which all of us should study. The Mother has said that the period between death and rebirth varies normally from six months to three years, at times maybe even a hundred. The more advanced the soul, the longer is the period after which it reincarnates. Also, an advanced soul can decide on its parents, on its environment, what it wants to do and can create its own environment before taking a new birth.

There is a second category where there is an element of accident. When a psychic being enters the earth atmosphere for reincarnation and if there are parents in family B who are more receptive, the psychic being which might have taken birth in family A, might go instead to family B. So near the earth level an element of chance – I do not say total chance – can also exist. What is even more interesting about the phenomenon of rebirth is that some children are conscious of their soul from their very childhood, but like foolish people we think that because he is a child, he would not understand anything. This is a very wrong approach. A child of two may be more conscious of his soul than a man of sixty because the child may have already lived many lives earlier. I remember, a girl of seven wanted to join the Ashram. I told the Mother, "Mother, this girl wants to join the Ashram but what would she know? She has never been in an Ashram." The Mother said, "Let her decide." I asked, "How can she decide?" The Mother said, "Even a child of three can decide. It is not a child's mind but her soul which decides, which says: 'My place is here.' "

One thing I would like to tell you about, before we continue with the phenomenon of rebirth, is suicide. The Mother has always been against suicide. If you cut your life short by suicide, you will have to start your next life under worse conditions. You should not cut short your life but you should, on the contrary, prolong it. About prolonging life, there is another interesting episode which I would like to share with you. When we find a person dear to us is suffering, we pray to God: "O God, it is better that he dies than he suffers like this." An aunt of mine had a paralytic stroke – this was some thirty-five years ago – and she was suffering a great deal. I told the Mother that it would be much better if she leaves her body. The Mother said: "No. You must not reduce life even by one breath, because till the last breath there is a chance to realise God." We must always remember this, that till the last breath there is a chance to realise God.

Now we come briefly to the phenomenon of immortality. Prolongation of life is one thing, immortality, another. In Sri Aurobindo's yoga it is a physical immortality that is envisaged. I remember when I was a young man – seventeen or eighteen – in Sri Aurobindo Circle in Bombay where I was the secretary, we had a discussion on the phenomenon of death, conquest of death. We had many scholars of Sri Aurobindo's teaching but they too can sometimes make mistakes. One of them said: "Physical transformation may even be undesirable." They said that by immortality Sri Aurobindo meant prolongation of life, conquering the fear of death, conquering death by realising one's soul and remaining in the immortal consciousness. But then I found that it was not so.

There is an old saying: "Mṛtyuṁ tirtvā amṛtam aśnute", which means that when you realise the Divine, you are in eternity, you are immortal. But in Sri Aurobindo's yoga this is not sufficient. In His yoga the goal is a physical immortality and that is what I want you to understand today. Sri Aurobindo has stated that there are three aspects of creation: First, there is the Eternal, the source of all. Second, there are the intermediate planes, the plane of gods, the planes of other beings, which He has graded as the Overmind, Intuitive Mind, Illumined Mind, Higher Mind. He has described all these different planes in great detail. And lastly there is the physical plane, the manifested creation. But what is important to know is that Sri Aurobindo considers the Supermind plane alone as a part of the Eternal and the perfect aspect of the Divine, where the powers of the Divine are not limited or diminished.

All the planes below the Supermind – the Overmind plane and below – are a part of creation. This means that if pralaya were to take place, creation would be dissolved right upto the Overmind plane and gods like Indra, Varuna, Maruts would all disappear, but the Supramental plane would remain. Now the Overmind plane is the plane which Sri Krishna manifested on earth. But he himself was a Divine incarnation. So we should not say that Sri Krishna belonged to the Overmind plane. He was far beyond the Overmind plane. But what he manifested in the world was the Overmind plane.

The Overmind plane, as I said, is a part of creation. So up to now, the highest manifestation on earth has been of the Overmind plane. Sri Aurobindo has brought down a manifestation of the Supermind plane. He has said that physical transformation and physical immortality are not possible by any descent from the Overmind plane or the planes below it. Prolongation of life can take place but physical transformation is not possible. But if the Supermind plane descends on earth and in the human body, the human body would then undergo a transmutation and become a body of light. The body itself would be immortal. This is one of the most fascinating aspects of Sri Aurobindo's yoga.

Let us try to understand in a simple manner what this body of light will be like. Sri Aurobindo was asked whether a man in the street would be able to see this body of light or only a great yogi. Sri Aurobindo replied that a man in the street would be able to see it. There would be no ambiguity once the transformation takes place. And once this transmutation and transformation come, then one can even go to the planets and the stars. Sri Aurobindo has said that a new element which did not exist in the world till today would be created by the Supermind descending in the material plane. He has further said that as you do yoga, you would gradually be able to transmit this consciousness even to things, for example, to this taperecorder or this chair when you touch them.

The Mother one day told us that She had seen in a vision the Meditation Hall of our Ashram, where the colour of the walls kept changing with the changing consciousness of man. Suppose you suddenly feel angry, you will find that the colour of the walls has changed. So you will no longer be able to hide your impulses when they arise in you. In ancient India people used to do "prāna-pratisthā" in an idol, by invoking the higher consciousness in the idol. In the supramental manifestation the new consciousness will be evoked in matter, in matter everywhere. This is the yoga of Sri Aurobindo. In every activity, in every being the Divine should manifest without any veil, without any curtain. This manifestation of the Divine, Sri Aurobindo calls *a divine life in a divine body*. And this evolution towards supermanhood will give rise to the superman who will have a body of light.

Sri Aurobindo has said that this process has also a collective aspect. You cannot sit in meditation alone in your room and invoke the supramental descent and say I will have transformation. Sri Aurobindo has explained the special features of this transformation from man to superman. The first is that you should work and work for Sri Aurobindo. You cannot say that I am doing this, I am doing that, I am doing public service, therefore I am working for the Divine and I will get transformed. No, you have to work for Sri Aurobindo; and in every action – whether you speak, walk, write or whatever else you may do – you have to open your physical consciousness to the supramental consciousness, and let it descend in your physical body and administer it.

Sri Aurobindo was once asked that if we remained in a very high level of consciousness, realising the Divine but did not work for the Mother, would we get transformed? Sri Aurobindo said, not at all. So you have to work and work for the Mother. Now what does 'work for the Mother' mean? One might ask why work for the Mother and Sri Aurobindo? It is because you get the consciousness of the person on whom you concentrate and that is why our shastras always say: "Ganaśa jay smṛti siddhi ho". So if you remember Sri Aurobindo, His consciousness will combine with yours and will give you the guidance for the thing to be done. That is why our shastras always insist on 'sumirana' (remembrance) because sumirana gives you the contact.

There can be many contacts but they are not all from the supramental level. The Divine is the same, but by meditating on 'Matsyāvatāra' you cannot get Sri Krishna's consciousness, you will get 'Matsyāvatarā' consciousness. So if you want a supramental change of the physical body and if you want the Supermind to descend in you, you have to concentrate on the Mother and Sri Aurobindo as they are the Supramental Avatars. Sri Aurobindo has never said that what He has taught is the last word. This is only the next step in evolution. So when you work for Them, you have a feeling that They are working through you. And with that feeling the wall between Their consciousness and yours will break for it is Their consciousness acting through you that can bring about the transformation. But you have to work; to work not only in a spirit of Karma Yoga but in a spirit of Karma Yoga concentrating on the Mother and Sri Aurobindo.

There is also another aspect. One day, the Mother explained to us the distinction between work *for* the Divine and work *of* the Divine. Any work you offer to Sri Aurobindo and the Mother you can say I am working *for* Them. But it becomes work *of* Them when the guidance comes directly from Them. Slowly and gradually you get Their guidance. And if you get a contact, even a little bit, Their consciousness automatically flows in you. It is like plugging in to an electric socket. The offering of your work automatically plugs you in to Their consciousness. Working for Them is the first step, and this leads you to the next one which is to *do* Their work, the work *of* the Divine, directly.

Another aspect of Their yoga is the manifestation of the Divine in the collectivity. In a collective life everybody tries to realise God and everybody tries to manifest Him. The Mother and Sri Aurobindo have said that this has two aspects. Let us suppose there are five hundred people or twenty or ten, practising yoga together. We start at level Z and we have to reach level A. When we start, all of us will not be at level Z, some will be at level X, some at level T. So we start at different levels but the goal of each one of us is to reach level A. Now, the man at level T will reach level, let us say K, a man at level Z will reach level X or maybe by some process he will come straight to level K – anything is possible. Now this ascent to different levels in the consciousness creates its own natural hierarchy.

Normally, in a hierarchy, a managing director of a company is higher than a clerk. But in a spiritual hierarchy it would be different. A man may be a managing director but this does not mean that he is spiritually more advanced than a clerk. So in this way, the Divine manifesting in all but through a hierarchy, the collective life will be different. How? Some people, as I told you, would rise to a higher level of consciousness, start working and the whole community would come nearer to that level. Again as some more people rise to a still higher level, once more the whole community would be lifted. This is what the Mother has described: each one will help the others by their very presence and the collective life will help the individual person.

Then there is another aspect of the collective life. There are some limitations in our normal life which come in the way of our spiritual growth. Economic worries, political worries, social worries – "ladki ki shadi karni hai, yeh kharcha chhahiye, doctor ko bolana hai." (We have to get our daughter married, we need money, we have to call for the doctor.) The new collective life will be organised in such a manner that if you fall ill, you will not have to worry; the doctor will give you free medicine, he will even arrange for your diet, as that will be his duty. If you are in charge of agriculture it will be your duty to produce the best fruits, the best flowers and offer these to the community. The Mother has said that in such a community, man, freed from different physical and psychological pulls, will be able to offer all his energies and concentration to the Divine, so that the process of evolution can be accelerated. This is the second aspect of the Mother's vision of the collective life.

The Mother's third vision is that as we advance nearer to the goal of transformation, a new social order will evolve which She calls the *gnostic society*. But before I come to this, I would like to tell you one more thing. A professor had come to Pondicherry to give a course in Business Management. He gave a talk on 'Management by Consciousness'. Now this is very important. You normally plan your day – you have to do this thing today, you want to ring up your friend, you want to go to your tailor, this kind of food is needed and so on. You even plan your life, your business, a little. In management by consciousness, which is completely different from this, you plan by consciousness. How? You plan nothing. You just remain in a higher consciousness. S comes and something is spoken. Suddenly M telephones and another thing is spoken, or A's programme is cancelled. Things start happening automatically if you live in that higher consciousness every minute of your life. Whatever the Divine wants to manifest through you gets manifested. You are not linked with the event which happened two minutes back nor are you thinking of what is going to happen to you two minutes afterwards. And, after a few days when you look back, you will find that there is a pattern of development in this, which is far better than mental planning. The new method has no relation to the old way of working, and it is a hundred times more effective.

Now, in the present society there might be handicaps. But in a collective life, where everybody is trying to do this, it will have a different dimension. No one will need to tell the other to do this or that. Each one will know that he will have the right guidance, that at the right time the guidance will come to him. Those who are doing Sri Aurobindo's yoga, are actually experiencing this all the time, all the time. I find people ringing me up, people coming, people writing, people speaking to me, just when I need them, just when I need them. It is most amazing how these things happen. This is what the Mother meant when She said that Auroville should be administered or developed by a new consciousness, by a new method. So every time you go to a higher consciousness you organise your life around it. Sri Aurobindo made His own life and work a part of this process. He wrote *Savitri* and when He reached a higher level, He revised it. Again He went to a higher level and again He revised it. So He made *Savitri* a means of His progress. Similarly, anything you do – agriculture, industry, farming, cooking – could be a means of realising the Divine and you will do your work better when you combine your consciousness with the Divine consciousness.

Suppose you are cooking at home and if you stretch out your hand for salt, something may tell you that you are putting the wrong thing and you will find that it is so. And later even with eyes closed you will find your hand going to the salt when needed.

When you need a thing your hand will automatically pick it up, because a new consciousness manifests in your body and in the objects. That is why the Mother was very strict. She would not allow our books to be touched by others, She would not allow some one else to sit in our chair. If you read Her old letters of thirty or forty years ago, you would find a lot of restrictions, like not meeting certain people. I remember some people had come from Bombay – I am telling you of an incident some thirty-five years ago – they were very important people. They invited me to tea. As I said, in those days the Mother was very strict. We used to ask the Mother's permission for everything. So I asked Her. She said, "You may go but don't give them more than four minutes." With Her everything was quite different.

So management by consciousness is another aspect of a collective spiritual life. As a result of all this, a gnostic society will evolve which Sri Aurobindo has described in great detail in His book, *The Life Divine*. What is a gnostic community? How will this gnostic society function? The first model is intended to be Auroville.

But Auroville is now facing serious difficulties. Accusations have been levelled against it by motivated persons. Accusations which are deliberately false. But the Divine had a reason behind it. And that reason is: we, who are connected with Sri Aurobindo were shirking our responsibilities, and trying to lead a peaceful life. What happens to India is of secondary importance to us. Sri Aurobindo wants us to understand that we are a part of humanity, we are a part of India. If we have developed, if we have progressed in anything, it is then our responsibility to work for a collective change. We have to fight falsehood and finally conquer it. In one of Her Prayers, the Mother says: *Give us a faith active and ardent, absolute and unshakable in Thy Victory.* So whatever the opposing forces may do, whatever be the situation, let us not forget that the Divine is with us. And it is a greater privilege to fight on His side and to conquer, because it will not be we who will conquer but it is He who is going to conquer. Sri Krishna tells Arjuna to fight; he then adds: "What is there, I have already killed them. Become simply 'nimitta' (instrument)." We must really become perfect instruments. That is the honour, the grace that has come to us. It is not trouble that has come to us, it is Grace that has come to us. So let us face this situation which in the world history will one day be recorded as a crucial situation for mankind. Auroville is a project of Sri Aurobindo, it is a project for realising His teaching, it is a project for establishing a gnostic society; as the Mother has said, *it will be the cradle of the Superman.* And if we believe that someone who does not understand Sri Aurobindo is going to come and administer it always and that the Divine forces are going to allow it, we are very foolish. But how is the Force going to act? This is not for us to decide. We have to do our duty towards the Divine. For us, it will have to be our sadhana. We cannot act like ordinary human beings. We have to remain concentrated in Sri Aurobindo's consciousness and let Him fight His battles using us as His instruments. It is a double fulfilment for us: to remain always on the side of the Truth, and not to have recourse to falsehood. Then the outer result and form do not matter. Our victory is to offer our instrumentality to the Divine so that His will may manifest through us.

Today is a sacred day for us because Sri Aurobindo left His body in a supreme sacrifice. The Mother has said that He will remain in the subtle-physical plane till the world is transformed. She has also said that He is constantly amongst us, helping us, guiding us, only we have to feel His Presence. He is with us, only we have to turn to Him.

Here I am reminded of a sentence from the Ramayana. When Vibhīśaṇa (brother of Ravana) comes to meet Rama, the monkeys cry out: "We do not know him, he may be a spy of Ravana. We must be very careful." In Tulsidas' Ramayana there are two beautiful sentences: "Sanamukha hoi jiva mohi jabahin / Janma koti agha nasahin tabahi." Rama says: "When Jiva (the psychic being) turns to Me, sins of a million lives, of ten million lives are destroyed." Sins are all those walls, those curtains we have created between our consciousness and the Divine consciousness. The mere act of just turning to Him wipes them out. Can you imagine a greater message of hope?

The thing needed is to turn to Him. Your past does not matter, for here is another interesting aspect mentioned in the Ramayana, which the Gita also endorses: "Koti bipra badha lagahi jahū / Āyen sarana tajawn nahi tahū". "Even if he has killed ten million brahmins I will not desert him if he seeks shelter in Me!" When you turn to the Divine He takes full responsibility for you. And here Sri Aurobindo not only takes full responsibility but promises us a life which we cannot imagine in our wildest dreams. I would not have believed it if anybody else had told me that such a thing is possible on earth. But after coming to Sri Aurobindo, I believe it. So it is Grace that has brought us in contact with Him.

Let us make a very firm resolution that the next four days will be for us days of intensive sadhana. Those of you who can give your entire time to Sri Aurobindo and the Mother should try to do so. It would be for your own good. Those who cannot, should try to remain concentrated on Them, as much as possible, in one's day-to-day work and thus participate in the transformation which They are already bringing about.

May the Mother's and Sri Aurobindo's Blessings be with you.

Fate, Free Will and Determinism

The question of fate and free will is a complex and difficult one, but let me begin by telling you that there is a lot of freedom given to man, a lot of things can be changed and more so at the present time, now that the Supramental descent has taken place. The old ideas that things are rigidly predetermined should be removed from our minds. How far things are predetermined, how far freedom exists, we can only know by reaching a certain level of consciousness. No amount of study, no amount of preaching is going to give us a clear idea – at least not till we raise ourselves in consciousness.

I will give you a simple example. Suppose you are in a very high place from where you can see everything. You see a car coming from one direction and another car from the opposite direction. And you realise that if nothing stops them, both the cars are bound to collide at a particular place and time. So this is one way of understanding what predeterminism means. But if there is a light, like you have in traffic regulations, where you stop one of the two cars, an accident is avoided. The same thing applies to the inner planes. If you have the inner knowledge events can be changed.

There are some major Forces or Powers acting in the world along with many lesser powers. First, there is the Divine Will. The Divine Will acts universally but acts within the limitations it has imposed on itself. It is a self-imposed limitation of cosmic forces for the play. The Divine Will in the world acts for man's evolution, for manifestation of the Divine. That nobody can change. We can delay its action but the Divine Will cannot be changed. That Divine Will is for the happiness of all, for the welfare of all. If you are in unity with the Divine Will, in unity with that current, with that flow, it can lead you to the highest good. This is the first thing to know.

Somebody asked Sri Aurobindo how to be a leader, a successful leader and He explained that the Divine current, the Divine forces work in a certain direction. If you are in unity with these forces, if you work in harmony with these forces, certain events are bound to take place. People are generally ignorant of these forces, so they think you have achieved it by yourself and they acclaim you as their leader. But when you work against the forces, you cannot succeed.

There are also cosmic forces at work. Cosmic forces work at many levels – levels of Overmind, Intuitive Mind, Illumined Mind, Higher Mind, Mind and Vital. They are more powerful than the physical forces we see around us and by the use of these cosmic forces the higher planes – can influence the lower. Each plane has its own law and the law of one plane does not apply to the other. If the law of the physical plane has to be changed, you have to bring the law of another plane – like the law of the vital, the mental, the psychic or the law of the higher planes to bear on the physical level.

Events can change if you bring the determinism of a higher plane to bear on a lower plane, either by prayer, yoga, puja or some similar method. We will try to understand today how we can bring down this higher determinism. We will also try to understand how we can remain in the highest possible consciousness so that the best always happens to us, the very best, not only the best under the prevailing circumstances but the best under new and changed circumstances.

There are many things which seem to imply that there is predeterminism. You see events in your dreams and they actually take place. You consult an astrologer who tells you certain things and these happen. But the Mother has cautioned us even regarding these events; we should, therefore, be very careful in what we accept. I remember a lady wrote to me that she had a particular dream and that her dreams always came true. She was very much worried because it was a bad dream about her family. I took the letter to the Mother and the Mother said that these dreams come true because she *imagines* that her dreams come true. If she got rid of her imagination, this dream would not come true. And by God's Grace, it did not. It is now almost thirty years that the dream has not come true.

In another case, I remember once a horoscope was shown to the Mother. One lady had written that an astrologer had predicted that something bad would happen to her husband (ladies are always worried about their husbands) and she was very much upset and had asked the Mother's protection. The Mother said, "Give me the horoscope." She took it, put it on Her lap, took out a pen, crossed it out and said, "Tell her that the destiny is wiped out. Send it. This is all finished now." It is interesting to see how the Mother dealt with these things.

I have suffered a great deal because of my old ideas and beliefs. In my young days I had read a lot of Hindu mythology and it penetrated my consciousness. This I had to first remove before I could absorb the new kind of thinking which Sri Aurobindo has given us. That is why I say we have to efface all we have studied, learnt previously if we want a supramental life. Those whose good fortune has brought them in contact with Sri Aurobindo should aspire not only to be perfect – in the sense of being highly intellectual persons, intelligent persons or good persons – but they should aspire to be something yet higher, yet greater and that can only happen if they become like a clean slate and allow the higher consciousness to descend in them and work in them.

The Mother once narrated an incident, a true incident, which took place when She was in France. She said that an astrologer had predicted that a certain person would die from the sea. After about six months, this person was eating in a restaurant and a fish-bone got stuck in his throat and, as a result of this, the man died. So the astrologer said that he had predicted that the man would die of something conncected with the sea. Now the fish-bone got stuck in his throat and fish is from the sea, so the prediction had come true. The Mother was present when the astrologer said all this and She looked at him and said, "You killed him. You planted the thought in his mind: 'I am going to die from the sea', and this thought which was constantly working created the circumstances by which the fish-bone got stuck and he died."

We are very fortunate to be in touch with Gurus who have completely changed our old ideas to which we are accustomed from childhood. Not only this, but even about death, about re-birth, about epidemics and accidents, the Mother has something new to tell us, Sri Aurobindo has something new to teach us. This does not mean that you can achieve what They say in one day. What I am telling you are some of the possibilities that you can develop in yourself, if you know the method. This can transform your life and lead you to a better one.

While speaking about death, the Mother one day told us – and it was very amazing to me – that death can be avoided. She told us something yet more amazing. She said that sometimes death comes to claim a particular person, but if somebody – a guru – has the power to give his protection or if something in the man aspires: "Lord, I have not finished with my life. I want to live", then he may get protection and death may leave him and take away another person who was not destined to die that day. So life is not as simiple as people imagine it to be. Life has many dimensions and many complications. You can organise your life properly if you know the method and you can be the master of your destiny by practising yoga, by a progressive growth in consciousness. There is really no other way.

The Mother also told us that when She started practising yoga, all the lines in Her hands disappeared. Her hands became blank, and then new lines started appearing. So it is very important to know that though events in your life are to a certain extent predetermined they *can* be changed. Also, you have many destinies. The Mother has said that out of several destinies, that destiny becomes applicable to you in which your consciousness dwells. If you can keep your consciousness *always* at the highest level, while walking, talking, working, always the best will happen to you. This is one principle, but there is also another. Always the best will happen to you under the existing circumstances. But the supramental transformation envisages a change in the circumstances themselves – transformation of the physical body, change in the collective life. All this we shall take up another time. Today we shall confine ourselves to the understanding of how these cosmic forces work, how you can get out of their grip and become the master of your life and the outer circumstances. When I say you can become the master of a situation you must know that it is not your ego that is going to control it. It is your 'egolessness' and through it, your unity with the Divine which is going to make you the master of outer circumstances, because He alone is completely free and you have a spark of His Divinity in you. Man has more freedom than gods, because gods do not have a psychic being. They are bound to their cosmic plane and cannot evolve and go beyond. Man is the only one who can go beyond and invoke the Divine power in his life on earth. Let me explain this further. Suppose you are going from Delhi to Calcutta by train. There are certain stations you will have to pass on the way if you are going by a particular route. So, unless you change trains these stations are bound to come. But within the compartment you have the freedom to do anything you like – reading, studying, eating, resting, whatever you want to do. So in the world an individual has a role to play, and that role he *has* to play, but it is played through his own will. Fate and freedom both exist.

Sri Aurobindo has quoted the interesting example of Napoleon. Napoleon was always talking of fate and always planning on a large scale – his army, their stores, everything. Somebody asked him why was he always speaking of fate and yet planning in such a big way. Sri Aurobindo said that Napoleon had uttered a great truth when he replied that it was fate which made him plan. His will was an instrument of Fate to achieve the goal. It is true that one's will can be a part of Fate, but it does not mean that everything is decided about you in detail before your birth. A lot of freedom is given to you. Predeterminism exists to a certain extent and a split-second before an event takes place, it is decided on a higher plane. Before that split-second, if something in you prayed and aspired for a change, if something in you offered yourself to the Divine, the event could be avoided or changed. The question may arise whether this aspiration in you was also predetermined, whether it was also destined that a particular event would take place but you would aspire and the event would change. Now this is a very difficult question to answer from our ordinary level of consciousness. At a higher level of consciousness the question does not exist, because you can know the answer for yourself. But I will yet try to give a practical answer at this level just for your understanding.

So long as you have ego, only an apparent freedom exists in you, and from a higher level, this freedom may appear to be notional. When you do not have ego, then alone does this freedom truly exist. But so long as you have ego, even if the freedom is limited or apparent, you must always try for the best and not say that everything is predetermined.

I will tell you what happened in my life. I had not joined the Ashram – this was in the early years of sadhana. God had given me everything I had asked for, everything. It was a happy life. But when I started doing yoga my attitude changed and I said to myself: "No, let the Divine Will prevail. I do not want to put my will in anything. Besides, when I put my will, things go wrong." So one day I told the Mother, "Mother, even if things are going wrong, I have taken this attitude that I should not put my will into anything but let the Divine Will prevail." The Mother said, "No, this is a wrong attitude. Your will is also a part of the Divine Will and you must positively apply it for the best. And all the time." So an indifferent attitude is not the best approach. You must positively put your will in tune with the Divine Will. The question is how does one know the Divine Will?

Now, so long as you have desires and preferences, you will not know the Divine Will. But if you can shake off your desires and preferences, not only will the Divine Will show you what to do, but it will show you how to do it. It will also at times show you what events are going to take place and how you can change them or accept them like Christ did. Christ knew he was going to be crucified, he knew it was the Divine Will and he had to fulfil it. When you come to that state of desirelessness this kind of awareness develops in you.

Even if the desires are not completely eliminated, it should be possible for you to meditate at least for half an hour or an hour and in that consciousness, you may have a glimpse of the past, present and future. Only when the desires are completely removed from your consciousness can you correctly foresee the future. And when you are totally desireless and surrendered to the Divine, He will also show you – He is the Paraṃ Guru – the way to change, the mantra to be used, the forces to be concentrated upon to change the events. Or, if it is necessary for you He will show you how to accept whatever destiny has in store for you and the wisdom to accept it gladly and the good that will come of it. So you will be happy, as either way or both ways you will benefit. He will show you the way to change not only your own life, but even the lives of others. If you are united with Him, even temporarily, even for a short period, He will show you how to change events in the lives of others. This is because the Divine works on the physical plane through human instruments. You must never forget that. You must be as good or as perfect an instrument as possible today, and try to become better and better everyday. This is the purpose of life: to progress everyday, to make your instrumentality – your mental, vital and physical personalities – better everyday so that you may become a perfect instrument of the Divine.

If you really want to foresee and influence events, try to go to a higher consciousness from where you can see everything and effectively change things. To bring about the desired result, there are two forces which are most important. One is will, prayer and aspiration – I put them all together – and the other is occult knowledge. When our forefathers said that for this you worship

Laxmi, for that you worship Shiva, they were not wrong. In fact this is what occult knowledge reveals. If you can combine your consciousness with the Supreme Divine, that would of course be the highest and the best; but that unity does not exclude an invocation to other cosmic forces manifested by the Supreme Divine. So you can combine your consciousness with both and when you are united at both levels, you will have the experience that you yourself are doing nothing but things are happening to you. For example, if the force has to go to somebody, it goes; if something has to be spoken, it gets spoken; if something has to be changed, it gets changed. A part of you is witnessing, another part is participating in the change or in the event. In this way you can lead a full life. And to live fully you have to have a deepening of consciousness and a universalisation of your consciousness and consciously manifest this through your physical personality. The union or the aspiration for the union with the Divine and occult knowledge, are both necessary if you want to be the master of events in your life or even of cosmic events. I will narrate an incident from the Mother's life which will give you an idea of how occult knowledge works.

After the First World War, an epidemic had spread in Japan. People would get fever and die. Doctors tried all possible ways but nothing worked. The Mother was in Japan at that time. She happened to call upon a friend about thirty miles from Tokyo. She spent sometime with her and when She returned She too had the fever. There were doctors attending on Her, but She refused to take any medicine. For three days, She had a high fever but She lay quietly in her bed, just united with the Divine consciousness. On the evening of the third or the fourth day – I now forget – She saw a being in a military uniform with only half a head, approaching Her. When he came near Her, She caught hold of him and there was a big struggle, but She succeeded in turning him back. From that day, people started getting cured in Japan. Later, when the Mother related this incident to us, She explained that he was one of those beings who had died during the War; one of those beings – and this is very interesting – who had not gone beyond, after death; 'gati nahin hui', as we say in India.

What I want to say is that man today is under the grip of several destinies. Your destiny on the physical plane is the result of your parents, partly of your environment and partly of yourself. The destiny on the vital plane is also partly the result of your parents though much less, more of your environment and yet much more of yourself. The destiny on the mental plane is very little from your parents, very little from your environment and a lot from you. As you go higher, the more is from you and the less is from the environment and the circumstances. When you go to the Highest, you can say it is from your soul, it is from the Divine, it is your true fate.

I now come to the most interesting part – how to avoid mistakes if you want to lead a fuller life. Many years ago, under the Mother's instructions I was having training from an Indian yogi. I went to his village to stay there and he had put me up in a small house, where the doors were extremely low, an old-style village house, with the toilet in a back courtyard, dark rooms and a kind of an open varendah in front – well, it was a village. I had to try to remain constantly in a particular state of consciousness. If, by some mistake or for some reason or by habit, I was not in the required state of consciousness and if I moved, my head would dash against a door, because the doors were so low – they came below my nose – or somehow or somewhere I would hurt myself. So I said to myself that this is how the Divine Teacher is teaching me all the time. You do not need anybody else to watch over you. He is watching over you, guiding you all the time.

When you start doing yoga the events which happen in your life take a different meaning. If you make the same mistake, a bigger blow will fall on you than on others and that is the sign of His Grace, that the Divine has accepted you. Blows are not a sign that the Divine has abandoned you, but rather that He has taken your responsibilities upon Himself. So if you want to become the master of your life and events and if you want to act always in the best possible manner, the first condition is an attitude of absolute surrender to the Divine and a constant aspiration that He may act through you.

The second is desirelessness which also is very important. You plan your day. Suppose you are working in an office; you have to be there at ten, you have to finish this work, finish that work today; you have to do this tomorrow, you must do that the day after. Now, this is a good way of planning but a mental way. There is another way which is not of the mind. Suppose you keep a diary in your pocket, and if you are open to the Divine, at the right time

He will tell you to pick up this paper, to pick up that diary and put them in your pocket. You must have no other desire but to remember Him constantly and be in touch with Him. Then He will send you the thought, He will make you write down in your diary what has to be written, He will make you go to the office. Though your conscious effort was not to link A with B, you would find when you look back at the end of the day that the link was established automatically.

I remember when I first went to the Ashram as a young boy in 1934 or 1935 – I forget now – in those days there were about three hundred people for the Darshan. Each one got one or two minutes, so every ten persons took about fifteen minutes. Since all of us were given a minute, we would know when our turn would come. Suppose my number was 150, I would know that my turn would come at about twelve noon. I need not, therefore, go to the Ashram early and wait there. I could go there at eleven-thirty or eleven forty-five. When the number of people for the Darshan rose from 1,000 to 1,200 to 2,000 the sadhaks asked Sri Aurobindo what should be done. Sri Aurobindo said that let there be a *divine anarchy*. No rules should be made – people may come at any time. Now those who have no experience of a higher level of consciousness may think that this would result in a total confusion, because everybody was allowed to come at any time they liked. But it was exactly the opposite that took place, exactly the opposite.

So you see if you remain in a particular level of consciousness your life gets organised from that level. Suppose you have fixed an appointment at five and if another important appointment comes also at the same time, you would normally refuse it, and make it at five-thirty or six. But if the guidance to you is to fix it at five, you fix it at five, although you know you already have another appointment at five. You may feel foolish, and wonder how this is going to work. But you will be amazed. After an hour or so the friend who had made the first appointment rings you up: "I am sorry I have a problem. May I change my appointment with you?" So this is how things work.

When you start living in His consciousness even things of material life and of the material plane take a different dimension. In the ordinary consciousness you can never organise life perfectly. You have to make your choice, whether you want to organise your life mentally or you want to be guided by a consciousness beyond mind. When you organise it from a higher consciousness, events take on a different quality. You see clearly the differences at the different levels of consciousness, and a higher destiny becomes applicable to you. Once you start doing yoga, and if you find yourself in a difficult situation, you concentrate and you put your difficulty before the Divine. Like a flash of light the guidance will come to you: do this. And when you do it, everything changes. Now, a doubting mind may question whether the same flash of light would have come to you from that higher level if you had not meditated. At the most, all that you can say is that the Divine made you meditate. He made you have this experience and that flash came because you were at that level of consciousness; it was not a part of predeterminism.

Getting guidance from the higher level of consciousness is not going to give you a worse life but materially a better life. If you create a wall between the two – spiritual and material – then the choice will be very difficult. The housewife may think: "If I do not cook today, my husband will be angry with me. How will the children go to school? What will happen?" But if she tried for a week to open to a higher consciousness she would find that she would come under a different predeterminism, in which the circumstances are better, events happen differently. But this choice has to be made. In which level of consciousness do you want to dwell? The Gita's 'guṇātīta' would have no meaning if going to the guṇātīta level, going beyond the three gunas, did not bring a new predeterminism or a new determinism in your life. If you really want to practise Sri Aurobindo's yoga, you should try to remain at your highest level of consciousness all the time, even during sleep, while taking food, and then let that consciousness manifest through you all the time. You will then go through life with confidence.

Once, my brother had gone on a tour of Europe – this was many years ago – and on his way back he had to attend a conference in Greece. At that time fighting was going on in Greece. He sent a telegram to me from Italy asking whether he should go to Greece at all. I asked the Mother and She said: "Remembering me, a man can go into the mouth of death and come back. Let him go to Greece and attend the conference." Now, *remembering me* – that is important. Things will not be the same if you do not remember the Mother. A man may get into trouble, but remembering Her, the consciousness will guide him: "now you do this, now you do that". There are any number of examples of persons not necessarily connected with the Ashram, who have received the inner guidance; for instance, when something told them: 'jump to one side', and the bullet passed by just where they were standing and they were saved. So there is a Higher Consciousness which can guide you at every moment.

If you know occult knowledge you can guide others and also you can put an aura around them, a consolidated, concentrated consciousness by which people can be guided. This can be done even without the knowledge or the conscious effort of the other person. When you come to occult knowledge there is no limit to the help you can give to others. You can even avoid or change events.

Occult knowledge is not bad, just like money is not bad. It is the bad use people make of it that spoils things. If you simply shun things, thinking they are bad you will never progress. If you are desireless, if you are in contact with the Divine, you cannot make bad use of this knowledge.

I will give you another incident. Once an aunt of mine got a paralytic stroke. (I am sharing these experiences with you just to show you that these are actual events that took place, not imaginary stories.) At that time I had not joined the Ashram, but used to go there on frequent visits and have regular interviews with the Mother. So I asked the Mother, "Mother, my aunt has got a paralytic stroke. She can't even move in the bed. Is it possible to do something for her through yoga? Can I do something?" She told me to recite a particular mantra, holding some grapes or other fruit in my hand which could then be given to my aunt to eat. The Mother also asked me to do certain invocations. I did as I was told and gave the fruit to my aunt. She asked me to put it in a cup and leave it there. She said that after the nurse gave her a wash she would take it. I left it in the cup. When I returned in the evening I found that she had given this to her grandchild instead of taking it herself. I said to myself that there must be something in her destiny which had worked it out in this manner. I also realised that I had made a mistake. I should have remained there and made her eat it because she was not in a state of consciousness where she could get the right inspiration. (I am narrating this incident to you so that if you are trying to work from a higher consciousness, you must give it your complete attention, from A to Z; otherwise, the other person may make a mistake and all your good work may get spoiled. I had to learn this lesson through this incident.) Anyhow, I said to myself that this is over. Let me see if she could be kept in touch with the Mother's and Sri Aurobindo's consciousness and whether that could protect her. The doctor said that at the maximum she would survive three weeks. I had to take a few days off because the Mother had given me a lot of work. But the method the Mother had taught me I applied to her. For three years my aunt survived and did not get worse; in fact, she became slightly better. She took a little food, a little more rice and I found that it was this consciousness which was keeping her alive, not letting her go. She was in Bombay. Once when I was in Calcutta, I remember one afternoon around four, I was with a friend – but a part of my concentration was constantly on her – and I told myself: "Oh, she has suffered enough. Now if she leaves, it does not matter. I am not going to keep contact with her." I returned home at about five. By five-thirty a trunk call came from Bombay that she had passed away at about ten minutes past four. So you can imagine how these things work. As long as the will was there that she should remain, for three years she went on. It seemed as if at four the Divine almost took your permission, took your approval: "It is better for this person to go, why are you resisting?"

From one angle, from a lower level, man has a lot of free will. But most of it is illusory. On the other hand, if you accept that the Divine is in everything, He is willing everything, then it becomes different – the freedom is there but of another kind. So let us understand that things can be changed, for ourselves, for our country, for humanity. Each one of us has some humble role to play in this world and those who are connected with Sri Aurobindo have a greater responsibility to discharge – for example, when a man is ill, it is the doctor who has a greater responsibility. And the best way is to constantly try to open to the supramental consciousness, receive it in you, assimilate it, surrender to it and become its instrument so that it can act in you, through you, around you, in the best possible manner. This growth, this constant growth, is the best thing you can do in the world, not only spiritually but materially. There is nothing better.

If you go to the Ganges but do not take the holy water; if you are in contact with Sri Aurobindo and the Mother but do not come in contact with the Supermind, you have missed – I would not say wasted, but missed – a great opportunity in your life. May Sri Aurobindo's and the Mother's Blessings be with you all.

If you have any questions, you may ask.

Will you tell us something about astrology?

According to Sri Aurobindo, astrology is founded on the knowledge of interdependence of things and is an occult science, really a science of intuition. Now, what do you find in astrology as it is practised? First, everything does not come true, because the astrologer has not applied his intuition and occult knowledge in casting the horoscope. Second, according to Sri Aurobindo, the stars are an indication, a notation, and things can be changed. Third, even astrology itself shows how things can be changed.

So I would say that the present-day astrology suffers from several handicaps. First, from the instrument – the astrologer – unless the astrologer is a yogi. The Mother sometimes used to see the palms of the sadhaks. One day She saw mine. I asked Her, "How do you read the palm?" She said, "When I hold a person's hand and if there is some good about him, his past, present, future, everything, is revealed to me." Astrology only confirms what you intuitively see. That is true astrology. When an astrologer sees you, he can feel the vibrations that bring with you your past, present, future, everything. When the Mother saw people, She would see emanations behind them. She would say: "Oh, behind A, I saw so-and-so person from his previous life." This also gave Her an indication of the future. So astrology is an incomplete science and when you come to yoga you should forget it all, unless you feel that the Divine wants you to make astrology your field. Then it will be an astrology in the supramental light. In the past, astrology was all right, but now it will be superseded by something new. And what that 'something new' will be, we do not know. It has to come. If we are going to be the instruments of the Divine, how to correlate the past with the new future will be revealed to us, because it has to be a leap, it is not a continuation.

Does each level of consciousness have its own destiny? The Divine consciousness is spiritual and there is no end to His consciousness. Does that mean that destiny can keep changing from one level to another?

Yes, yes. You have a freedom from the lower angle and from the higher, also; but from another point of view. You may be concentrated on the Divine or your consciousness may dwell on a lower plane, in your mind or in your vital impulses or in your physical functions. And that destiny will become applicable to you in which your consciousness dwells. So we must make our consciousness dwell where we want to. Most people never consciously make this effort – events just happen in their lives. In yoga you make a conscious effort to remain always on the highest level and to open your lower personality to the highest. Suppose your psychic is already in contact with the Divine, your mind, body, vital should also open and keep the contact. At the same time, you should act as a screen by meditating on Light all around you, so that undesirable forces do not enter. And this has to be a constant effort. Once it gets established, you do not have to make an effort, it then becomes a habit.

The True Role of Women

The question before us is, how women in general and the Women's Commission of Sri Aurobindo Society in particular, can play their role in realising the great teaching of Sri Aurobindo. We will try to deal with this question in two aspects: what women can do in collaboration with men – that is a woman's total work – and what is the role which women alone are qualified to fulfil. We must first understand what is the true potential of women. The Mother once told me that the Shakti, the Power, is in the ladies, in the women. What does it mean? How is it that the power is in the ladies? What is this power in the ladies and how can they best utilise it for the maximum benefit of mankind?

The power is really the spiritual power, the psychic power, the Divine Presence. This probably, according to the Mother, is a little more easily concentrated in women and they are perhaps a little more naturally qualified than men to manifest this power but which uptill now they have not manifested to the extent needed or expected of them. It is against this background that we will try to understand how women can evoke this power, this supramental power, this Divine power in their mind, life and body and, in its light, reorganise their individual life, their family life, their social life and play their true role for their own benefit and for the benefit of mankind.

This power permeates our entire being – mind, life, body and psychic. It is awakened by aspiration and invocation and grows through surrender. The important thing, the first thing, for a woman is to become clear in her own mind that she has to mould not only her own life, but the life of her husband, the lives of her children, the lives of her relatives, into a supramental life. Her whole life has to be organised from that angle – that is the first principle.

How is she going to organise her entire life and the life around her for the supramental manifestation? I have heard women complain that they have no time, that from morning till night they have to do household work, that even when they want to, their husbands are so ill-organised that because of this, they cannot organise their own lives, that the children take away all their time. I have also come across women, very few, very few indeed, who are exactly the opposite, who are working, earning a living, who have a husband, who have children and yet they are able to organise all their life. So it is not the husband who is to be blamed for what happens. The Divine creates conditions which are necessary for the growth of every individual and the Divine puts the individual in that particular situation which is most conducive to his growth.

The first principle you have to be clear about is not to complain about your surroundings, not to complain about relatives and people with whom you are in close contact. Ask yourself what is the kind of relationship the Divine wants you to develop with others and in what way. What is the kind of life the Divine wants you to organise – your food habits, your sleep habits, your social life, your work needs. I can assure you that once you make this kind of appeal to the highest source of knowledge and power – the Divine within you – He will not only guide you but will give you the necessary power to help you organise your life. So the first thing is not to feel deterred, not to feel yourself crushed under the circumstances but to be sure that if you truly turn to the Divine and invoke His help, and if you want to work out a programme for the Divine manifestation, His entire help and support will be with you. And when His entire help and support are with you, there is nothing that you cannot overcome.

You must be very clear that your aim in life is to become a perfect instrument of the Divine, that you are not to be cowed down or bogged down by your external problems or your psychological problems but that you have to face them, have to solve them and you have the necessary strength, wisdom and power in you to solve them. These powers exist in you – only you have to invoke and develop them.

It is against this background that we shall look at work and consider what should be done and how it should be done. First, I will tell you what a woman should do, individually. Then I will come to her family life, her social life and her working life. Individually, the first thing a woman has to do and to know is how she can always act in the right manner, how all her decisions – about the clothes to be stitched for the child or a particular dress she has to put on, on that day – how all her activities, can be guided by a higher state of consciousness instead of her mind.

Let us now take up the woman's routine in India and see how she can apply it to her everyday life because if she cannot uplift herself, if she cannot progress herself, it is idle to think that she can make other people progress, make other people become conscious of their true being. Not only has she to become conscious so that it may help her, but her very act of becoming conscious will communicate to others, and even without speaking, the environment around her will start changing. She does not have to speak, she does not have to impose herself on others, things will start changing – everything will get uplifted.

So the first thing is to remember the Divine. And not only to remember but to feel the presence of the Divine in mind, life and body and to pray that you may become conscious of the Divine's working in you, around you and through you. Three things are important: to become conscious of the Divine Presence and His working *in* you, *through* you and *around* you. Every thought that arises in you, every impulse that comes in you, you put it, remembering the Divine, before His light. You will be surprised to find that if it is not in keeping with the Divine's Will, it will automatically dissolve. You do not have to make any effort. If it is in keeping with the Divine's Will, it will receive additional strength, additional impetus and you will be able to realise it. This is the first step – the working of the Divine *in* you.

Through you, means the words you speak, the work you do, the clothes you select, the house, the furniture. Every time you touch anything it should have the Divine's touch. In order that everything should have the Divine's touch, you should abdicate the thought, "I am working." You should think, "The Divine consciousness is working through my fingers, the Divine consciousness is moving through my feet, the Divine consciousness is speaking through my mouth." If you remain in this consciousness, whatever you constantly and continuously touch will come to have a Divine impact, whether it is your child, your husband, the furniture in your house, or the food – everything will acquire a new touch. If it is food, it will have a new taste; if it is the children, you will see a new light shining in them; if it is your husband you will slowly see a change in him without his knowledge of how the change has come about, because of your constant communication with the Divine consciousness. Whatever the work may be, whether it is dusting a photograph, cleaning a pillar or sweeping the floor, it would be an act of invoking the Divine Presence and establishing it.

Once you create this atmosphere *around* you and remain in a house surrounded by this atmosphere, you can imagine the service you are doing to your family, to your children and to every person who enters your house. It is this atmosphere which you are giving to all as a bath, this purifying bath, this bath of upliftment which is one of the greatest things. A man cannot do this. It is the woman who can do it, who can create this atmosphere in the house, create this kind of a climate. Man cannot do it, just cannot do it. So this is the first thing you do in your immediate surroundings.

The Mother has said that if you speak less, if you always try to keep yourself in the highest consciousness so that the right words can come through you, if you plan your day as guided by the Divine Presence, you will find that gradually you establish a new connection with your environment, with objects and with people. This means that your husband knows you are going to deal with a situation in a particular manner – that is a part of your personality. So instead of your always having to adjust yourself to him, you will see that he will start adjusting himself to you, because remembering the Divine, you are carrying a higher consciousness, a higher force in you and he himself will start adjusting. Whenever you have a problem, aspire, aspire for harmony, aspire for a change in the other person and you will see how everything falls in line.

I remember a small incident about which the Mother told us. She said that when André, her son, came to India, K, who is in charge of our Bureau Centrale accompanied him to the airport when he left. He asked André when did he realise that his mother was the Divine Mother. André said when he was a child of nine. The Mother once told me that when André was a child some people were speaking against Her. The boy told them not to speak against his mother because she was the Divine Mother. You have to build that kind of relationship with your children so that they will respect you, they will love you.

I have seen in a family in Madras, that if the mother showed the slightest disapproval, the children felt uneasy. It is this kind of a rapport she has with her children that whenever they enter a competition they try to do their best. It is the relationship you build with your husband, the relationship you build with your children that makes all the difference. All the usual talk about both hands having to work together, otherwise no work is possible, all that is true, but at the lower level. In the higher sense, one hand can lead. If you can really rise to a higher consciousness, one hand is enough. If you are in the lower consciousness, two hands become necessary.

For bringing about a change in your immediate surroundings, two things are essential. First, your house should be in order. I have seen this with the Mother. Once I saw the things She had brought from Japan – that means in 1920, so you can say She had them for about fifty years – the seal, the shellac, the lac on which the seal has to be put, were all kept in their proper place. She may be drawing out the things after two years, after three years, and just using them once. She told me once when She was taking out an object, that if we knew how to stop wastage, we would be multi-millionaires. We go on wasting everything. She wasted nothing. When a parcel arrived, She opened the string and kept it in a box so that the string could be used again, and the wrapping paper She either sent to the Hand-Made Paper unit to be recycled or it was stored somewhere for future use. If we do not waste, there is enough for everybody in the world. The habit which you give to your husband you will see it reflected in your children. If you live that life, everybody will follow. It may or may not be today, it may be tomorrow, it is only a question of time and patience. But if you yourself do not live this kind of life, nobody else is going to follow it. So the first thing is not to waste anything.

The second thing is to try and know your best potential, your husband's best potential, the best potential of each of your children, and to help your immediate colleagues to advance towards the goal. Be very tolerant, be very helpful to them, for that is your duty to God and towards your immediate surroundings and even beyond. How are you going to be at your best, how are you going to cultivate in the people around you the power which you are developing in you? I tell you that you do not have to cultivate it. It gets cultivated by itself, if you remain in that consciousness, if you remain as God's instrument, if you abdicate the ego, if you remove the feeling that it is I who am doing and instead invoke: "O God, You act, You speak, You see through my eyes, You speak through my mouth, You listen through my ears." This abdication itself will create a change in you and the people around you.

I tell you from my own experience that whenever we act in haste, howsoever good it may appear to be, the result is never satisfactory. But if we remain concentrated, howsoever difficult the situation, the result is the best. The doors which were closed, automatically open and everything changes. Do not act in your present state of consciousness. Always act in unity with the highest consciousness you are capable of at present. You can always try to increase the reach of this highest consciousness, to increase its total field of action. Always act from the highest consciousness and totally, even in your physical body, even concerning your food, all around you. You should feel you are surrounded by His consciousness everywhere, and not feel it only in the psychic centre.

Another important aspect of woman's work is the preparation of food. In the Indian traditional yoga, the guru used to make his disciples eat in his presence. He would touch the food, he would concentrate on the food – the idea of prasad – and then let them eat. Every time you cook food, you should concentrate thus: "I am cooking food for the Divine. It is my offering to the Divine. May the Divine consciousness awaken in this food." The priest offers prasad for only a minute, you are cooking for an hour, you are preparing for an hour and a half or two hours. If for these hours you are concentrated in this consciousness, I can give you the assurance that anyone who eats your food, will begin to change in his consciousness – purity will come to him, wisdom will come to him, tolerance, peace and even health will come to him. So, this should be in addition to the normal knowledge about nutrition and all the scientific knowledge to be applied – an invocation to a higher consciousness which will also be instrumental in changing the consciousness of people around you through the medium of food.

The third important thing is the decoration of your house. You should be a living model of what a child of the Mother should be. That speaks ten thousand times more than giving a lecture. There also, the best way, the only way of doing anything is to concentrate on what you are doing. Suppose you are having your house painted. You will be surprised to find as if the walls are speaking to you, the walls are telling you that they want this colour here or that painting there. You look at your garden. Be quiet and concentrate. Concentrate on the garden, on the land around you, the plants around you, on the Divine in you, the Divine in them and ask yourself what you should do. You will feel as if your surroundings are speaking to you and you will know that this plant should go there, another kind of chair should come here.

Another important thing is not to keep useless things. Remove them from the house. Useless things are almost like garbage that create problems for you. Sell them off, give them away, do whatever you like. Do not store useless things. Keep beautiful things, nice things and you will see how beauty and happiness grow around you.

Now about your social life and your economic life. We forget a very important thing about our economic life. One day I was sitting with a person who was teaching me yoga, the traditional yoga, and we were talking about the Tirupati Temple. I asked him how was it that the Tirupati Temple was so prosperous and other temples were not? He told me that the yantra called the Dhanākarshana yantra, the yantra that pulls money, has been placed under the idol. Do you want to solve your economic problems in an occult-cum-material manner or do you want to solve them in a purely material way? Let us take the example of an animal. The poor animal runs about the whole day just to get a little food. A man with his intelligence works hard, sets up industry, works eight hours everyday for his living and earning. A yogi can get money even when he seems to be merely sitting at one place doing nothing, because he invokes the power of wealth and this invocation itself creates a channel for the wealth to come to him.

So if you really want to lead a higher life, you must know that you have to rise above the ordinary life. You cannot lead an ordinary life and say your life is of the highest. No, the pattern, the character, everything of the higher life is different. So for the economic problem there are two important solutions – the occult and the material. In the occult there are mantras, there are invocations by which you establish in yourself the consciousness that brings in the money, that opens the door for the money to come in, with very little effort. But everything has to be done as guided by the Divine.

The material aspect would depend again on the Divine guidance. If the Divine guidance tells you to do a particular work, you do it as His command. But if there is no guidance, then wait. The Divine will look after your economic needs. You do your duty. It is not for every soldier to say that he wants to arrange the food, also; it is for the commander to decide who will hold this front, who will hold that front, that food will be arranged by these people, medicine will be arranged by those people. The supreme commander is God Himself. So if you are surrendered to Him and if you do exactly what He tells you to do, you do not have to bother about other things. It is for Him to send you the means for carrying out His work. He provides ample means if the openness is there. If you want to do His work, you have at every moment of your life to do an active sadhana.

This principle has then to be extended to the organisational work. In organisational work you must first meditate and become clear in your vision with regard to the economic aspect of Sri Aurobindo's yoga, its psychological aspect, its social aspect, its educational aspect and its spiritual aspect. All have to be integrated in a total vision; a total vision of the welfare of mankind.

Here, you must remember two things. Sri Aurobindo has said that if a higher supramental life has to come we have to be progressive, we have to practise progressive self-perfection and expansion of consciousness. If your consciousness is narrow – the Mother has said that people have such small consciousness that they are filled only with petty ideas and desires – how can the Supermind work in you? If the Supermind has to work, your consciousness has to be universal and has to gradually progress towards self-perfection. This progressive self-perfection means opening more and more to the supramental force and light. To open to the supramental force and light means constant remembrance of Sri Aurobindo and the Mother and to be united with Their consciousness.

What I would like to suggest to you about your social work is to apply the same principle. You have to become clear in the vision which God will give you. You see, you have to prepare the conditions to receive all that He wants to give you. You are not going to cultivate the land and grow things. Things are already grown, you have only to receive them. You have to receive and learn to use them. As you progress you will find that the force brings you in contact with the right people for every kind of work. If you are in the highest consciousness, even before the person comes, you will know that so-and-so person is coming and that he is meant for so-and-so work. You just have to talk to him, you do not have to use your head and you will see how the Divine organises through you. But there has to be a dynamic surrender. You cannot say: "Oh, now I am tired, seven is my time for retirement, I am not going to see people at seven-thirty." Then you are closing the door on the Divine's Grace. If He wants you to work at twelve at night, He will give you the necessary strength; if He does not want you to work at two in the afternoon, He will give you the necessary rest. You do not make conditions. When you make conditions, you close the door to the highest progress. If you really remain in this consciousness, in one sentence I will tell you: He will do everything for you.

I wanted to cover the subject of bringing up children which, according to the Mother, is the true role of women. But I think I will leave it for the next meeting. This talk here is only a part of what I wanted to say – the rest can wait.

New Education

We should have a new thinking in education because the present systems of education all over the world have failed. And this new thinking has to come from India. Why? This is what we will try to understand today. In this new thinking, there are three basic things we have to consider. First, what should be the goal of our education as suited to the needs of the present and the future. Second, what should be the method of realising it and third, now that the world has become a global society, the educational institutions should not only impart education but develop community services, to realise the goals which they initiate through the educational programmes. I want to place all these before you, in the light of Sri Aurobindo's and the Mother's teachings.

To begin with, we must realise that so many religions have come, so many political thoughts have come, so many social thoughts have come, so many educational programmes have come but the human problems remain unsolved. If we continue with the old ways repeating the old methods, howsoever good they may be, but which have failed in the past, how can we expect them to deliver the goods now? So, we must discard the past and open our minds very wide to a completely new thinking.

The second thing to understand is that the goal of education cannot be different from the goal of creation, the goal of life. Why has the world been created at all? What is the purpose behind it? Education should fulfil that purpose and education isolated from that basic thought will never be able to fulfil itself.

There is a basic need in man, a basic search since eternity — the search for Happiness, the search for Knowledge, the search for Power, the search for Immortality. If the search for Immortality has eluded mankind, would it mean that man will always remain unfulfilled? Will he never have this Immortality which he has been dreaming of and which he has tried to pursue through the realisation of his soul? Would this realisation bring us Immortality? But the soul is already immortal. Then what is that Immortality which we can get by the realisation of the soul? The Immortality has to be a physical immortality. Sri Aurobindo has said that death asks us a question: have you fulfilled the purpose for which you have come? That is the question death poses to every human being. What is the purpose of our coming here, why are we on earth? That is a question our education must answer.

To this question, Sri Aurobindo gives an amazing answer. Till I read Him, nowhere did I get that answer. It is this answer that I want to place before you. It answers three questions simultaneously: it tells you what is the purpose of creation, it tells you what is the highest you can do individually, it also tells you how the whole world can be happy – not merely one individual but how the whole world can be happy. It is this message which has to go from India to the world.

Sri Aurobindo uses three phrases continuously in His writings: *The Divine Body*, *the Divine Life*, *the Divine Perfection*. Not human perfection. All along we have been thinking of human perfection. Our education system is geared to the best in human perfection but human beings, being imperfect, our mind itself being imperfect, the concept of perfection itself is imperfect.

Sri Aurobindo says that the world is in evolution – from matter to plant and plant to animal, life develops; from animal to man, mind develops. Our Hindu Shastras have spoken of the same thing in a different manner as propounded by the ten Avatars. It is the descent of the higher consciousness that results in the evolution of all. This is the double vision of descent and evolution. Sri Aurobindo has said that if it is an evolution, why should it stop with man? It will go from half-animal, half-man to superman - the divine man on earth. A divine man does not mean a goody-goody man, telling the truth, doing good service to others. No, a divine man means a divine man. His body will be a body of Light.

When I first read Sri Aurobindo's *The Life Divine*, I was amazed, I was startled, I thought I had misunderstood Him. How could He speak of physical immortality? There must be something wrong in my own understanding but later I found it was true. And what is more amazing is how I first heard of it. I had to go to the West to get this knowledge! On BBC a lady gave a talk, 'The Divine Becoming' and there she said that according to Sri Aurobindo, in the next step in evolution, the human body would undergo a change - there would be no blood, skin or bones in the body - it would become a body of Light. So long as you have a body of blood, skin and bones, death, decay and disease are inevitable. But if you have a body of Light, (the gods have bodies of Light), it will be heaven on earth. Christianity dreamt of the same, Islam dreamt of the same, Hinduism dreamt of the same, but here comes a man who wants to realise it and that man comes from India. That is the great honour Mother India gives to all of us.

What Sri Aurobindo has said is that the new body will be luminous, it will be light as air, it will be adaptable, it will be plastic, no food and water will be needed for its sustenance and it will not be vulnerable. If somebody shoots at it, it will not get shot. He has further said that this is also not the last word in God's creation - from superman something new will develop. He does not say that what He says is the last word.

If the human being within the small span of a lifetime has a choice to realise something, why not realise the highest? I cannot dream of anything higher than this on earth. At that level even the man-woman relationship will disappear. Sri Aurobindo says that once the supramental body is created, once this new substance is created on earth, the soul will take up a body straight from that transformed matter without the normal process of procreation and birth. All human values change when you read Sri Aurobindo. Now, this is the first thing: His concept of a divine body. When a number of people try to realise this, there comes the divine life. A life guided by the mind, a life guided by the intellect, howsoever high, is a human life; it becomes divine only when the Divine guides you and the Divine manifests through you without restriction, without limitation, through a divine body, not through a human body.

Indian thought is continously evolving. According to the Indian concept there are four Ashramas. The Indian concept has always been an integration of spiritual and material life – you have the best of both. But the Gita went a step further than the four Ashramas: all your actions should be guided by the Divine. That means the Divine realisation should be the beginning. Sri Aurobindo goes a step still further: not only the realisation of the Divine, not only to be guided by the Divine, but a divine life in a divine body to manifest the Divine perfectly. Without this even if you realise the Divine, the manifestation will be limited by the limitation of your body, by the ignorant laws of the government, by the collective economic life of today, as is seen in the present economic society. Sri Aurobindo calls it *economic barbarism*. Economic incentive is an old story. Under the economic system, you can never realise the highest. It is a society of competition, and in a competitive society, some people are bound to suffer. So, all our dreams of Utopia and Sarvodaya will never get fulfilled.

Sri Aurobindo's second vision is to evolve from an economic society to a spiritualised society, of which we are trying to make a model near Pondicherry; a society where money will not be in circulation, where there will be no private property. All the needs of a person will be provided free at the best possible level, free house, free food, free medical attention, free library, free tennis, free cinema, and there will be no difference between a labourer and a director of a department. You will be free to choose your work and to do it in a spirit of dedication to God. Then everything will change. We had a very happy experience of a gardener. He was telling me that one day, while watering the garden he felt as if a plant was telling him "I am not watered" and, when he turned back, he found he had actually forgotten to water that plant! In India it is said that when the Rishis touched a herb, knowledge of its properties came to them. So all this knowledge of India that comes under psychology, we have to give back to mankind as suited to modern science. This is the Divine perfection - when the Divine descends and acts through a human body.

Our goal is a complete, total transformation of life - social, economic, political - based on the Divine guidance. If that is not the base, then our Gita is false, our Indian culture is false and we are not fit to call ourselves Indians. Only that person can claim to be an Indian who is willing to seek the Divine guidance and follow it. That is also the true meaning of Hinduism.

By God's grace, I had the best education which could be given under the present modern system. Before I joined the Ashram I was the chairman of more than a dozen companies and industries. I found that all that we received in education, all the things that we learnt about cost of production, sales, planning never worked - always new factors were cropping up. Because we had large profits, people thought we were very wise and we were very competent, though honestly, we were not at all competent, we were not at all wise. The profits came because they came; the circumstances were such.

I used to go to Pondicherry and ask the Mother not only about how to meditate, but sometimes also to seek Her guidance on mundane matters: "Mother, so-and-so is ill. Doctors are unable to diagnose what is wrong with him." At that time I had no intention of joining the Ashram, I must tell you. I was seeking how to perfect human life, I was seeking how to dedicate myself to the welfare of mankind. But I did not know that *spirituality* was the path for material perfection of mankind. I used to ask the Mother's advice even in my business matters and She used to guide me. I used to differ with Her sometimes but I found She was always right and I was wrong. So I asked Her, "How can we get this knowledge? This was never taught to us in our education." She said, "Everybody can have this knowledge." I said, "How, Mother?" She said, "This knowledge comes to you when you have no preferences and no desires." The Gita says do not have preferences and do not have desires. I had studied the Gita since I was a child that if you have no preferences and no desires, intuition will develop in you. I did not believe it, because the poor teacher who taught me the Gita did not have the intuition. But when the Mother told me, I immediately understood. So I asked, "Mother, how does one have no preferences and no desires?" She said, "Whenever you have an important decision to take, meditate in your heart-centre, pose the question, do not think of the answer. Wait for the answer." And I honestly tell you I tried this in my directors' meetings and it worked. If I deferred with the foreign technicians, I would find I would be right and they would be wrong, though I would not know the reason. So I thought to myself, it works! If a little practice can develop human faculties like this, what will a Divine contact do?

So, the second step followed. I asked Her, "Mother, is everything predetermined in life?" There are so many questions which our education never answers. If God is everywhere why is there falsehood? If God is everywhere why is there misery? He is Satchitananda, He is All-Delight, He is All-Knowledge, He is All-Power and yet there is misery, yet there is falsehood and we say God is everywhere. How do we reconcile all this? Are things predetermined? If not, what is the freedom given to man? This was all before I joined the Ashram. I used to run away every fortnight to Pondicherry, meet Her and come back in the evening. It is better if all of you know about predeterminism. We Hindus are accustomed to saying that everything is God-ordained. Yes, it is God-ordained, but it is God-ordained under certain conditions. You change the conditions and God's working in you will change. The Mother has said that each person has many destinies and that destiny becomes applicable to him in which his consciousness dwells. By lifting the consciousness to the highest level which means in union with the Divine, everything changes. Then She said that even a prayer can change destiny. She gave an example. Suppose a fruit is falling from the tree and you put your hand out to stop it from falling on the ground, its destiny has changed. So, like this, prayer can change destiny. After a few days I asked Her, "Mother, was not putting the hand out a part of the destiny that made it so?" She said, "You have to decide. If you are looking from the top, yes. But when you are looking from below, you cannot say that it is so. Things can change." Then She added, "My child, you are hypnotised by Hindu mythology. Everything can change. I tell you everything can change."

Now I come to another interesting point. I said, "Mother, this is all right, but I have decided I want to follow the Divine's command. I do not want to follow my ignorant and limited mind. It does not lead me anywhere. But how do I know the Divine's command? I could be doing something very foolish thinking it is the Divine's command." So She looked at me and said, "My child, you must give credit to the Divine for being at least as wise as you are." I said, "Mother, what are you saying! He is Omniscient!" She said, "Yes, He is Omniscient, He knows your problems, He knows you are relying on Him and if you rely on Him and act, thinking that it is His command, even if you are mistaken in guidance He will give you protection. You can be sure of it." This, I must tell you, helped me greatly.

Why I am mentioning this to you – you, who are in the field of education – is because you have to make a simple choice: is it you who are going to teach or is it the Divine who is going to teach through you? Is it you who are going to give something new to mankind in the field of education or is it the Divine, through you, who is going to give that new thing to mankind? And if this is so, the way is very simple. You do not have to recite mantras ten million times, you do not have to sit in tapasya, meditating on Him and going through all kinds of austerities. The path is very simple: aspiration, surrender and rejection. Aspire - He is everywhere - and pray to Him: "Guide me, O God! You teach through this body, You listen through the students, You manifest in our lives." And you will see the result. Offer your mind to Him, offer your body to Him, tell Him: "I belong to You, the ball is in Your court, You guide me. If You do not guide me, it is no longer my fault if I commit mistakes with my human limitations for which I am not responsible. You are responsible. I will make mistakes, for I do not know how to lead a perfect life. But I offer myself to You. You are on test, not I. You can possess me, transform me, speak through my voice, act through me." You will see the difference.

You must make your surrender complete. I am reminded of a short story by Tagore which I would like to relate to you. I do not remember it in detail, but its essence has remained in my mind. It is a story, it is not true but it has a great meaning. A man went out begging. He found the Divine coming in His golden chariot. The Divine looked at him and smiled, so he said to himself: "Now is the time to take my begging bowl to Him and my poverty will disappear." The Divine stopped the chariot and got down. The man advanced towards Him, but before he could stretch out his bowl, the Divine Himself stretched out His hand. So when the Divine stretched out His hand, he thought, now the Divine is playing a joke. How can the Divine ask anything from me! He took out a grain of rice from his bowl and put it in the Divine's hand and came back very dejected to his hut. When he turned his bowl upside down, he became even sadder because a grain of rice had turned into gold. "Why did I not give all of me to the Divine!" the beggar lamented.

So you see, the secret of life is to have nothing that you can call your own. Anything you call your own is dust; anything you offer to the Divine is purified in His fire and becomes gold. This is the decision each one of us has to make. And once that decision is taken, the Divine Himself will descend on this great land and everything will change. When the human will is united with the Divine Will, there is no limit to what it can achieve. But when the human will is not united with the Divine Will, there is no limit to the follies it commits in the name of the Divine or without the name of the Divine.

The most important thing is to offer your will with all its limitations, all its shortcomings to the Divine. Do not look at your shortcomings. His power is far greater than your shortcomings. Look to His greatness, His omniscience, His omnipotence, His compassion and offer yourself. That is the first step for every teacher. A teacher's life itself has to be an example, has to be an influence. Teaching is a very small part of it. If you can do that you will be able to communicate with your students far better. You will get new ideas for your curriculum and everything will change.

Now we come to physical education. The aim of our physical education should be to attain a divine body. People say asanas are merely postures; I say asanas are only physical exercises. They become yoga asanas when you perform them in unity with the Divine. In the morning when you get up, you say to yourself, you will do every action only in unity with the Divine – you will not speak unless He speaks through your mouth, you will not walk unless He walks through your feet, you will abdicate yourself. Let Him see through your eyes, let Him listen through your ears and you will find how quickly the ego vanishes; you will see how the curtain between you and the Divine is torn apart and how He manifests Himself in all His splendour. The path is very simple, but the desire, the aspiration, the need to do it should be cultivated. This is India's message to mankind: to be perfect, to be divinely perfect, to have a divine life in a divine body. Offer yourself to the Divine, He will give you the divine body, He will manifest the divine life. His manifestation will be the divine perfection. This should be the objective of our education system.

Education is our only hope in this life, in this political life of fear and favour, in this life where ignorant political laws govern our life, where the most ignorant people make them. In ancient India, the Rishis used to make the laws. It was the luminous men who made the laws and now in the name of majority, in the name of democracy, all kinds of cheating and fraud are committed on the whole nation. How long will this great nation tolerate it? Are our ideals those children of Gurugovindji who sacrificed themselves to uphold the Indian culture? Are our ideals that galaxy of great Rishis who gave us such great knowledge and taught us fearlessness? Or are our ideals the present politicians, our leaders whom we call upon to inaugurate meetings, we garland them, we call them leaders. Are they our ideals? We are fools, not they. If we accept them and say, they are our leaders, we are free to do do so. Who stops us from that? In this, who has brought it upon us? Have we not ourselves done so? Become true Indians, become truthful, become fearless, have faith in God, He will do everything for you.

A friend of mine was a junior secretary about ten years ago in a very big organisation, perhaps the biggest in India. The post of the managing director fell vacant. There were many men senior to him and another man was already appointed to a new post of acting managing director. My friend said to me, "Bhaiji, I do not want to try for this post. My life belongs to God. If God wants me, He will take me there, if He does not want me, I am not interested." I said, "Your attitude is correct." At that time, Mr. X was the Finance Minister. Mr. X called the ex-chairman of this organisation and asked him who was the most competent man in the organisation. That chairman gave my friend's name, saying that he was the man most competent – very honest, very competent, but because of this people thought him quarrelsome also. He told Mr. X, "If you want a competent person, this is your man." Mr. X had never heard of my friend, had never seen his face. So he sent for him and said, "Young man, we want you to be the managing director of this organisation." My friend replied, "Sir, there are other men senior to me. They should be given the chance." (He did not say, Sir, I am so glad that you are appointing me.) So Mr. X said, "No, it cannot be. The work cannot depend on any such seniority. It is a very important position. And whenever you have any matter of importance to discuss you can come and meet me." He said, "No Sir, I am not going to meet you. You may talk to my chairman. Let him bring me to you." Mr. X looked at him and thought here is a young man who stands by his principles even today. Mr. X told him, "We will make you the chairman of the organisation, not the managing director." Within two months he was made the managing director and within one year, the chairman. Then there was a strike in that organisation. Mr. X said, "Dismiss those on strike." The State Finance Minister said, "No, yield to their demands." My friend said, "I am going to do neither. I will do what is right and true." If I continue it will be a long story, but what I want to tell you is this, that even in the ordinary life, if you rely on God, He is the only one who will never let you down. And if He lets you down it is a pleasure to be let down. There is nothing to regret. Rely on the highest force on earth. Why rely on small human beings and make your life miserable? Rely on the Supreme, work for the Supreme. I remember when Vinoba Bhave came to our Ashram he said that the Mother had given him a message: "Live for the Divine, work for the Divine, aspire for the Divine." The goal of education should also be the same, a divine perfection on earth.

Now let me tell you a little about the programme which we have decided for education and on which we would like to have the close collaboration of your organisation or any other institution that may wish to join it. To begin with, we are dividing it into two parts. I must tell you that at the Ashram we have broken new ground in education - no examinations, no fixed terms. We have 500 students and 100 teachers and more than 50 physical instructors. We call the whole system free progress system. A student may be in the fifth class of French, the eighth of English, the third of Sanskrit, the seventh of Mathematics, and every student decides which subject he is going to study that day. One student may go to the History class, another may go to the Geography class, a third may go the Mathematics class.

We are keen that every community bloc - there are 6,000 community blocs in the country - and every town should have a centre for total education and community services. We have divided the programme into twelve parts.

You know we carried out certain researches when the Auroville project came up. I will share with you one or two of our experiences. We went to the Patwari (here they call him Karnam) just to see how they kept the records. I saw only a part of the thing and we found that the fellow had not kept records for three years. I asked him, "Our whole statistics are based on the information you provide – so much rice, so much wheat, so much land under rice and wheat and how is it that you have not kept records?" He said, "It is very simple. In the first week of March I receive word from my Director of Agriculture to increase five percent from last year or decrease ten percent from last year and I send him the reports." I said to myself this is how the thing is done. I never knew till we carried out our researches that this is how our statistics were built.

Then we undertook a survey of the dispensaries and we found that ninety percent of the people were ill due to malnutrition and all along while the medicines were being distributed, nothing was being done for nutrition. So we decided that we ourselves will carry out the nutrition programme. Until we carried out the nutrition programme, we did not know that nobody was interested in nutrition. People were starving, they were coming only to eat something. The solution is that there should be a community kitchen. (You must come to Pondicherry and see how beautiful our community kitchen is, where two thousand of us take food every day.) So why not set up community kitchens everywhere in India where you can get food on a no-profit, no-loss basis. The people who eat there could work as volunteers so you do not have to pay them. Life of the country will change. The programme we envisage will enable us to increase production by more than one thousand rupees an acre, over a period of six to seven years.

We feel every community bloc should have a small town of thirty to forty thousand people. A number of people will be in the periphery, in the Green Belt and, as a collective family, it should meet all its needs; like in our Ashram, we make many things ourselves - our own cream, our own powder, our own oil - and we use these ourselves.

The Mother was very strict. When I needed an eye lotion (we make beautiful eye lotion from the lotus flower), She gave it to me. I had just joined the Ashram. The next time I wanted it, She said, "No, you do not know the rules here. You must return the old bottle before I give you a new one." I said, "Yes Mother, I will bring it to you now." It is a very interesting experience. We are wasting life, we are wasting energy. If we really start working with our own hands, everything will change. So in every community bloc we should begin a basic-need training programme. All the items of basic need should be manufactured there, to be given on no-profit, no-loss basis, so that people can have a high standard of living without a corresponding increase in the cost of living.

Then we come to construction. Construction needs architects. We want the local people, the local masons to come forward to whom we will give training in architecture. We will upgrade the local carpenters as skilled carpenters. We can even bring in good instruments. Each department will be research-oriented - research in education, research in education extension services. Such community blocs could be developed throughout India. We could start with, say about ten to twenty or thirty acres in a community bloc, with a nucleus of people leading a spiritual life which will serve as a model and develop their area. And this would mean total employment. We have made a programme for total employment and for the job suited to each person. In the beginning we want to take up two blocs as models which in themselves will become training blocs. Simultaneously, every community bloc will form a nucleus. This is not the time to go step by step - one, two, three, four! This is the time to just upgrade the whole thing and together we can do it successfully. If we all pooled our resources we can do it. This programme covers all aspects, even leadership training.

What should be our national programme? The other day, a very important politician was dining with us. I asked him, "What is the goal of your party?" He said, "It is socialistic democracy." I asked, "Is socialistic democracy the goal or the means?" He replied, "Bhaiji, I never thought of the goal." So I said, "You have been fooling the public all these years. You have never thought of the goal. The goal can only be the highest welfare of all, and it can never come from socialistic democracy." And he agreed, "That is true."

Let us do some deep thinking, some new thinking. Let us forget the past. Let us pray to God. Let the revelation come from within. And let us give something to mankind. If in this session we could pray to Him, silence our mind, seek His guidance, talk less, take decisions more and implement them, I think we would have broken new ground in starting a new education.

May the Divine's Blessings be with you.

The Ramayana, the Mahabharata and the Gita

One question about the Ramayana which I have often asked myself is, was Valmiki telling merely a story – because if it were just a story it would have no meaning. Let us take the example of 'Sundarkāṇḍa', that is, Hanuman going to Lanka in search of Sita and after finding her, giving a fight to the Rakshasas, letting himself be bound, burning Lanka and returning and narrating his exploits. I wanted to know how a person like Hanuman would recite his own exploits.

Or let us take the last chapter. After the return of Rama a boy in the kingdom dies very young. So his father comes and tells Rama that because of the sins of the king, his son had died. And the king is Rama himself. So the question is, what actually happened, how much of the Epic is true, how much is mere imagination.

I believe that Valmiki is giving us some essential truths though in the story he may have dressed up his statements, his descriptions or his narrations; that part is O.K. My approach to Valmiki is different. I believe many of the things narrated in the Ramayana are not just stories or symbols but events that actually took place. If they could have happened at that time, they can happen more surely now, because man has also advanced his possibilities of progress.

What do you really have in mind, Bhaiji?

Well, let us consider Hanuman's fight with the Rakshasas. When Hanuman started for Lanka he became very big and flew in the air in a physical body. Patanjali's yoga says it is possible; many yogis say it can be done. And these books are in the form of 'sutras', that means they are very small crisp sentences which describe certain things – say, in five words, they will describe the whole philosophy of life. So, in those words if they say that it is possible that a person can fly, I also believe that this is possible not only theoretically but in practice as well. But I admit I also wonder how this feat can be possible.

Then when Hanuman jumped on a hill, a small hill in the ocean, by the pressure of his feet the hill went down. Now, we could dismiss the prowess of Hanuman as an exaggerated description, just to create bhakti among the devotees. This kind of devotion I really would not subscribe to, since it is born of, I am sorry to say, false exaggerations. Why would a person like Hanuman go to great lengths to describe his prowess? I personally feel that they are not false. When a great man like Valmiki whom I would call an embodiment of Truth, narrates the life of Rama who is *the* embodiment of Truth and describes the prowess of Hanuman who is another embodiment of Truth, how could he be speaking what is not true and merely telling a story? This is beyond me.

So then Hanuman meets the mother of the Nagas – Naga is not necessarily a serpent but a kind of a serpent – and she tells him, "Well, I have come to eat you up." He answers very politely, "I am a messenger of Rama and I am going for his work. Let me finish the work of finding Sita and report to my king, then I promise you I will come back and you may eat me up, since my work would then be finished." She answers, "Nothing of the kind. I want to eat you now." So Hanuman says, "Then you eat me." He becomes big – he was big but he becomes bigger – and she too becomes bigger than him and then bigger and bigger, each one goes on expanding. Suddenly Hanuman becomes very small and enters her mouth and comes out and says to her, "I have now fulfilled your wish." She then smiles and says, "No, I did not want to eat you up. I only wanted to test you, because you were going for such a great work. Now, I am sure you will succeed."

Then Hanuman goes to Lanka and after meeting Sita, he destroys the garden and gives fight to the Rakshasas who come to kill him. I find that in the fight he would contract his body, he would expand his body, he would fly in the sky, he would uproot trees, throw big rocks. Throwing big rocks or uprooting trees cannot be only a physical prowess; it has to be a combination of physical, vital, mental, psychic and spiritual powers. And what is important is that when Ravana comes to know of it, he tells his generals, "Hanuman has already killed my very prestigious and seasoned warriors. We should not take him to be a mere monkey. Either he is some God personified or the gods have given him all their powers so as to create problems for us. We should not take him lightly." Now, here is the crux. Hanuman is supposed to be the son of Vayu, the God of Wind. The God of Wind here does not mean the physical wind. The God of Wind is a luminous being and the

God of Wind seems to have produced him by a lady monkey, 'Anjani'. So his name is 'Ānjaneya'. Now, how could this be except by will, because gods do not have physical bodies. Hanuman was a 'bal brahmachari' which is another of his great aspects.

What does it mean, Bhaiji? He never married?

He not only never married but he never had a sex desire at all from his childhood. This is only possible if one is in a very high state of consciousness from the very beginning or if God has not thought it necessary that he should go through the usual process and marry and have children.

It is very interesting that when he goes to Ravana's darbar and when he is accosted by the Rakshasas, he tells them about the great Rama and Sugriva, his friend. He says that he is one of the soldiers of Sugriva. He makes himself so insignificant, so humble. He does not even say that he is one of the soldiers of Rama. He tells them that Sugriva is a friend and a servant of Rama and that he himself is a servant of Sugriva. This is an extremely interesting theme and Valmiki tells very clearly that when Meghnada, son of Ravana, shoots a 'Brahmastra' at him, Hanuman of his own will submits to it because he says that if he did not submit, it would be dishonouring Brahma. So, in many ways, Valmiki, I think, is a good deal different from Tulsidas, a good deal different, in his narration, his way of presentation, and so on. Even the story is different in some places.

Is his interpretation very different?

I do not know. Interpretation of what? He has not interpreted things, he has narrated them.

There is interpretation also, is there not?

Tulsidas sings the praises of Rama like a Bhakta. Valmiki does not praise Rama like a bhakta; he leaves it to the readers to judge. But he describes Rama in such a way that you can see that you are in the presence of somebody really great, somebody really very extraordinary and he cannot but be God, the way Rama fights or does things or reacts to things. So Valmiki does not praise him directly as Tulsidas does, but he narrates things in such a manner and puts such words in the mouth of Rama, that you cannot but admire him; not only admire him but feel that he is divine. Even then, with all his godly qualities, his occult powers, you find Rama very human. Valmiki's Rama is very close to you, very near to you, you do not feel him as a distant figure.

Could you give me a reasonably elaborate but still a brief review of the Gita? What is the common man expected to understand from its ethics, what it means and what you think is its purpose?

The Gita, like many other great books has been highly misunderstood. People take one or two sentences from the second chapter and present it as the whole teaching of the Gita – 'Niṣkāma Karma' – where it says: "Karmaṇyevā'dhikāraste mā phaleṣu kadācana." "Thou hast the right to action only, to the fruit of action thou hast no manner of right at all." I often find people repeating these words as the entire message of the Gita. It is not so.

To me, the whole crux of the Gita's teaching is this: Arjuna, a friend of Krishna requests Krishna to join him in the battle, even though Krishna had told him that he would not bear arms nor would he fight. Krishna gives Arjuna a choice between taking his whole army of great warriors and taking himself unarmed. Arjuna chooses Krishna as his unarmed guide and friend – to me, this is very crucial. Krishna then agrees to be Arjuna's charioteer. This means that it will be Krishna who will direct Arjuna's fight and look after him.

Now, Arjuna, Bhima and Yudhishthira all accepted to fight for a number of reasons. First, because they were Kshatriyas and a great injustice had been done to them. Their kingdom had been usurped by the Kauravas and they could not submit to such an injustice. Moreover, their wife, Draupadi, had been very badly insulted by the Kauravas – she was pulled by her hair, they had tried to disrobe her – and the Pandavas had vowed vengence. So they had to keep their word of honour. They had tried every peaceful means; they had asked for only five villages, not even their kingdom, but even that was refused. And almost a challenge was thrown at them which, as Kashtriyas, they could not refuse.

So they came to the battle feeling very self-righteous, they felt they were on the right side, that they knew what to do, that they were doing their duty by fighting and that the fight fully fitted in with the ideas of ethics of their times and their own notions of what was good and bad.

Now comes the crucial situation in the beginning of the great battle, where Arjuna tells Krishna, "Please take the chariot between the two armies so that I can see who are destined to die at my hands." So Krishna takes the chariot in the middle of the two armies. When Arjuna sees his grandfather who loved him very much and who had brought him up in his lap, as the Commander in Chief of the opposite side; when he sees his own guru who had taught him archery as the second-in-command; when he sees his own maternal uncle, Salya, on the other side; when he sees a number of people whom he loved and who loved him, but because of their sense of duty and even much against their wish, they were obliged to join the other side, Arjuna becomes despondent. He realises that in the battle, in this bloodbath, people would die on both sides, and even if the Pandavas were to win there would be a great loss of men. He reflects that the women who are left widows would go astray, and when they went astray the children who would be born, would be illegitimate, and the children would not be able to perform 'piṇḍadāna' for their forefathers, and the forefathers would not go to heaven. He also felt that after such a bloodbath, after killing his own grandfather, his own guru, how would he enjoy the kingdom. What would be the charm of winning a kingdom in this manner by killing his own guru and his grandfather. So his sense of ethics, his whole sense of approach to life, his attitude to life which he had built, is shaken.

Arjuna represents the Sattwic-Rajasic man, the best man, the most ethical man, the most courageous man who always stood for Truth as understood by the mind, and now his ideas are shaken. His old ideas of good and bad fail him and he is left with two choices – either to fight and kill the Kauravas and take the throne soaked in blood as he says, or not to fight at all. He says, "I would rather that they killed me, I would take to sannyas, I would do anything, I do not want to have the kingdom by killing my own kith and kin. What is the sense? Spiritually it is wrong, morally it is wrong." He advances a number of arguments to Krishna why he should not fight. And he feels confused.

Now, this is the situation of not only Arjuna, but of every man who comes to a stage in his life when his attitude to life and his own notions of life are shaken. In this situation what does Arjuna say? He says, "I am confused." Though Krishna is his friend, for the first time Arjuna tells him, "I am your disciple." He does not say, "I am your friend, help me." He says, "Śiṣyas te'haṁ' – "I am your disciple." 'Śādhi maṁ' – "Please command me." 'Tvāṁ prapannam' – "I seek refuge in You. You alone can guide me. I really do not know what is the right thing to do."

Krishna gives Arjuna many reasons why he should fight and Arjuna puts counter-questions to him. Arjuna is not fully satisfied with these answers as they are not complete and do not reveal the ultimate truth. In the eleventh chapter, Krishna ultimately shows him the working of the world and his own 'Virātsvarūpa', the Supreme Form. Then for the first time Arjuna finds that Krishna, his charioteer, is not only his friend but the Supreme Lord Himself. A very beautiful thing he says: 'Sakhe'ti matvā prasabhaṁ yad uktaṁ he kṛṣṇa he yādava he sakhe'ti ajanatā mahimanaṁ tave'daṁmayā pramādāt praṇayena vapi.' – "O Friend, O Krishna, O Yadav, I have called you by all kinds of names as a friend, out of confusion, out of 'pramādāt', out of ignorance. Please pardon me." For the first time, Arjuna realises that the Supreme Lord Himself has been his friend.

After the eleventh chapter, Arjuna's questioning takes a different approach. He is now more receptive and less argumentative. He wants to have an experience. Finally he comes to a great conclusion. What is needed is not just 'niṣkāma karma'; what is needed is Karma Yoga'. And what is the final conclusion he comes to? When Krishna asks him, "Has your confusion gone?" what is the reply Arjuna gives? He says, "Yes, my confusion has gone." Then what will he do? He says to Krishna, 'Tvayā hṛṣikeśa hṛdi sthitena yathā niyukto'smi tathā karomi.' – "According as I am appointed by Thee, O Hrishikesha, seated in my heart, so I act."

Now this is the whole teaching of the Gita. It starts with 'śiṣyas te'haṁ'. Arjuna tells his friend Krishna, "O dear Krishna, I am your disciple, please guide me. I will do as you command me to do." And later when his confusion leaves him, he again says, "Yes, I will do as you command me to do." In both cases the answer is the same but the first time it was given to Krishna who was standing in front of him and the second time to Krishna 'seated in the heart' – 'hṛdi sthitena.' "You must guide me constantly, all the time, in small matters and in big. I am fighting because you want me to fight. All my earlier reasons for fighting are gone," says Arjuna.

How can one be guided constantly?

You must create the conditions which the Gita gives you. Equanimity is one, desirelessness is another.

But before that, Bhaiji, one more question. After all, the Kauravas and the Pandavas were cousins, right? What do you have to say about the Kshatriyas and their beliefs and their ethics and things like that. Why stop the other side from having the same beliefs and ethics? Are we talking about politics or are we talking about spirituality?

You see, the other side, the Kauravas, did not believe in those ethics. There is an interesting statement of Duryodhana about how the nature of man compels him to do wrong even after knowing what is right. He says, 'Jānāmi dharamam na ca me pravṛittiḥ' – "I know what Dharma is, but somehow I do not feel like practising it." 'Jānāmyadharmam na ca me nivṛittiḥ' – "I know what adharma is, but I cannot get away from it."

So there are people who by nature are like him, even like Ravana. Ravana was a man of great askesis, a man of great will power. He could move mountains with his will power. Even that man, why did he abduct the great Sita? So there is a play of the Divine in the world in which He gives you the unfortunate role of villain.

What is the purpose behind this?

The purpose, the real purpose of the world is to manifest God. You see, in God everything is latent – all sounds, all colours, all temperaments, everything is latent.

But how can God have anything bad in Him!

He does not have anything essentially bad, because for Him it is all a drama, a 'lila'. If you look from a certain height, you will see that there is nothing fundamentally bad. How? In a drama, if someone acts the role of a villain he does not actually become a villain. Rather he has done his duty to God, he has done his duty to the director. He cannot say do not give me the part of a villain. I will play only the role of a hero.

No Bhaiji, how is His purpose served, God's purpose?

How is God's purpose served in that man? Let us see. God's purpose in every man is to make him grow in godhood. Now, suppose there are two men – I am giving you a very theoretical, a hypothetical example; in practice it may be slightly different – and one of them is very virtuous and the other is full of vice in his thoughts and actions. It is very surprising that often it is men with vices who are strong and the virtuous who are the weaker ones – or most of them. Such is the drama. Now, there are two categories of men with vices: men who are weak and men who are really strong, like Duryodhana and Ravana.

Duryodhana was a great man. When the war was over, he was saved. People said: "You are saved." "No," he said, "my friends have died, why should I live?" You see, he was not an ordinary man. He was a man of great courage, he was a great warrior himself; but certain actions of his were bad. We must realise that he did not misrule his subjects. Perhaps Yudhishthira would have ruled better but Duryodhana did not misrule, as such. However, he did misbehave with his brothers, the Pandavas, cheated them, and all that. Now, why did he do this? When a man is ultimately going to die, why this greed for a kingdom he is not going to take with him? Why fight for something which is not going to remain with you? Why give blows and take blows for nothing? No, there is a purpose. The purpose may apparently be the kingdom, but spiritually, the reason, as I told you, is to move godward.

Let us take three examples: Duryodhana, Yudhishthira and Arjuna. Arjuna was the favourite of Krishna, though it was Yudhishthira who was looked upon as the embodiment of Truth. And to Arjuna, inner illumination came from Krishna. If there was no Mahabharata, no war to be fought, how could Arjuna's own progress be possible? Where would have Krishna given him the message of the Gita? Arjuna would not have even asked him the questions, he would not have even been receptive to the answers. He would probably have said, "It does not concern me. You are giving me a very hypothetical answer." But because he was in the middle of a battlefield, the answer could not be hypothetical. He wanted a practical and a direct answer urgently.

I will make a little deviation and tell you a very interesting episode in the story as commonly told – though some of the popular stories are not part of the original Mahabharata. When Arjuna returned after the first day of the battle, Draupadi, his wife – he was her favourite husband – received him and said, "My lord, I heard you refused to fight. But I am sure you remember how I had been insulted and I am glad you have now decided to fight." Arjuna replied to her, "Draupadi, when I went to fight, it was because of these reasons. But now I am not fighting because you were insulted. Let me be very frank with you – I am fighting for no other reason except that it is Krishna's command. Even if you had not been insulted and if he had commanded me to fight, I would have fought, and if he had told me not to fight I would not have fought. So for me, I have no other reason except to obey him in the world and whichever role he gives me, I will fulfil it. My human reasons for fighting are gone." Externally the work was the same but the motivation had changed.

You must know that the man, Arjuna, who wanted to fight and the man, Arjuna, who was fighting now, were really psychologically two different Arjunas. So this is the important answer. That event made him grow godward though it took the form of a bloodbath which is normally abhorrent to men. But this happens.

Now, let us take Yudhishthira. Yudhishthira, the incarnation of Truth, was obliged to tell a lie – just *one* lie. I am sure he must have thought later: "What is this life? Why did I tell a lie? What was the real result? Even my son Abhimanyu has died." Ultimately, when the Pandavas go to the Himalayas, all the brothers die. Perhaps at one stage Yudhisthira must have told himself: "All this has no meaning except my unity with God. United with Him, whatever role He wants me to play, I will play. All other motives must go." Moving godward means replacing all other motivations by only one: God's command.

It is the same thing with Duryodhana. After enjoying such a vast kingdom, he became the cause of the death of all his kith and kin; of the young men, his son, his grandson, who were great warriors, great people, and he became the cause of the death of all. He became the cause of the ruin of an empire. What did he do during the last stage? I feel he might have told God: "I do not know if I did right or wrong. I did my duty where You put me and according to the consciousness You gave me. Please in future guide me and tell me what I should do. If it has served Your purpose by giving me the villain's role, and if it made the Lord give the Gita on the battlefield, I am also fulfilled, not only Arjuna, because it is not Arjuna who is the cause, I am the cause of the Gita." So everybody grows out of experiences, good and bad, and the more evolved one is, the greater is the experience. Even Ravana knew that Rama was an incarnation of God and yet he fought him.

But does the Gita say all this, in so many words?

The Gita does not say all this. The Gita is meant to give the philosophy of life and the way to right action and the way also to *successful* action. You see, right action in the eigthteenth chapter is not an unsuccessful action, because the last thing which Sanjay says is: 'Yatra yogeśvaraḥ kṛṣṇe yatra pārtho dhanurdharaḥ // tatra śrir vijayo bhūtir dhruvā nītir matir mama'// "Where there is Krishna who is the Lord of Yoga and Partha, the holder of the bow, there the victory shall always be."

You must be a man with a bow and arrow but that does not mean a material bow and arrow; but a man of action, a warrior ready to fight, willing to face any challenge that God commands you to do, regardless of the consequences. So the Gita only covers the philosophy of life, of action, successful action. The Gita does not cover everything, though it may briefly cover many other things like death, rebirth, karma, food, but only as far as it is relevant to the main theme.

What is your view about the drinking of the Soma wine, which is a part of many yogic practices?

What could be the' rasa' of Soma? People say it was a herb. How can it be a physical herb? Anyhow, the important thing to know is that whatever be the meaning of 'Soma rasa', the normal wine is very harmful. You see, wine, gambling and women are an invitation for the hostile forces, for the wrong forces, that bring wrong influences in one's life. These cannot bring spiritual progress. Right forces bring right influence, wrong forces bring wrong influence. If you bring a rose, you will have fragrance, but if you bring a foul-smelling object, you will have a bad smell. So it is like that.

I do not understand how women can be an invitation to hostile forces!

By women I do not mean your wife or a woman for whom you have real love and affection. It is indulging in all kinds of passions – that is what I meant. I must correct my word and be more accurate. I do not mean women as such or in the sense of your wife or a woman you love or your mother, your sister or even a friend. I mean 'woman' in the sense of womanizing, dissipated sex and all these things connected with wine and women, as they say. That kind of life attracts the asuric forces.

But then why is it that drinking is not only permitted but even encouraged in some spiritual practices?

This is not a simple question to answer. There are many reasons and many possible misinterpretations. Also, the same laws do not apply at different stages of a man's consciousness and growth.

The question arises that if a man did not take wine, would he be greater than the one who drinks? I would not be able to answer this point. In the ordinary ethical sense, he would certainly be more virtuous but whether he would be greater spiritually, I cannot say, because I have known of men who not only drank wine but having got drunk, turned towards God. The wine takes away the mental control of your life. If you are already inclined towards God, maybe in some rare cases, it may help you. If you are not inclined towards God, the lower nature that has been put down by the control of the mind, will come up and get the better of you – the side of ego, the side of drinks, the side of womanizing, the side that runs into passions. So, whatever is dormant in you and kept under suppression by the mind, with drinks, the control of mind goes and then all these come up. There may be some rare cases of men in whom spirituality is dormant and after taking wine, spirituality awakens. So this is a question that is difficult to answer with a yes or a no.

But in any case in the first stage – that of a normal, average man who is not aspiring for a spiritual life but who leads a mundane life, a normal life – we have to look at the question purely from the physical point of view and there, wine does harm.

The second stage comes when you have made one of your goals or *the* goal, to realise God in life, to become His instrument or even to become God. This, I call the stage of a 'sadhak', a person who is on his way towards realisation of God, who has taken a route to reach this stage. I personally feel that in the 'sadhak' stage, wine is definitely harmful. There can be exceptions but as a general rule, wine must be avoided.

You may say that there have been instances where a guru has made his disciple drink wine in his presence. Now this type of yoga comes under 'Vāmamārga'. It is called 'Vāmamārga', which means that he will take meat, he will womanize, he will drink also, but in his guru's presence. Now this is very important. I have heard of people who indulge in this kind of life. I have heard of them, but I have never seen them indulging in this kind of life.

I find that there are two sides to this. It can happen that a guru who is already realised, comes across a disciple who is addicted to drinks, addicted to this kind of life and if he finds it difficult to rescue him by explanations or persuasion or an inner communication, what he does is, he asks his disciple to do it in his presence. The result is exactly the opposite. The man really cannot do it. The man gives up drinking, gives up that kind of life. There is a kind of a liberation as soon as he feels his guru's presence. This is one kind. There can be the other kind of gurus, the false gurus, who actually encourage this, because the practice puts them in contact with some vital beings and some small siddhis which they can display before men. And men, ignorant of the deeper forces acting from behind, accept them as great spiritual gurus, which they are not – in fact, they can be very dangerous.

What is your own opinion of that kind of a person, Bhaiji, that is, guruwise?

Speaking from a deeper spiritual angle, God permits this because somewhere a necessity for this kind of experience also exists; that a man may undergo this experience and if he is sincere, he may realise that it does not lead him to spirituality, does not lead him to fulfilment, but to dissipation and ruin. Even that experience may be necessary for some people and maybe God allows some gurus or some people to follow this because for that category of people this kind of an experience may be necessary as the only way for them to turn godward. But these, as I said, are exceptions. As a rule, it is to be avoided.

Can the guru know what kind of a disciple he has, what are his inner propensities?

A real guru would know, a really realised guru.

Otherwise should the disciple tell him or would the guru just know?

You see, the disciple should always lay bare everything before the guru. When the disciple tells his guru, three things happen. One is that the wall between him and his guru thins and the guru's grace and consciousness flow to him better. Second, this kind of a confession – you may call it a confession before God or before a guru – is enjoined in all religions as a way of washing away your past. And I fully believe in it. A kind of purification does take place, I have no doubt about it. This is the second benefit.

The third and the greatest benefit is that it invokes a Grace from God, a Grace which not only wipes out the past, not only strengthens you, but wipes out even the result of the wrong karma; a Grace which almost undertakes to lead you to the goal and also helps you get over the habit. This is the biggest advantage of this kind of, as I said, an opening or a confession or a kind of placing your problems before your guru in a very candid manner. And this always good. If there is something you want to hide from him, it means that you want that corner to remain in the dark. Somehow you do not want to get rid of it. One part of you wants to get rid of it but some other part does not. That is why human conduct is sometimes difficult to understand and to change.

Does not the Gita also analyse the complexity of human nature and show the way to overcome it?

First, I must tell you that the Gita is the most deep, the most practical book you could come across. It is the most positive, the most sincere book on life.

But are there not parts in the Mahabharata which seem to be contrary to it?

I am not talking of the Mahabharata, I am talking of a part of the Mahabharata – the Gita. Now, if we are taking the whole of the Mahabharata, let me tell you that the whole of it is not originally from Vyasa. Only ten thousand slokas are from him and there are a lot of additions from others.

What Vyasa has written, I accept; but what others have added, I may or may not accept. My attitude will be critical. My attitude will not be an acceptance of a gospel, thinking that the person who has written it is a realised soul and we cannot reject it but must try to understand it. What the others have written, we can understand in our own way and if it does not fit in with our ideas, we may say no, we do not accept.

So the author, the man behind an epic is very important for books of this nature. What the author has said is important but his personality is more important, whether we should accept his word or not. These realised souls are very few, very, very few. Vyasa is one of them, let us accept him; Valmiki is another, let us accept him, also. So it is like this. Let us see and then decide. If you take the Mahabharata in its totality this point arises. When you read the Mahabharata, you must read it with a certain amount of critical attitude. You cannot read the whole of it with an attitude of total acceptance – that you cannot do. But with the Gita, you can. That portion is pure. It is as Vyasa wrote it.

But there are many instances in the Mahabharata where corrupt or wrong practices seem to be encouraged.

You see, in the story there is a lot of mixture added to it. In spiritual life you have to always leave out the mixture. Even more than the moral, the spiritual thought behind it, is more important, because the basis of our moral thought, the basis of our ecomonic ideals, the basis of our political ideals, social conventions, is all spiritual. If there is anything contradictory between the spiritual ideals and other ideals, then it requires a second look. In ninety percent of cases I feel it would be immediately clear that the spiritual basis would be right and the other ideals would be wrong. And in the remaining ten percent also, if we go deeper, the spiritual would be found in any case to be right and the others would be found to be temporal, suited to a particular time and place.

Now the spiritual vision is that there is a Divine Consciousness pervading the whole universe. This Divine Consciousness by a process of involution became the various inner planes. And then by a process of evolution a portion of each plane combined with the others to produce an external creation – plant, animal, man – and this evolution is going even further. The aim of our political, economic, social or ethical life should be to further accelerate the evolution. Anything which retards it, is wrong. If we go even a little into detail, we find that all our highest political ideas, like democracy, communism, socialism, all have their roots - even roots which we are not conscious of – in the spiritual ideals. If we try to correlate them, we will find that those who preach them – Rousseau or Karl Marx – were somehow influenced by the basic ideal, the spiritual ideal of the welfare of mankind. They might have missed the details in certain things, because the spiritual basis was not clear to them in its totality. But there are many things Karl Marx has said, with which one can agree. His followers may spoil it as the followers of religions have done.

So the important thing to know is that whatever be the stories in the Mahabharata, it is quite possible that our interpretation of them may be wrong. We have to learn to have a correct interpretation, and that can only come about when we are united with God. Any level of consciousness lower than this will always be subject to revision. It may or may not be correct, or it may be partially correct, but you can never say with surety that the interpretation is correct. Only when you are united with the Divine can you say with some certainty that the interpretation is correct.

So we must realise our limitations while interpreting any book, any story, anything. We must know that whatever interpretation we give it, it is our own. It may be good for us, but good only at that point in time; as we grow in consciousness, we may give it another interpretation later.

This should also be our attitude to everything in life. So long as a person has not realised the Divine, he must accept the fact that his attitude is imperfect, his knowlege is imperfect, his interpretation is imperfect, his reaction is imperfect, and he should not impose his views on others, under whatever garb. And this holds true for everything – whether it is a political dictatorship, a religious dogma, a social pressure or an economic power which makes people employed by him follow his line of action, right or wrong.

Broadly, there are two forces in the world – the Divine force and the undivine force; and many intermediate forces, also. The greatest opposition to the Divine force is the Inconscient in man. Now when the Inconscient becomes partly conscient, that part which has become conscient comes under the influence of the Divine force and the other parts which are still inconscient remain under the influence of the hostile forces. Then one can say that that person is partly correct. When a person is totally conscious and under the influence of the Divine force, then only can one say that he is totally correct. Now given this situation, how can a person presume that his interpretation is correct, so long as he has not realised the Divine.

How can one realise the Divine?

There is a process, a process of realising – and that is yoga. And the process of integral realisation is called Integral Yoga.

How can one know that one is ripe or ready for realisation or for spiritual life?

You see, nobody is ripe completely from the beginning. But a part is ripe from which one can make a start. Besides, you should try to do your best all the time under the prevailing circumstances and that will be good enough. If you do your best you become a little better; again you strive and you become still better – it is always an ongoing movement. So instead of wondering whether you are ripe or not, your attitude should be that there is a Divine Presence in you, that there is a seed of the Divine in you and it cannot but be that this tree of the Divine consciousness will grow and flower because the seed is divine. In between there may come certain problems, but the seed is very powerful. "If I collaborate with it, the obstructions will be removed. Let me, with all my weaknesses, shortcomings, lack of resolution, surrender to the Supreme, the all-knowing Consciousness, the 'antaryāmin', the One within me, and relying on Him, let me do my best." That is enough.

Why does a guru accept a disciple who is not yet ready or ripe?

If he is a real guru, it is not he who accepts a disciple; it is the Divine in him who accepts him. So long as a guru has a feeling of 'I-ness' – 'I accept, I do this, I do that' – then he is not a real guru. The Divine knows what is best, that is why he accepts. And He has made a commitment that "whosoever needs My help I will give it." He does not impose, He does not interfere but once you turn to Him, He stretches out His hand to you through a physical guru; that is all.

I will be very honest about my shortcomings. I have done many wrong deeds, I have my weaknesses, I am unable to leave them. Can I still turn to God?

God does not take into account all these things. He is God; in whatever form you worship Him, He is God. These things do not matter to Him. The greater your problems are the more He enjoys lifting you up, so long as you are willing to be uplifted. That is the only thing expected of you, that you should be willing to be uplifted. If you are willing to be uplifted and if you pray to Him: "Please take charge of my life", He will accept your prayer. He will even give you two slaps and take you back. It has happened before! Then He will not leave you. Once He has picked you up, He will not leave you. But this is not dependent upon these outer actions. It is dependent only upon the aspiration of your soul.

In that case, Bhaiji, why do you say that one should not drink or do similar things, if the inner aspiration is what matters?

In nearly all cases, spiritual aspiration does diminish by drinking but not, as I told you, in every case. Spiritual aspiration is there but dormant and while under the influence of drink, in some rare cases, it has awakened. I have heard people speak of this, and I do not categorically reject it. Removing mental control and replacing it by a spiritual control through yoga, is not the same as replacing mental control by impulses. Everyone will naturally agree that the control of impulses cannot be better than the control of the reasoning mind. So the drink removes the control of the reasoning mind and increases the action of all impulses, good and bad, in man. Very few people unfortunately have the spiritual impulse and most of them have only the unspiritual impulses which then manifest themselves.

To what does the Gita lead us?

The Gita shows you the way to realise the Highest Consciousness in you, that is the Divine in you and to become His instrument of action in the world.

Does not the Gita claim that it will deliver man from all evil?

It is not the Gita that makes the claim, it is Krishna who makes the claim in the Gita. The Gita is the name of the book which is a dialogue between Krishna and Arjuna. There are assurances given in the Gita in a form which expresses an eternal truth. Says Krishna in one sloka: 'Kṣipraṃ bhavati dharmātmā Śaśvacchāntiṃ nigacchati / Kaunteya pratijānīhi na me bhaktaḥ praṇaśyati.' Krishna speaks about 'my bhaktaḥ' and the meaning of bhaktaḥ according to Krishna in the Gita is, "he who remembers Me, he who really puts his consciousness in Me, he is My bhaktaḥ." Krishna says in the Gita: 'Ye yathā mām prapadyante tāṁs tathai'va bhajāmyahaṁ.' He says, "As men approach Me, so I accept them." If you believe Krishna is your elder brother, he will treat you like his younger brother; if you say Krishna is your father, He will treat you like his son. It is very interesting, God responds to you according to your aspiration for Him. Now, having given this background, Krishna says: 'Kṣipraṁ bhavati dharmātmā,' – very quickly he becomes a 'dharmātmā'; 'Kṣipraṁ' – very quickly, speedily; 'Śaśvacchāntiṁ nigacchati' – he gets eternal peace; 'Kaunteya pratijānīhi' – O Kunte, O Arjuna, know ye for certainty; 'Na me bhatkaḥ praṇaśyati' – My disciple, My devotee cannot be destroyed, he does not perish, he is not vulnerable; 'Na me bhaktaḥ praṇaśyati' – this is a great assurance he has given; once a person has turned to Me, he has become My 'bhaktaḥ' – he will not perish.

If one has turned to the Divine, the Divine Grace descends and acts in him. Then the progress becomes quick, because if man had to travel all the way by himself, he would never reach the goal. But once you open the window the sun comes to you. So similarly once you turn to Him, He reaches out to you and holds you. But the turning to the Divine is important.

But at places the Gita seems to be very vague.

In no place is it vague. It is very clear. It was told to a man who was constantly doubting. Arjuna is the prototype of the questioning man, a man who is questioning constantly and is trying to reason. Where do you find it vague?

Now let us see how the Gita begins. In the first chapter a description of the two armies is given with Duryodhana assessing as to who will win the War, who is on their side, who is on the other side, what is his prowess. In the first chapter itself, Arjuna asks Krishna to take him between the two armies. So the stage is set.

As you know, the Gita and the War are narrated by Sanjaya to Dhritarashtra, the father of Duryodhana. I think it was Vyasa himself who gave Sanjaya 'divyaḍriṣṭi', the faculty of being able to see and hear at a distance even through a wall – what we would call in modern psychology, clairaudience and clairvoyance. Sitting in his room, Sanjaya describes to Dhritarashtra the whole War as it takes place. So it is the opposite side that is describing it and you can be sure that they would not put unnecessary points in favour of the Pandavas. If it had been told by one of the Pandavas, the chances are that they might have exaggerated things in their own favour. But here it is being told to a person who has everything at stake – his own sons are fighting, he is a king – and he is aided by Sanjaya, who is an honest man and who is trying to present a true picture without any exaggeration.

In the first chapter we find Duryodhana going to his guru, Dronacharya and telling him: "Acharya, let us take an assessment of the situation." Now, this is an important point. The assessment is made by Duryodhana – not by Arjuna or Yudhishthira – a man for whom the whole Kaurava army has assembled to fight for his cause, who is a sort of a symbol of their coming together. And his assessment is: "We are far superior to the other side because my army is protected by Bhīṣmapitāmaha, by you, by Karṇa, by such great warriors. Though the other army is led by Arjuna, Bhima and others, compared to you and Bhīṣmapitāmaha, that army is nothing." This is absolutely true. The whole difference is made by one man – Krishna.

There is one thing related in the first chapter that is very interesting. The 'Śaṅkhanāda', the blowing of the conches starts on the Kauravas' side. Sanjaya says that conches were blown by the Kauravas, the conches were blown by the Pandavas. 'Devadatta' and 'Pāñcajanya', the conches of Arjuna and Krishna, were even named; and the sound of these conches created a tremor, a fear, in the hearts of the Kauravas. He does not say – and this is very significant – that the sound of the conches on the Kauravas' side created a fear on the side of the Pandavas. Sanjaya, as I told you, has the faculty of clairaudience, clairvoyance and has the power to feel the consciousness of the people and he finds that the fear was created in the hearts of the Kauravas, although they are the stronger army, while no fear was created on the Pandavas' side. There is a Divine action behind the whole thing and the Divine power is on the weaker side – weaker, if considered from the angle of the number of warriors. So the action of the so-called weaker side is creating a fear in the hearts of the warriors who consider themselves invincible. This is ominous – a kind of a premonition of things to come.

Now, Arjuna reflects on the result of the War. What will be the result? In the battle, his own children will die, his brothers will die, his friends will die, the children of the Kauravas will die, their friends will die, their relations will die. And after this holocaust, I will sit on the throne and enjoy it? Arjuna thinks of all this. How can this be possible for a man of his ethics, a man of his morals, a man of his great capacity. How can he dream of such a thing! So he says, "I do not see one good reason why this War should be fought." In this vision, all his earlier reasons for fighting the War seem invalid. The background is thus set for the great message of the Gita. Here are two armies assembled; one, consisting of men who think that right is on their side and who are willing to stand up and fight for the sake of righteousness, but who find that fighting for their right is not reason enough, because the consequences are evil. So what kind of right is this when the consequences are evil? What is it that they are fighting to preserve? What is the issue at stake? What will they gain if they win? This is the most important question which every man has to ask. A man seeking money might make millions but is money the issue? What would a man gain if he became the king of the world? The issue is not only becoming a victor in the Mahabharata War or a king; it is becoming victorious in any walk of life. What is this issue?

Therefore, Krishna shows the true issue. And this is the crucial point in the Gita. The motive with which the Pandavas started the War was to regain their kingdom and to right the wrong as they imagined or thought it to be. But Krishna shows that the issue is not righting the wrong; it is not winning the kindgom, either. The issue in the Gita is: do you want to carry out God's command or not?

Symbolic, is it?

No, not symbolic, it is very real. Suppose you are a writer. Do you want to write to please yourself and earn money or to write because God wants to express something through your writing? Now, there is a difference between the two. You write because He wants to express something through you. You write it as perfectly as you can, you are not worried whether the book sells or not, you are not concerned whether people will understand it or not. Your only motive to write is because God wants to manifest something through you and you allow it to manifest. Besides, what you write could be a Gita which is read through centuries or it could be just another book which is thrown away after two days. That is not your concern. God made you write and you wrote it, and that is enough.

So the issue, the constant issue, that God brings before you, before every man, is whether man wants to surrender to God and become His instrument in carrying out His command or whether he wants to work for some egoistic reason. Is every action of his, even an ordinary routine one like taking a bath, done because God wants him to do it at a particular time in a particular fashion or does he want to do it in his own way. This is the issue which the Gita stresses. And the ultimate conclusion to which Arjuna comes, is: "I do not care whose side wins, I do not care whether I win the kindgom or lose it. I am fighting because Krishna wants me to fight. He has given me that role and I must fulfil it." This is the whole teaching of the Gita: How to receive God's command and act as His perfect instrument. And the way is shown by the Gita.

Did you say that the Gita is not a symbol but a moral lesson?

It is not a moral lesson, it is a spiritual lesson; and you must make a distinction between spirituality and morality. They are not contradictory but there is a difference. Morality is mental – speak the truth, do not hurt your neighbour, love your neighbour, and so on. This is the external aspect of morality, but psychology is its base; the external is the result. So morality is mostly psychological and mental.

According to Hindu philosophy, moral laws must be observed by men. But some people can transcend the laws if they get a command from the Divine. If you do not get a command from Him, it cannot be superseded. This is the whole difference. The moral laws can be superseded by a spiritual law. But if you do not have the spiritual contact you have no right to break the moral laws.

How could Krishna have spoken to Arjuna for so long on the battlefield?

This question has occured to many people, including me. Considering it from a purely physical or material level, perhaps the dialogue of the Gita would take almost a whole day or at least a good many hours. How could it be possible to argue and explain in this manner? I do not think the dialogue took place in so many words – literally – as given in the book. You see, this is all Vyasa's elaboration of what Krishna must have communicated by his consciousness and thoughts to Arjuna, all in a short time. And it is quite possible in yoga to communicate this to others without saying much.

In the dialogue Krishna sometimes seems to contradict himself. Why is it so?

I will tell you. Arjuna himself says to Krishna, "You are saying one thing at one time and another thing at another time." But then Krishna explains to Arjuna that his viewpoint is wrong. This is how the mind of man interprets. Even Arjuna interpreted it in this way till the eleventh chapter. But after the eleventh chapter he does not talk in that trend.

Now, let us take the life of Krishna. Krishna was born in prison.

At the time of his birth the guards somehow fell asleep and the chains fell off. His father put him in a basket, took him across the Jamuna to the other side, left him at Nanda's house, brought back the daughter born there, as their new-born child and the chains by themselves got tied again. This is very amazing. And throughout Krishna's life we find incidents more or less of this nature. So a very basic question arises, whether all these things could have happened physically, whether they are symbolic, or are they mere stories? I personally feel these could have actually taken place. I do not say that they did happen but I cannot say that they are impossible, also. When we see materialisation and dematerialisation of objects, when we see a number of siddhis, many of which I also had the good fortune to witness in my life, then to me these kinds of siddhis do not seem to be very great or impossible, but rather very much possible. Further, they have been conceived by people who have this kind of power. So let us suggest that they were possible. While accepting them, if there is a symbolic meaning useful to us, there is no harm in taking that also. So we can take an integrated view and accept both the good points, the symbolic and the actual, for our benefit.

To come back to our story, Krishna grows up. Like any other child he has his childish pranks – many might have been exaggerated by men and poets and many might have been the creation of their imagination. But every child has his pranks. When God accepts a human form He accepts human limitations, also – both in body and nature – yet He remains God at the soul level and the highest level. So Krishna, having accepted a human form and a human nature, naturally limited himself. And what were his pranks?

They are innocent ones.

Not only innocent, but also amazingly powerful. It rains and he lifts up the Goverdhana mountain on his finger. Again the question arises, how did he do it? Did it really happen or are these all exaggerated stories?

Is it symbolic or real?

I think it could be both. And why not accept it as both, for our benefit? It encourages us. Can we not also lift the Goverdhana mountain on our finger? Is there a way to do it? I think there is a way, because it is not the finger which lifts the mountain, it is the vital force, the spiritual force that supports the mountain. The finger is only symbolic or an instrument. Actually, in some occult practices, you take a broom and you do this (gesture) to ward off some disease. The question arises whether without the broom and doing this (gesture), a man could remove the disease. There are other methods by which you can remove the disease but this also, is one of them. And I found that when some people practise this, a kind of a force really goes out to the broom. It is not without meaning. So there is no reason to disbelieve the various incidents in Krishna's life. But if we believe them as possible, it does not mean that they happened that way. Now let us accept two things: the symbolic reason behind it and this possibility in man which he can develop and not live his life below the level of his potentiality as he is living today.

To continue, Krishna then one day comes to Mathura from Nandagaon with his brother, fights an elephant, fights a strong muscular wrestler, kills both and ultimately, kills the king of Mathura, Kaṇsa, his *mama* (maternal uncle), who is the symbol of evil, who represents the evil force. Now this killing of Kaṇsa, creates a lot of political problems. Another great king – Kaṇsa has some close relatives – becomes Krishna's enemy. Krishna fights a host of kings, defeats them and makes his father the king of Mathura. Later, he goes to Dwarka. I do not know if it is the same Dwarka as of today.

As king of Dwarka and ruler of the Yadavas, he is related from Kunti's side to the Pandavas, who are his cousins. A new chapter opens in Krishna's life – chapter one: Nandagaon and Mathura – chapter two: Dwarka, where we see a new Krishna, as a king, who is involved in politics, involved in war, involved in a number of activities.

What is the message he came to give? He tells in the Gita two very important things. In the fourth chapter, Krishna says: "Yadāyadā hi dharmasya glānir bhavati bhārata abhyutthānam adharmasya tadā'tmānaṁ sṛjāmy ahaṁ." This is a very important sloka. Most religions say that God has come and gone finally; no more is He going to come. But this is very peculiar, very unique to Hinduism, that God comes not just once, but again and again. The problems are never wiped out permanently! 'Yadā-yadā hi dharmasya glānir bhavati bhārata' – whenever 'dharma' goes down and 'adharma' comes; 'abhyutthānam adharmasya tadā'tmānaṁ sṛjāmy ahaṁ' – 'I create Myself'. Now, this is very important: 'tadā'tmānaṃ sṛjāmy ahaṁ' – 'I create Myself, not that I am born of a particular father and he created Me'. The father is only a 'nimitta', a mere instrument. 'I create Myself'. And what do I do? "I remove the evil forces". That was the time when the rule of ethics was becoming fossilised. Most of the people had lost their spiritual ways and were merely clinging to certain laws given at a particular time, regardless of the time that had passed, regardless of the water that had flowed. Some of them were even using these laws for their evil designs, a kind of misinterpretation.

Whenever God comes as an Avatar, He establishes a new and a higher level of consciousness, a new approach to life. In the Rama Avatar, it was a new kind of ethics which was established upon earth. I believe it was the same Krishna who had come earlier as Rama and established sattwic ethics. For example, Kaikeyi tells the king that Rama should go to the forest and Rama agrees: "Yes, I will go, since it is my father's command;" a man says that his son had died because of the sins of the king; something wrong happens and Rama starts searching for the cause; some men criticize Sita and Rama leaves her. So there were certain very high standards of so-called ethics at that time. We may today disagree with the ethics which were established in those times. And Krishna breaks all these ethical laws. He makes Arjuna kill Bhīṣmapitāmaha and when he found it necessary he put Śikhaṇḍī in the middle, during the fight.

But don't you think Krishna's actions were wrong or foul.

No, that is what I was coming to, that neither are Krishna's views wrong nor his actions foul, as they apparently look. I am trying to show you Krishna from a higher level of consciousness because an action, when you see from a particular level, may look as you say; but that same action, if you see it from another angle, it does not look at all like that. That other angle is a higher and more integral view of life than the earlier one. The angle itself, the window itself is different. And this window which is higher and has a greater view will naturally predominate over the window with a limited view. So from an external point of view, he seems to break many accepted laws, and in doing this, what was he trying to establish? What was he trying to reveal to us? What was his message?

If you look only at the outer action you have again the example of Dronacharya, second-in-command of the Kauravas, killed by a foul deed, by giving a wrong report of his son. This is the second incident. And all at the behest of Krishna. He prevailed upon Yudhishthira to say this lie. First, let us put Krishna's case as the devil would put it: "You fellows who have done all this mischief, what kind of gods are you?" And then we may examine the situation from a deeper angle.

The third was the example of Karṇa. He was also killed by foul means when the wheel of his chariot got stuck in the mud. Fourth was Salya who fought for only half a day – I forget now how he got killed – but by that time the Kauravas had already weakened. Salya was their own maternal uncle who was always sympathetic to the Pandavas. He was the charioteer of Karṇa and he was putting down Karṇa's spirit all the time, because of his affection for the Pandavas. He was on the Kauravas' side because he had given his word to Duryodhana. But he had also given his word to Yudhishthira that he would dampen Karṇa's spirit, so he kept his word. These ethics to our mind are very confusing.

Now this is the crucial point. Krishna, finding that his side was in a tight corner, did not hesitate to adopt means, the so-called external means which some self-righteous people would call unethical. Now what is the justification? The justification comes from both, the spiritual standpoint and from the external, ethical angle. Suppose a woman is being molested on the road by two or three ruffians. You go to her rescue, but find that the ruffians are stronger than you. You have a pistol with you. Will you say I won't use the pistol because the ruffians do not have one? This would be the old ethics. But the new ethics of Krishna is, no, they are doing a wrong act, and you are free to use all means to stop a wrong act. This is the justification of Rama killing Vali, a person who was infra-human. You cannot stand before an elephant and tell him, I will fight you in an ethical manner. Your having to take this recourse is not unethical because you are trying to protect a truth. So, from an ethical angle this would be the explanation.

From a spiritual point of view, the Gita gives a higher explanation, that it is not the action itself, but the consciousness that decides whether an act is spiritual or unspiritual, whether a thing is ethical or unethical. So if the motivation is not to win the kingdom, but to remain united with the Divine, if the motivation is purely to establish the truth as commanded by the Divine, then you do as commanded by Him and the sin will be His, not yours.

If you are one with your soul, your soul does not partake of the sin. Sin is at your level of consciousness, it is not in the action itself. So we must become very clear that in the Krishna Avatar, the Divine establishes a new standard of approach to life. Sri Aurobindo writes in *Essays on the Gita* that the path shown by the Gita is the only way of right living and there is no other. The only way to live rightly is to realise the Divine and to follow His command. If you have not realised Him you can never be sure that you are living the right life. So the whole teaching of the Gita is to find the highest consciousness in you, the total consciousness in you, which takes an integral view of life, in which everything is contained and which knows what is right and wrong and to follow it completely.

Why is the Gita not written in modern terms instead of the way it is? Also, why are there so many interpretations?

It was because Krishna was speaking to Arjuna and not Navajata (laughter). He spoke the language which Arjuna would understand, the language of that time. We are now talking in the language of the twentieth century. The world has advanced, priorities and values have changed. The problems which were faced by one Arjuna are now being faced by thousands of Arjunas. So in the present times, it is told to them in their language, in their way of understanding but the basic points remain the same. It is a bigger world. After a hundred years, the interpretation of the Gita will be different to what I am saying now. That does not mean it is contradictory or false. It may be even more deep, who knows?

Yes, it will not be contradictory; it will be evolutionary. A transcendental attitude. It will transcend this approach; it will not oppose this approach. Transcend – more total, more complete.

But do you really think that the Gita is literally true?

Literally? What do you mean? Spiritually, yes; physically also, yes. This kind of a message was preached and without it, the Mahabharata would have no value. The life and soul of the Mahabharata is the Gita. Though the Mahabharata is a great epic, has many great things, its life and soul is the Gita. Vyasa who wrote the Gita, was a contemporary of the Pandavas and the Kauravas – we must not forget this. And it was Vyasa who compiled the Vedas also. The Vedas were oral before Vyasa wrote them down. It was again Vyasa who wrote 'Śṛimadbhāgavata' (the life of Sri Krishna); it was Vyasa who wrote most of the Puranas, the great Puranas. So it was Vyasa. One day we must visit Vyasa's place near Badrinath. I saw it only from a distance when I went to Badrinath.

When Vyasa wrote the Mahabharata, he did not want to give a record of what had happened like a legal treatise or an archaeological document. He wanted to make people understand the forces behind all those events and what these were leading to and what was the lesson humanity should draw from the whole epic, although it is historical. The Mahabharata and the Ramayana are considered by many to be historical books, epics.

What is the moral lesson one can draw from the Mahabharata War or the World War?

We have seen the Second World War. Moral lessons have been clear, very clear and I have drawn some moral lessons from the War. Another person may draw some other moral lesson. So what I say only applies to my own approach. The moral lessons which I have drawn from the War are: one, if you allow the evil to remain and grow, one day it will become so big that you will have to fight it at a great cost. That was what Chamberlain did, that was what the British did, despite Churchill's warning they allowed the evil to grow. But if the War had not taken place we would not have learnt these lessons. So many people died, there was such a great loss, that it compelled us to understand things in a deeper way.

The second lesson – I have not yet come to the greatest lesson I have learnt from the War – the second lesson that I learnt from the World War is that when two sides fight, one may have a little more truth on his side, another may have a little more falsehood on his side, but none is completely false. And the fighting is bitter. You see, if one was completely true and the other completely false, the fighting would not be bitter. It is like this.

The third and one of the greatest lessons I have learnt from the War, by reading some of the chronicles, records, is that it seemed as if an invisible hand was helping the Allies. Like, when Rommel wanted to send a crucial message to Berlin, the electric wires went dead and the message did not go through in time. A number of such incidents occured during the liberation of France, the battles fought on the Normandy beaches, and the rest. When I read the narration of the various battles, I found that some invisible hand was helping the Allies. But before that, some invisible hand was helping Hitler, too. That means there are forces that exist beyond man, as during the Trojan War or the Mahabharata War or any other great event and these forces help both sides.

But at a certain stage this evil force abandons one. Hitler could not get proper guidance from this force. Upto a certain stage, the force was guiding Hitler and he was winning. Then it abandoned him.

Was it the right thing at that time? I mean was he doing the right thing at that time?

No, not the right thing. One cannot permit oneself to be guided by the evil force but, from an inner viewpoint it is not a question of right or wrong at all. It is a question of the Supreme director, the Divine, giving the responsibilities or the roles to different people which they are supposed to play. The roles are decided a good deal in advance in a general way – like, Hitler would come, wars would be fought, but through it all the world would progress. This is the real explanation. My first explanation is from our present practical level. The same thing can be seen from many levels. In the Gita, Krishna gives various explanations as each time Arjuna is not satisfied and wants a more complete explanation from a higher level.

I find you are clearer than the Gita.

No, no, don't say that! I have only learnt from the Gita. I may appear to be clearer, because I am not commenting on the whole of the Gita. I am only telling you those aspects of it that may be useful to you at present. Actually, the Gita presents a deep, many-sided truth which can only be understood by experience and practice. It is the way to a new life upon earth.

Social Transformation

People think yoga is meditation, yoga is sitting in a posture. This is a very wrong impression. In ancient India, when a student went to a teacher, he did not tell him he had come to learn chemistry, medicine, physics, administration or astronomy. He said he had come to receive the fundamental knowledge of creation, how it happened, how it operates. So the teacher gave him both – the fundamental knowledge which is called 'Brahmajñāna', the knowledge of the Brahman and also the knowledge in chemistry, physics, astronomy, medicine, and so on. All these were very highly developed. The concept of 'zero' came from India. And when the spiritual endeavour began to die down, India also went down in every field.

It is an 'intuitive' group which has to develop in every country. It will always be in a minority, at least for one hundred years to come. I do not know what will happen after that but for one hundred years, it will remain in a minority. But even if it is in a minority, it will play a very important role.

I am keen that in Canada such a group be formed, because I find that some of the writings of the Canadians are full of spirituality. It is a fertile soil for yoga but not, as I said, yoga in the old sense of the term but yoga in the new sense, yoga of the future. We need not call it yoga; we may give it some other name.

I was discussing yoga with Madam H, Director of the Philosophy department of UNESCO. I asked her the definition of philosophy, because I wanted to make a deeper study of it. She said philosophy is an integrated view of life. People in the West normally think that philosophy is separate and life is separate; it is something a professor goes on explaining, very confusing to himself and to others. But when she told me that philosophy is an integrated view of life, I was surprised, because that is also the Indian viewpoint. Philosophy is a complete vision of life, it is the basis of life; it is not something outside of life on which you meditate and try to reason out. Madam H said that Greece also had the same vision. When I asked her why the West does not have this vision now, she said that in the West, while scientific knowledge is of a high level, the philosophy taught is not very useful as it is eighty percent imagination. On the other hand, Greek and Indian philosophies were not based on imagination but on experience. She hoped that the time would come when this approach to philosophy would be accepted by all.

I mention this because there has to be a group throughout the world working for a new way of life in every country and co-ordinating the activities.

Philosophy and psychology should be a part of all education; but not this present-day philosophy. New books will have to be written, new explanations will have to be given and today with the scientific advancement many new approaches are possible. What you can explain about the deeper levels of human psychology through television and films, you can never explain by word of mouth or through books, because in the visual media you can show the range of colours, the aura, in the consciousness of man. This has to be made a part of scientific knowledge. I am thinking of scientists, because the scientific mind is very accurate, very exact – we know this, we do not know that; there is no confusion. They may revise their ideas later on. Science is cumulative, it is mathematically cumulative. Today you find something, tomorrow you find something is wrong, so you deduct that; the next day you find something new, you add to it.

And now science must add a third dimension to its search, a third inner dimension. Every branch of science must have a third dimension. If science does not have a third dimension, it is defective. How to bring about this third dimension should be the aim of all those who are doing scientific research. What we can do is to try to develop faculties beyond the mind through a growth of consciousness. For their application, each one has to try out for himself and co-ordinate his own activities.

A Canadian once explained to me the difference between science and yoga. He said that if you want to go from here, from Montreal to Ottawa you go straight, that is yoga; if you go round the world and come to Ottawa, that is science. So science goes round, making circles and ultiamtely it comes to God. There is no other way because God is within us. Though the scientists are looking for forms of energy, ultimately they will come to the Truth. Science is bound to come.

My hosts with whom I was staying in New York were Jews and their library was full of books, mostly on Jewish literature. In America people get up late, have a late breakfast, while in Pondicherry, I normally get up at three in the morning. So what to do? I would read the books from their library. It is amazing how every religion has been misinterpreted, even by its own followers. I found much similarity between Judaism and Sri Aurobindo's thoughtsand vision. So I told them that they had misunderstood their own ancient teachings, that they were giving them their own interpretations. It is the same with Christianity.

Now about rebirth, a Christian clergyman (you must have met him in Pondicherry; he preaches in churches) was telling me that upto 500 A.D, the idea of rebirth was accepted by Christianity. It was after 500 A.D. that it was put aside. He is doing researches, he is lecturing and many of his sermons are based on Sri Aurobindo's teachings, though he never uses His name. He just says what Sri Aurobindo has said. And he says people accept him readily; they are so happy. He told me that after two years he will tell his people that whatever he had been telling them was really what Sri Aurobindo has written in His books.

The same thing is happening in America. There are quite a number of churches, Methodist churches, other churches, where they are arranging talks on Sri Aurobindo but there they directly use Sri Aurobindo's name – both, Christ's name and Sri Aurobindo's – and they try to correlate the two.

So the time has come for some kind of a rapport to be established between what Sri Aurobindo has said and all the spiritual thought that has come into the world. People say it is contradictory. It is not so. You quite often reject a thing without trying it out. Many people are not even interested in understanding anything else. Take this lady with whose husband I was staying. When she came to Pondicherry her mother was very much upset, because she thought her daughter had left her Jewish religion and had taken up some other religion. It was the same with me. When I joined the Ashram, my cousin-sister was annoyed with me. She thought I had become a Christian. And the Christian thinks this fellow has become a Hindu and the Hindu thinks that this other one has become something else. This is a very foolish approach. You know, all yoga, all religions have many common basic principles. The difference is in the details and the ultimate result. Sri Aurobindo accepts the truth of all and adds a completely new dimension to them.

I am reminded of a story told to me by an Indian yogi. He said some people came to the house of, let us say, M. Now, M made beautiful lemon squash. She had tumblers of different colours, red, green, blue and yellow and she served that lemon squash in them. Somebody said that the drink in the yellow tumbler was very tasty. Another man said no, the one in the green was better. And the third said no, neither green nor yellow; the red was far tastier, though it was the same lemon squash. So this is how human nature creates the differences.

Now a stage has come when separatist religions as propounded by churches and temples and mosques will go. But religion, as a basic seeking, will grow in spirituality. It is exactly the opposite movement. Instead of creating divisions it will bring people together. Let us take an example from industry. Suppose you are manufacturing cloth. The man who keeps accounts thinks the future of the company depends upon him; the man who purchases wool or cotton thinks that unless he purchases the correct yarn, the company will flop; each man thinks everything depends upon him. Very few take an integrated view. It is the management that takes the total view of the company. It is the same problem with the world. Everybody thinks that the future of the world will be according to his vision and will depend only on him and nobody else. All this will change. A big change is coming in the world. And we must all work together for the big change, for the future.

Once you take the decision that you want God to take charge of your life, He will guide you in everything; even in your business. People do not know this simple secret. You try this and see what happens. This will be a means for your own progress.

Yoga is always taught individually, never collectively. Each case is different. I am not talking of Hatha Yoga, but the higher yoga. Ninety-nine percent of yoga is taught through a silent communication; only one percent is explained by words. A guru links his consciousness with the person whom he wants to help. It is a very powerful and effective method.

You know, I was learning traditional yoga from an Indian yogi, many years ago. When I first went to him I told him, "Tell me what I should do to co-operate with you for my own progress." He said, "Nothing. I have accepted you, I will do everything for you." So I asked him, "Tell me what I must do in order not to hinder your work." He replied, "Your hindrance does not worry me." In yoga, you see, once a guru accepts a disciple and if he has the power to link his consciousness with yours, there is no limit, no limit to the action.

How long have you been doing yoga?

A very difficult question to answer. Everybody is doing yoga in the world, some consciously, some unconsciously. I have settled in Pondicherry now for the last eighteen years. I have been in contact with the Ashram since 1929, which means forty-one years now. It is a great institution. I will explain to you something fundamental which will help you.

Training in yoga can be divided into five parts: physical, vital (what is vital, I will explain to you later), mental, psychic and spiritual. Physical you know – eyes, nose, ears, and so on. Vital is the life-body in you which is connected to the physical through the nerves. The aura is actually in the vital body. It is normally so much outside the body, so much (gesture). It is inside the body also and that can expand, contract, even separate from the body; it can be brought into the body. When it permanently separates, it is death.

Life is not only in the physical body. So long as the life-body which we call the vital body, is using the physical body, it is living. It is like electricity which is connected to the fan, for example. You remove the wire from the socket and the fan stops. The whole mechanism is there but the electric current is missing. So when the life-body separates from the physical body, men call it death. It is the separation of the two bodies.

The vital body has its own instrument of hearing, seeing, tasting, smelling. It can use the physical body for seeing or even without the use of the physical body, it can see. When the Russian scientists said that man could see from any part of the body, they did not know that man could see, not from any part of the physical body, but from any *point* of his vital body. In the physical body he can see from only one point. But because a man can close his eyes and concentrate and see, they thought he could see from any part of the physical body. It is not the physical part, it is the vital part. Your emotions, your instincts, your desires, are all a part of your vital body.

And now the mental. Mental is not limited by space; it is limited by time. A thought disappears, another comes. Mental is like the tuning of a radio or television. You tune in to Montreal, you tune in to Ottawa, you tune in to New York and you will get the programme on your radio or television accordingly. If you are very greedy by nature, you are always tuned in to greedy vibrations. All the time you keep thinking this will bring me so much money, that will bring me so much money; if I buy this, it will mean two dollars more, so I better save. The whole mind of that man is like that. If you are very generous by nature you will say, "Oh, it does not matter." You are not calculating at all, rather it is the other way about, you are extravagant. If you are very angry by nature everything will make you angry; if you are very fearful by nature, everything will make you afraid. So the thoughts respond according to your tuning. The mental plane contains logic, memory, thought formations and in the higher sense, intuition. So this is the mental plane.

Between the mental plane and the Supramental plane, there are many higher planes – Higher Mind, Illumined Mind, Intuitive Mind and Overmind. (These, we will not discuss today). A man can be in the Higher Mind, he can be in the Intuitive Mind, he can be in the Illumined Mind. Beyond the Intuitive Mind, he can be in the Overmind and beyond Overmind, he can be in the Supermind and he can go even further than that.

Let us try to understand this in a broad sense. Now, just as life is inside the physical, the mind is inside life. So the mind is also inside the physical. It is like saying water is latent in ice, vapour is inside water and inside vapour, there is hydrogen and oxygen. So it is hydrogen-oxygen that becomes vapour, that becomes water, that becomes ice. Ice has water inside it. So similarly, the physical body has life involved in it, life has mind inside it and mind has the psychic inside it. So everything is inside the physical body – outside, also. It is very important to understand this. How can the capacity of the body be developed by concentration? Once you know the basic principle you will know why taste comes to the tongue, why smell comes to the nose. The mind only gets the cognisance – this is bitter, that is sweet. But why does it feel bitter, why does it feel sweet? The chemical process only shows how it feels but not *why* it feels. Why it feels, yoga gives you the answer.

The third, as I said, is the mental plane and the fourth is the psychic. The psychic plane is extremely important. If you get in contact with your psychic, you will know everything. There will be no problem in your life that you cannot solve. You just have to concentrate and the answer will come. Psychic is the seat of all knowledge within you, the seat of the Divine in you. When you get in contact with it, you can always refer to it and be guided by it – that is the psychic. The psychic's attitude is love, love for the Divine, love for the whole creation; it always thinks in terms of giving, in spreading out.

And the fifth is spiritual. When you go beyond the mental, vital and physical, and you become one with the Supreme in which there is no movement, then, that is spiritual. Each of these five parts of a human being has its own personality. Poor man! he has not developed any of them properly. He develops his physical body by some exercises from time to time; his mind, a little by education, by reasoning, by observation; a little development. But there are immense possibilities awaiting him. And to develop them, is the real aim of yoga. Yoga means 'to join'. Yoga does not mean sitting in a posture and meditating; yoga literally means to join, to integrate. Once you develop your psychic and the spiritual personality, you also get integrated with the whole world. Suppose you are in contact with your psychic and if, with this psychic contact, you look at a child or somebody, you will give him a psychic contact without him even knowing it. If you have a psychic contact even for ten minutes and, if you concentrate on the other person who has no psychic contact, you will find that he gets a contact with a higher consciousness for those ten minutes. This is very simple. Electricity is everywhere but you generate it somewhere and then you put in the wiring, and you switch on and the light comes. Psychic consciousness is everywhere and once you develop it in you, it communicates to others.

If your psychic is well developed, your concentration also is powerful; but if your psychic is not powerful, your concentration is weak, it is not very strong. You get a psychic contact when you have no desires, when your attitude is: "I want to do what God wants me to do. I want to be guided by my psychic." In such an attitude you get the contact, because, as I told you, one is behind the other – psychic, mental, vital, physical. Also, one is inside the other.

Now let us take the example of cinema. In cinema you project a film on the screen. Suppose someone walks in front of the projection, his reflection will come on the screen. So also with the psychic; when the psychic light tries to express itself, your thoughts, your desires come in-between.

Psychic is within you, it does not come from outside. Then, why are you not feeling the psychic contact? It is because your mind is very active. We will take an example. Let us say the light is coming from here. If you put a transparent glass, the light will come through..If you put a blue-coloured glass and then a red one, the light will first become blue and then red. That means you are colouring the light, you are obstructing the light. So your mind is obstructing, your vital is obstructing the psychic light. The mind is obstructing it by continuous thinking, the vital is also obstructing it by its incessant desires, emotions. When these become quiet, the psychic light manifests in your life.

If you want a higher consciousness to guide you, you must quieten your mind and your vital. Quieten them first, then you will use them better. What you are now doing is constantly putting thoughts in the atmosphere – good, bad, right, wrong. Your wife does something wrong, and you become angry. You may not say anything but you have put out an angry thought in the atmosphere. It influences her without her knowing it; it influences you also, without your knowing it. But in yoga, this does not happen. You project only those thoughts which you want to put out: otherwise, you control them. An action does not bring any reaction in you at all. You create an action which you want to create. Nothing makes you angry, nothing makes you happy, you do what you have to do. In that consciousness, you can develop a good psychic contact. And then you use your mind, your vital, your physical body, as guided by the psychic. You do not want to be guided by the mind, but by a consciousness higher than your mind. That is the first step in yoga.

The second step in yoga is taken when the psychic or spiritual consciousness comes down to your mind and starts acting on the mental plane. When it starts acting on the mental plane, what will happen? It will change the mental plane. If you look at a person he will start changing. You do not even have to concentrate, it is automatic at that level, because it has become a part of your life.

Now suppose that the same high consciousness has descended to the vital plane. Then wrong desires cannot arise in man. Whatever is the Divine's will, only that will manifest. Sri Aurobindo has said that if it could descend into the very cells of the body there will be a change in the physical body. There will be a mutation and a transformation from a body of blood, skin and bones to a body of light. How many years this process will take, is very difficult to say; but, it is possible. If you can bring it down to the physical level, even the physical difficulties will disappear.

You have to decide whether you want to do this kind of work for your transformation. It can be done even while working in your office; you do not have to give up your work. Do you want to use your concentration for improving your life or do you want to live without a contact with the highest consciousness within you? This is the important question. Each one has to make his own decision. Do you want to be guided all the time by the highest consciousness and act accordingly or do you want to be guided by the lower consciousness? This choice you have at every minute of your life; it is not just once that you have to make this choice, but all the time. Once you have integrated your personality, once the highest consciousness has become a part of your life, you do not have to make any effort. But till it becomes a part of you, you have to make this effort all the time.

An American lady who is a playwright and an actress had turned to Sri Aurobindo. When she met me in New York, she told me, "For me, it was very simple. The life I was leading was no solution. I will do anything, except lead that life. This book, *The Mother*, came in very handy to me. There was no question of a choice. I did not want to lead that life anymore. That was no solution at all."

So, someday, man has to come to a solution. But what is the solution? Man is a link between God and earth, and he must become conscious of that link. *All the time*. When something is said to him it should be the Divine consciousness in him that should listen, it should be the Divine consciousness in him that should act, and that can only happen by an attitude of surrender. Even when you are repairing a machine, you say: "Lord, You use these hands." Like this, it is so simple. But you have to make a start. Talking is very simple, you know, practising it, is difficult. You must do it all the time, till you start feeling, understanding, then everything becomes simple. All this is not against any religion, against any belief and yet it is very scientific.

Man must know what he wants from life. You see, we go on living in ignorance. How old are you, M? thirty-one? So for the past eleven years, at least, you have been quite conscious – let us forget the first twenty years. In these eleven years how many times have you asked yourself: What do I want to do?, what is really worth doing? I am sure you must not have given more than, say two hundred hours, if at all. Two hundred hours is what? eight days? In eleven years it is eight days – even thinking like this, even making your mind clear. Where am I going? Where is my direction? What is the best I can do? What is the highest I can do? Let me strive towards the highest, let me try to achieve the best. What can be the best for me and the best for all? This is extremely important. People should concentrate, fix a goal and work for it, to begin with, later, it would be different. Once they start getting guidance, it becomes easy. You must have a goal in life. The Mother says that upon the quality of your goal will depend the quality of your life. If you want the quality of your life to be high and wide, your goal should be high and wide. And never be worried about your incapacities or the lack of means; God will provide them once you are ready to work for the new life.

I remember once a person wrote to the Mother: "Mother, I am working in a brewery. I do not drink. If I leave my job, my children will be in trouble. What should I do?" The Mother said that it was not a question of working or not working in a brewery. The question is, have you decided to live for God? If you tell yourself resolutely: "I do not know God, I do not see God, but I want to live for Him, let Him create conditions where I can live for Him", then He will change everything.

Man is too egoistic. He wants to rule the world. He does not want to be ruled by God. He wants to rule God. Man would like God to be his servant. What does man want? What does he desire? He wants that the Divine should be his servant always. If we think a little more profoundly, we will find that consciously or unconsciously man wants the Divine to do everything for him. He does not want to do anything for the Divine; he wants the Divine to be his servitor, he does not want to be God's servitor.

Man does not know what he wants, whether it is money, music, painting, drama, he does not know what he wants. He is always jumping from one thing to another. How can his life be good and happy and fruitful? He is always going zig-zag, zig-zag; he does not go in a straight line. Today it is the cinema, tomorrow it would be the theatre, the third day at a night club and the fourth day it would be a party at a restaurant and on the fifth day, cleaning the house! The same life, the same problem! There is no solution.

We have to reorganise all the aspects of our life, economic, social, aesthetic, and so on and organise life in such a way that it will help us in our integral development. How to organise life in this manner? It is already being tried in the Ashram. Auroville will try to do this on a bigger scale for fifty thousand people. Industry, education, health, agriculture, music, cinema, sports, everything, will be organised differently, without the objectives of an economic life. Material things will be there, but the objective will change. The only goal will be perfection of life, to manifest the Divine in every work, in every aspect of life. Then what will be the result? With this objective before you, when you teach your students Hatha Yoga, what will you do? You will say to God: "Lord, You teach, You are this body, this mind, You are in the students." You will find that the Divine will start helping you and the students, also. The Divine is in you and also in the students.

This is the consciousness we have to develop. The whole life has to be reorganised. People have need of money for food, for medicine, for a house, for so many things, and all their lives they clamour for money, money. How will they realise that their true goal is to find the Divine and to manifest Him at every moment? How is a man – whether he is a poet, a writer, a musician or an artist – going to move towards the realisation and the manifestation of the Divine in his life, if he is going to spend all his energy in earning money to procure the few things he really needs and the many things he desires in his life? So we must reorganise life in such a manner that all of man's needs, his basic needs, are provided free. Everything will be provided without a man having to spend money – his food, his house – so that he can choose and concentrate on his work which will give him a sense of fulfilment. Everyone will choose his work in this manner and only then, will something worthwhile happen – collectively, also.

A great and permanent change will come when each person will take up the work for which he is best suited and will do it in a spirit of dedication. This is what we want to try in Auroville. There will be no government, nobody will work for money, there will be no essential difference between a managing director and a labourer, because a managing director can somewhere be even a labourer. Then there is no quarrel, no social problems. This is actually a spiritual concept – all working towards further evolution. And somewhere in the world we have to make a beginning; we must start in some corner of the world. It does not matter which corner it is, but somewhere we have to start. It can even be here, in your own home. We waste a lot of time, a lot of energy for things that are useless. If we waste twenty percent of our life to earn some money to build a house, of what value is it? What is its use? It would be better if we were given the house where we could stay and do some work which would be useful to the entire world. At present we have great dreams, great ideals, but life does not give us an opportunity to realise them. This is what Auroville will provide to everyone, to reach his highest goal – the highest goal individually as well as collectively, at the same time. So we must become clear in our own minds and also carry the message to others who are ready, so that a cohesive group may be formed.

Let us first become clear about what we mean by spiritual law. What do you mean by spiritual law? If you want to make spirituality your aim, it is better to be clear about a few things and what I tell you now, may help you later in your work.

First, spirituality means to reorganise life in the light of a consciousness that is higher than the mind; not to be organised by the mind, but to develop in each one of us the consciousness beyond the mind and reorganise our life in the light of that consciousness. That consciousness is the consciousness of unity in diversity. In that consciousness, an individual will not be subordinate to communal life. Each one will try to realise the consciousness beyond the mind and in that light reorganise the external life. That would mean unifying the consciousness where people will be guided by the same consciousness, and automatically, harmony will come.

But the stress should be on getting the guidance beyond the mind; otherwise, sooner or later you will be in difficult waters. Because if the stress on the mind remains, after sometime everyone starts imposing himself on others: "What you say is true but I think it is like this." Another person may object: "No, I think it is like that." That is human nature – even with goodwill. Then it comes to almost the same thing, that is, you have to subordinate your individual growth to the community's dictates; it comes to that. It will mean that the majority will decide and it will be the same confusion that we hear of today. You must very clearly tell the people who join you, about this.

We are starting to create an environment where all can grow. Instead of thinking of your place as a place of competition you should think of it in terms of collaboration. When a person comes to work there, he does not work for money. A new way of life will start. As you grow within, the spiritual city or the spiritual community will grow with you.

A spiritual commune should really be a spiritual commune. There is a big difference between a religious commune and a spiritual commune. A religious commune would mean 'do this, don't do that'. But a spiritual commune is not like this. A spiritual commune will not subordinate an individual to the community life. How it can harmonise both, is the great challenge to spirituality.

Man through centuries has tried this. Sometimes, it is to eulogise the individual and put him higher than the community; sometimes, it is to bring up the other side and put the community higher than the individual. But they have never been able to find a true balance. Spirituality alone can find that synthesis. And Auroville will make this attempt, as the city grows and develops with the growth in consciousness of its inhabitants.

Karma Yoga

The question that arises, is, how and where does one start on one's spiritual path. Speaking personally, my process started with Bhakti Yoga and Karma Yoga; meditation came much later. But when it came, it came so naturally and so intensely that I did not have to make any effort at all.

Several things are common in Karma Yoga and Bhakti Yoga. In Bhakti Yoga you love the Divine and offer yourself to the Divine's work regardless of the consequences. You do not ask anything from the Divine, except that He may use you and that your life may serve His purpose. It is a self-giving without condition. This kind of approach was very natural, very spontaneous to me. I wanted to give myself to the Divine, I had nothing to ask of Him, really nothing to ask of Him. What can you ask from the Divine? He knows everything, He does everything, and much better without your asking Him. But that does not mean that when you feel like asking Him, you should not ask; that would not be natural. He is your only true friend to whom you can confide your problems and ask His help. And when you pray to Him, He is there to listen. But, as far as giving yourself to Him, giving yourself to His work is concerned, it is without condition, it is just for the love of it, for the joy of it. And this is how in my case Bhakti Yoga and Karma Yoga got combined. I wanted Him to give me His Divine guidance in all my work, in the clothes I should wear, in the people I should meet, in the books I should read, which part I should play and for how long, what meditation I should do and when, when should I go to sleep. In all my duties I wanted to be guided by Him, and I found that it worked.

Once the Mother gave me a very important assignment in Calcutta. I did not even know Bengali. She gave me a power of attorney and instructions for immediate disposal of a large piece of land which was offered to Her, as She needed the money. This was at the time when refugees from East Bengal had squatted on this land, so nobody would buy it. Though the Government was thinking of regularising and paying the money to the people, nothing had been done and the refugees had occupied the land. I am relating this to show you how Karma Yoga operates in one's life in every detail. At that time I was not in Calcutta, I was in Bombay, but the Mother gave me instructions to go and do this work in Calcutta. So I went there with only one or two days at my disposal, and I did not know what to do. Somebody suggested that I should meet the Chief Minister. I went without an appointment to meet him at the Writers Building. At the gate I sent in my name to the Secretary and somehow, I was allowed to go in. When I went there I said, "I want to meet the Chief Minister, Mr. Y." I was asked if I had an appointment. I had none. They told me that I could not see him in that case. So I sat in the reception room and prayed. Why did God bring me here if an appointment had to be fixed in advance? It was in response to His guidance that I had come here. Just then, a special officer came out and asked me if I had come from the Ashram in Pondicherry. When I told him that I had, he said, "The Chief Minister will see you." So without an appointment, without any influence, without any contact, I was taken in to see him. (I think it was 1951 or 1952.) I told the Chief Minister that Sri Aurobindo had left His body, that we were building a memorial to Him, and that it would be known as Sri Aurobindo International University. I also told him that since he was the Chief Minister of West Bengal he should help. He said that he would like to help, but added, "You know businessmen; if I ask money from them today, they will come to me for a favour tomorrow." I told him that I was not asking him to collect funds. He then asked in what way he could help. I told him he could take the land which we had in Calcutta and on which the refugees had squatted, and make the payment to me. To this he agreed and immediately sent for his commissioner for acquisition. The commissioner said, "Sir, this cannot be done, there are legal problems." Mr. Y told him in my presence that he had given his word to me and a way had to be found to do it.

This is most interesting: if I had gone through the regular channel, this proposal would never have been recommended, but because I went to him directly (and Mr. Y was a man of his word), all along he saw to it that it went through, even though there were many hurdles. The government officials said that the price I was asking was very high. They said that they had a ceiling. So I asked them that subject to the Mother's approval, would they be willing to give me the same price for all the lands. They agreed. I said I would stay a day and confirm it. The meeting finished in just seven or eight minutes. I then sent a telegram to the Mother and She confirmed it. I told the Chief Minister that the acquisition proceedings normally take several years, but that I wanted the money now. He said that they would immediately notify and, if I would give them an indemnity bond and let their people examine the title deeds, they would give us ninety percent in advance. I asked Mr. Y, "Why ninety percent? If you are taking an indemnity bond, why not give me hundred percent? Why make me run after the Government for the balance ten percent?" So he said, "All right, as a special case I will give you hundred percent." The land acquisition collector was instructed to issue a notification. I went to the acquisition collector's office. Let me tell you what happened there.

A man came out of his cabin and asked me what I wanted. I told him I had come from Pondicherry and explained the nature of the work. He told me that he was the additional collector and a devotee of the Ashram and would be happy to help but it was his colleague, another additional collector, who looked after this work. (You see, I would have normally gone to the other man. Just then why should this man have to come out?) He introduced me to his colleague who asked me to have all the documents listed – the survey numbers, area details, and so on – after which the officers would examine the papers and then proceed. I had not briefed any lawyer because I wanted to save all the money for the Mother's work. The other additional collector whom I had first met, told me on his own that I need not waste money on a lawyer; he himself would list all the documents and submit them to his colleague and let the office examine the papers. So he sat through the whole night examining all the title deeds. Wherever he found any mistakes he corrected them and those which he found absolutely clear, he listed them. I took the papers to the office superintendent. The superintendent was busy and would not examine my documents. The Mother had sent an urgent message from Pondicherry that She needed the money soon, so I tried to persuade this man but he would not listen. I said to myself, this is beyond me, I cannot persuade this man. I prayed and left it to the Divine, and went home a bit dejected; I would not say I was totally dejected, but I had this feeling I could not persuade this man anymore; I had tried my best. The next day when I again went to his office I found he had already examined and cleared my documents. So this was a new experience for me. When I was trying my best, nothing happened; but when I left everything to the Divine, the work got done. And the first cheque went to the Ashram under his signature. It was amazing to witness how these things worked out.

I was staying with my cousin and had the documents in the house. I had also some other legal papers connected with this. At about eleven or two in the night somebody or something would wake me up, make me open the bag and take out the documents which were relevant; it would make me read them, say for fifteen minutes to half an hour or even more, and then I would automatically feel tired and put them back and go to sleep. To my surprise, I would find that only those documents I had read were needed the next day. I would go to meet some friends and suddenly a voice would prompt me to go to the collector's office. And, when I would go there I would find the collector waiting for me with some documents. So I realised that something was constantly guiding me. The Divine has His own way of working. We complain all the time about corruption, but I must tell you, nobody even charged me a paise. On the contrary, they spent time looking after me, bringing me a cup of tea or a cold drink and otherwise seeing to my comfort. None of the lower staff ever asked me for a favour, except one person and the favour was to give him a photograph of Sri Aurobindo. They did all my work on a priority basis. Whatever darkness there may be in man, there is something that is responsive to the Light, too.

To continue with this episode, one of the top men in the land acquisition department, for some reason of his own, was not sympathetic towards the Ashram. Some of the lands had some slight discrepancy though the titles were honest. These had to be cleared. Now this man, out of spite, rejected them. But in order to show that he was not rejecting the whole package he passed the smaller lots even though the titles were defective. Soon after he passed these, he got transfered and another man came. When this new officer found that the other titles had been cleared, he passed the rest, also.

This was another amazing experience for me to see how the Divine uses even the wrong side of a human personality for His work. But the man of ill will does not benefit. I know of another case where a letter was sent to the Government regarding some work of the Ashram. The Mother later changed Her mind and did not want the work to be done. Now the person to whom the letter was sent for recommendation, had for some reason some annoyance with the Ashram and he did not recommend it. So I was very happy, and told the Mother that he had not recommended it. The Mother said that he did this not with the intention of helping the Ashram, but out of spite. It did not benefit him, but the Divine's purpose was served. So you see, the Divine's work is always done; only the person doing it does not benefit if his attitude is not right. This is extremely important for us to understand.

Karma Yoga has four stages. The first stage is Niṣkāma Karma – desireless work. You say, whatever be the result, I am doing this work as my duty to the Divine, I am offering it to Him, let Him guide me. Even if there is only one percent chance or no chance at all to succeed, this thing is worth doing and I must do it. And you find you usually do succeed. So this attitude is helpful in the work. You take up the work not because you are interested in it but because you feel it should be done. This way, the work is done much better. But still this is not Karma Yoga; it is Niṣkāma Karma. A second stage comes as a result of the first when something in you starts guiding you. Then you get a direct guidance. Karma Yoga means work done in unity with the consciousness of the Divine. In the second stage the Divine guides you and you are no longer the doer, you are the instrument. This is the real Karma Yoga. When He descends in you, speaks through your voice, moves through your feet, writes through your hands, sees through your eyes, listens through your ears, then, it is true Karma Yoga. In Sri Aurobindo's Yoga, even this is not the final stage. There is a next step. But these preparatory stages are necessary to lead to a higher stage. The next step is the result of this descent becoming more and more constant and your surrender becoming more and more complete. You receive the Divine guidance more and more, assimilate it and, as a result of this, your body and mind are transmuted. They become transformed into their highest. Your body becomes a body of light, your mind becomes a mind of light, it has perfect knowledge. Then Karma Yoga becomes Purna Yoga. That means a complete inner union with the Divine; the heart, the mind, the body are one with Him. The final stage comes when this happens not only at an individual level but in a collective life. This is the result of Integral Yoga.

The vision of spirituality of today becomes the spiritual reality of tomorrow. And if one wants to lead a spiritual life, why not keep the highest as the goal? This is the highest. If one wants to do

Karma Yoga, one has to be very clear what it exactly means. Karma Yoga is work surrendered to the Divine, work done without care or desire for the result, work done with perfection, for you cannot offer imperfect work to Him. It is your offering to the Divine. You do not doubt, you do not think, what will happen to me? Will I lead a happier life than what I am leading today? Will it become poor, and would I have to put up with it? Or will it lead me to a richer and fuller life? We must be very clear that the reason for our downfall is due to our creating or erecting an artificial barrier between spiritual life and material life. People have this wrong idea that if they want to lead a spiritual life, they should give up the material world. And if they want to lead a material life, all that is needed is to do some worship or puja in the morning, or say a little prayer to Him for their well-being.

Now this truly is the cause, the basic cause of all the problems we are facing today. Because all these problems have their root in ego. Ego can be eliminated by the Divine Presence. There should not be even a trace of ego. Either there is ego dominating life or there will be the Divine Presence in its place. Now, ego cannot go till the Divine Presence is awakened in you or you become conscious of it. And when you become conscious of the Divine Presence in you, ego cannot remain. Ego is a formation in consciousness which automatically dissolves and disappears in the Divine Presence. There is no solution to human problems till the higher consciousness becomes active in you and gradually replaces the lower consciousness (the egoistic consciousness). Envy, jealousy, greed, lust are all ingredients of the lower consciousness. You cannot get rid of them without losing the ego. You cannot say I will have the Divine Presence and still continue to lead an egoistic life. While the ego is active in you, you can only partially control the emotions. Even the great Rishi Vishvamitra succumed to it. There was an occasion when the great sage told a lie. So this lower nature will go on troubling human beings at least to a limited extent, till ego remains. When it disappears totally, then in all magnificence the Divine manifests in you, then there are no more limitations. There is an ever-widening, ever-deepening manifestation of everything you can dream of, and of many things even beyond your dreams. Everything heightens and deepens – a love you can never experience in the egoistic stage, a generosity you can never imagine in your egoistic stage, a power that does not exist in the egoistic stage, a wider knowledge which always was in you but only partially manifested in the egoistic stage. You enter into the realm of absolute knowledge, absolute power, absolute love. You receive these to the extent you are open, to the extent you are ready. The more you surrender, the more you become receptive; the more you deepen your consciousness, the more you receive according to your capacity. So, in yoga you naturally extend your personality both vertically and horizontally.

In Karma Yoga, there is a constant progress, a constant progress towards the Divine perfection, not a human perfection. Human perfection is a mental perfection, Divine perfection is an integral perfection. It has its own law, it has its own symbolic language. If you see in your vision an elephant of a particular colour and size it means something different. If you see a particular number, if you see a plane fly, it has its own symbol, its own interpretation. Whatever is mechanical is imperfect. So, as you keep opening to this higher consciousness many new chapters, many new openings come to you. You combine this physical plane with the other higher planes, you combine your lower consciousness with various powers to achieve a particular result. The result may be anything – it could be a particular outcome in a war, it could be the writing of literature and poetry, it could be just the arrangement of a meeting. There are all kinds of powers within you that are represented by various gods. People have seen these gods in their visions. You can combine your consciousness with them and channelise it. You know, yoga and meditation are like a steam engine. You generate the steam and direct it and the movement takes place. So here you learn to put the consciousness in union with a particular power and direct it with a force in a particular direction. But these results can be obtained only if you combine your consciousness with a higher power. When you combine it with a higher power, there is no limit to its working. It is almost invincible. But you must know the conditions of Karma Yoga.

As I told you the first stage in Karma Yoga is Niṣkāma Karma. It is not the last step, it is only a beginning. What does it mean? Does it mean you are not to have a desire even to find God? No, that does not come under desire. That is aspiration, the basic movement of the soul. Desires are the normal human vital feelings, for example, the desire for money, for fame, for name. And all the enlightened people, did they care for fame, for name? They did not care for such things though these came to them. They aspired for the Divine. If they were meant to do some work which needed finance, even finance came to them – many things came to them. As soon as you ask for a thing, you become a slave to it; you are willing to do anything for it. This often happens in life! But when you do not ask for it and the Divine gives it to you, you accept it but you must use it properly. You must not misuse it. It does not belong to you, it belongs to the Divine.

In Karma Yoga things come to you, many things, but there should be no attachment. You feel that they have been given to you, that whatever you need for a particular work will be given to you at the right time. For example, you want a ticket for a particular flight but there is no seat available; if you are really doing Karma Yoga you will somehow get a reservation. If the guidance comes to you for a particular work, you will see that the money also comes for that work. It will come. But it comes according to His plan. You cannot say you want it at eight in the morning when He plans to give it to you at two in the afternoon. So He has His own plan of working. And on your part you do not have to act, but to remain united with Him, so that He can act in you. It is a long process, an inner process.

You must know that the effort in Karma Yoga is vertical. It is to be united with the higher consciousness at every level even in your body, by concentration, by meditation, by constant practice.

Karma Yoga is the only purpose of human existence. Not to do Karma Yoga is not to use the body and mind for the service of the Divine. Then there is wastage, there is decay. When you work for the Lord you prolong life. You can progress only in the body; and if life is cut short then the work can continue only in the next life.

When you include in Karma Yoga your entire life, then only your viewpoint changes. What may look like misery to other people is not misery to you. It is happiness. Nothing matters to you. You have the sense of power; you have the sense of richness. You do not have money because you do not need it. If you need money, it comes to you. And really the consciousness is purified by the Divine. You love the creation because everywhere you see the Divine and you work for Him. Your life comes to have only one meaning; to be more purposeful, to be more enlarged and to be more widened. You have a true sense of fulfilment which does not exist in normal life. So this is Karma Yoga.

Bhakti Yoga can be elaborated in two parts. Karma Yoga itself opens to Bhakti Yoga. A concentrated Bhakti will help you to come more quickly in contact with the Divine. In India we perform 'sashatanga' pranam, that means all the eight parts of the body touch the ground. You have seen people lie flat in front of a deity in a temple. Unfortunately, most people do it as a ritual. But if you really lie down for a little while and offer each part to the Divine, from the tips of the fingers of your outstretched hands to each part of your body, one by one, and go right down to the toes of your feet, then, when you get up, you become a different man. From one 'sashatanga' pranam done sincerely you can become a different person. You can feel it, but not if you do it as an exercise. It should be an imperative urge in you, an aspiration in you to offer your entire self, an aspiration that you cannot remain separate from Him. There should be a feeling in you to just merge in the Divine. You will see how easy it is and, as you continue, it will become a part of you. You will feel the change, you will feel the Divine Shakti and Power.

Bhakti purifies the emotional side of your personality, purifies it rapidly. Bhakti takes you to the Divine and the Divine knows and loves you more than any human being can ever do. He is the only one who will never fail you, never betray you. You are relying on someone who is Omnipotent and Omnipresent. What greater person could there be? So, in the spiritual life there is a combination of Jñāna Yoga, Bhakti Yoga and Karma Yoga. The beginning may be in any direction, but they all ultimately converge.

Meditation in Life

There are many kinds of meditations. All kinds have to be practised. We do several kinds of exercises for developing the body; so also for the development of consciousness, a variety of meditations has to be practised. In meditation we learn how to deepen and heighten our consciousness, that is, we get in contact with deeper and higher planes beyond the mind, the Intuition plane, for example, and finally unite with the Divine Consciousness. Through meditation, we also learn to widen our consciousness so that sitting in one place we can be effective even at a distance. These are only two among many. A third type is to unite our consciousness with the guru's consciousness – if we have a guru – so that when we direct our consciousness towards an object, an event or a person, it is not only our consciousness but our consciousness combined with the consciousness of the guru, which is directed towards the object, event or person. We must also know that meditation is done for purification. By eliminating selfishness, anger and greed through meditation, one is better able to control one's lower nature as one develops the higher qualities. So meditation is of many types, of many varieties and has boundless result. In some meditation you can recite a mantra or concentrate on a form or an idea, while in others, you remain still and allow the Divine Consciousness to work through your enlarged and deepened consciousness. Besides purification, meditation can also teach you self-observation.

Meditation, as I told you before, is like exercises; exercises in consciousness. Meditation done during work is of one kind, meditation done during worship is of another kind. But now I am talking of pure meditation. That means you are sitting quietly and are trying to develop an action of consciousness with the help of meditation. Silencing the mind is one kind of meditation. So meditation has to start according to the need of the person, but I will tell you things in general that can help in the beginning. The first thing in meditation is to aspire for peace, calm and purity, as if you are invoking the highest to descend in you, in your mind, in your body. This descent in you of peace, equanimity and purity forms a solid base for you to meditate. If the consciousness is not still, it fluctuates. If there is no purity in the mind, a descent gets distorted. A patient man may become more patient, but an angry man may get more angry. This is because the descent of power has come but the purity has not come. Everything becomes more pronounced and acute. That is why certain people who attain some powers but are not purified, have their downfall. So peace, equanimity and purity should be cultivated first before the descent from the higher levels can take place. While doing this, meditation helps to enlarge and deepen your consciousness, to feel the Divine's presence, light, or whatever you may call it.

A very good meditation is to lie down or sit down and try to imagine the Divine light in your body, in your room, in your city, in the world, in the air, in the ocean, in the whole universe and even beyond. You should go on imagining light, light, and more light and keep enlarging your consciousness. Just do this and see what happens. Try to see the light *in* everything. Lights have colours in meditation and the colours have a symbol. It is better to meditate on a golden or a white light. Once you have become accustomed to meditating on light, you see everything saturated with the light, you know there is light in everything. The second stage is when you feel *everything* is in the light. You feel as if everything is enveloped in light. Nothing can move unless the light sanctions it. Then wrong thoughts cannot come, they cannot penetrate your consciousness. Everything is in the light.

The third stage comes as a result of the first two where you see everything *as* light. This is a meditation which is enjoined in the Gita and the Upanishads. Many spiritual leaders have spoken of it as a very effective meditation. Though they have used the word Divine, I am using the word, Light, because many people find it hard to have a concept of the Divine. But if you have a concept of the Divine as Light that is omnipresent, it is so much easier and better. People also try to meditate on the form of Krishna, on the form of Christ, and others. To begin with this kind of meditation, is also good. But finally each one has to find his own way, to have a little uniqueness in his meditation. Generally speaking, we may start by concentrating on the Divine Consciousness *in* everything, then *everything* in the Divine and finally everything *as* the Divine. When you see everything as the Divine, everything wrong disappears; hatred, jealousy, greed, all the wrong feelings in you disappear. It is this growth, this purification which ultimately leads to the higher power, knowledge, love, happiness which are always latent in us and which now can manifest. This is how meditation helps.

There are meditations for healing, meditations for prosperity, for many other things. People meditate on Laxmi, people meditate on Ganesh. I want to tell you these are effective and true. They are not imaginery. What has been told in our Sastras is true. It is because we do not do them in the right way that they do not work. If done correctly they do work. Meditating on Hanuman and invoking his presence, does work. The other day a lady told me that in her meditation she saw a light. She said it was so strong that even in her vision she found it difficult to look at it. Now, how did this vision come? How did this happen? This light is always there. It is only when the inner eye is opened that you can see it.

So meditation opens you to your inner self. It opens windows, doors, inside you. And there are planes of consciousness. One window gets you to the next room, another window leads you to next gate or door, whatever you may call it. All these things go on happening in meditation.

Let us not talk too much of advanced meditation. Let us first make a beginning. As we progress, the inner vision opens. Another interesting aspect of meditation is that a stage comes in spiritual life when the inner guidance starts working. Then the functioning of the mental being decreases and finally the inner being takes over. Meditation is an aid to get in contact with the inner being, and when the contact begins, the guidance starts and all your problems get solved. In the beginning the guidance is best received during meditation. But we have to learn to receive it all the time. That is why I say that those who start with work have an advantage because if we can remain open during work, it comes easily during meditation. Once we are accustomed to meditating during work, the exclusive meditation also becomes easier and more intense. So we must establish a balance between several types of meditations, each helping the other. All the meditations are included in Purna Yoga, I may add.

A question may arise that in case of meditation during work how does one concentrate on whatever one is actually doing. It is very simple. You do not have to concentrate. That is the charm of it. The Divine Himself does everything through you. Suppose you are speaking and I am listening to you – that is the normal process. But in spiritual life I do not try to think, I only try to meditate on the Divine. Then if He wants, He may speak through me and listen through you, or whatever has to be communicated may get directly done to your mind. You may go back feeling luminous, without even a word being spoken. When you get in contact with the higher consciousness, it expresses itself in a logical manner. So to the listener it may look like logic, but to the person who gives it, it is not a thinking process; it is given without thinking. That is the charm of it. All those things that the mind would have done, get done better without thinking and by opening to the higher consciousness. In spiritual life everything works differently, mostly inwardly. People may not realise this because externally there may not be much change. Of course, some change will be visible but inwardly there is a big change. It will slowly manifest itself, even physically, for example, in the expression of the face, in the eyes, and so on. As the inner power develops, its outward manifestation also increases.

Once the Mother asked me to take a person to a physician and said that the man will get cured. And this is exactly what happened. It was amazing. I found out later that this physician had this siddhi. He believed that God is everywhere and there is no illness in God. This had become such a part of his consciousness, that when he saw a patient, he saw God. He had full faith that there is no illness in God, so there can be no illness in the person. When he looked at a patient with this faith the patient got cured. When you realise a certain siddhi and when you direct your concentration to a person, it works. One can realise God through any one of His aspects and attain siddhi in that field. It may be the siddhi of dance, the siddhi of drama, the siddhi of music, a man may develop the siddhi of expression, the siddhi of telepathy. All human beings have some powers which are a part of the personality. Through the physical body, a man works on material things. He plants seeds, grows grains, cooks food, he writes an article or does a painting. Now, this is normal. He does not need spiritual powers, but even such activities or occupations can be done better with spiritual powers.

There is a soul in us, a soul which is directly a part of the Divine. The Divine is realisable in His true form at the soul level. By certain processes, by yoga, you can get in contact with your soul. When you get in contact with your soul, it is a contact with the Divine. That means this Divine contact becomes real to you, and this is what we call realisation at the highest level. For easier understanding, we can compare it to a house which has a first floor, a second floor and a third floor; but it is at the top floor that you can get a certain contact. So when I say the Divine is realisable, I say there is a way in which you can become aware of your soul, your consciousness can realise the Divine. If a man is not aware of his soul, he is living a life of ignorance. Once you have contact with Him at the soul level, you come to a stage where you melt, you spread out in consciousness and as a result of this, it becomes a universal condition. After having realised it at the highest level, you bring that consciousness down to the lower level. At the mental level it creates a kind of mental universality which is open to the Divine.

Now, there are several kinds of openings. One opening is like a clear mirror reflecting the light. That means your mind is so pure, so clear that the highest consciousness is reflected without distortion. It descends in your mind and divinises it. If you have brought your highest consciousness down, you automatically influence the minds of other people even without their knowing it. This is the greatest service you can do to humanity, to bring down this higher consciousness which is yet unknown to most people. You can bring the consciousness to the vital level. But on the vital level, it is more difficult, because there the forms are more firm and hard. On the mental level there are also forms, but they are flexible and fluid, not so rigid. On the vital level, forms become more gross and on the physical level, the forms become yet more gross and rigid. If you ultimately bring it down to the physical level, it is more at your level and at the level of the people with whom you come in contact. It is often by touch that a spiritual person transmits the higher consciousness to others. Just as he can, by the eyes, give it to the soul, so also by a physical touch, he gives it to the body. That is how a guru helps a disciple to become more and more united with the Divine, to become a vehicle of His manifestation on earth. So I tell you that this is the greatest service you can do to mankind: bringing down the higher consciousness and becoming a channel for its distribution and manifestation.

And this distribution can be done even if the receiver is not aware of it. It is such a pleasure for the instrument to observe how things happen, how things get spoken through him, how things get done, without a physical contact with a person. Now this is not your willing. If you want to be His instrument it is His willing in you. So long as you have willings, you are weak. That is what Sri

Aurobindo has written in a beautiful aphorism: *When we have passed beyond willings, then we shall have Power.* I must add that at some stage, the preparatory stage of evolution, your will, your ego, is a help because you work harder – my house, my family – you try to build, you try to conquer. But at a later stage, as you grow – not in a physical sense, but in spirituality – it becomes a hindrance, it becomes an obstacle. We have to ultimately go beyond the ego and surrender ourselves to the Divine. This is the only way.

Occult Knowledge and Religion

Hinduism is a practical and comprehensive religion. Its aim is perfection of life, the greatest welfare of all mankind. It is a religion which is almost like the universe, expressed in great detail and covering many aspects. It contains the love of Christianity, it embodies the faith of Islam, it embraces many aspects. Yet, it is a religion that is truly the most misunderstood. And that is unfortunate. People do not follow it, or are following it only in a very limited way.

In Hinduism a thing can have many aspects, internal, external or the combination of both. Let us take the common example of 'havan' (sacrificial fire). The internal havan is with aspiration, to light the fire of aspiration. And in that fire you offer your feelings, desires and impurities. You want the Divine, you want to remove all these impurities. In the physical havan when you offer the mantras and a particular 'ahuti' (offerings in the sacrificial fire), you must also simultaneously, internally, offer a state of consciousness, in the fire. That is how it works – it is a double action. You bring it right down to the physical plane. But in many cases the internal aspect disappears, and only the outer shell remains. It is this meaningless outer crust that people go on following day after day, repeating the same Gayatri mantra and doing the same havan. After twenty years of doing this, even then one might not be purified at all. On the other hand, in just half an hour and with the right approach one can make a great progress.

Bhaiji, what about organised religion?

Whatever may be its origin, organised religion as it is practised today, is mostly social customs. You cannot even call it religion. You go for prayers at nine in the morning, you do pooja at a particular time and fast on a specific day. It has become very socialised. It is a religion based on fear and desire. It may have been started by an enlightened man full of love, full of good will. So its origin was for the good and well-being of all. It is the lower consciousness in man, the egoistic consciousness in man, the impure consciousness in man, that later gave it its present form.

I will give you an incident. The son of a friend of mine had become a sadhu. When he came to the Ashram, we made him shave his beard, got him to cut his long flowing hair, to remove the ashes from his forehead and made him wear new clothes. We also asked him to work in the Ashram press. He was a good boy. After sometime he told us that his whole life had become far better. When I asked him how it had become better, he said, "Before, I would have my bath, put some ashes on my body, sit near the temple and money would come, food would come to me. I had to do nothing. In your Ashram I have to work from morning till evening and I only get food and clothes". He was tired of his earlier life. He had no intention of becoming a sadhu as such, but that was the only alternative he saw to the life he was then leading. There are some people whom you may call seekers. They are seeking, searching for something of lasting value. Religion today does not satisfy the spiritual hunger of man. Or rather, it does not satisfy it adequately. All the distortion is a wrong thing that has happened to religion. There is a need for correction. I have come across people who really have a contact with the higher planes, who are following the spiritual path. So the question for each one of us should be: how can I be transformed in the true way? Religion to be useful has to find its true way. A spiritual man has a contact with the highest level, and in the light of that contact he tries to organise a socio-political life. This is very important. Political and social life can never be properly organised unless you have the inner Divine light.

So, religion should have two aspects: an inner highest light and, with the help of this light, an effort to organise the external life. Anyone who is interested in bringing about a change in mankind should start with himself, instead of trying to convert more and more people. The change in others will take place naturally and gradually as the higher consciousness descends in you and, through you, it will influence and benefit others even without their knowing it. And it will spread as more and more people manifest the new consciousness. The world is looking for a new religion. I have met people of the Islamic faith, I have met people who practise Christianity, and from their talks, I have come to the conclusion that they have now come to a stage where they are looking not for a new religion as such, but a more spiritualised way of life. Rituals form only a very small part of religion. Sri Aurobindo Himself has condemned this aspect where rituals are performed without the inner consciousness. If prophets like

Moses, Christ, Mohammed, were to be among us now, they would be shocked to discover what man has done to their teachings. The religion of the future will have to be spiritual. Spirituality means knowledge of God, knowledge of the inner self and its manifestation in life. You can say that spirituality is the soul of religion, it is the essence of religion. Without spirituality there can be no religion. There would be only superstition and fear.

I will give you an example of how superstitions and rituals arise. There was a priest who had a pet cat. Every time a ceremony had to be performed, he would tie up the cat because the cat would drink the milk to be used in the ritual, even before the ceremony started. After some years both the priest and the cat died. When his turn came to perform the ceremony, the disciple did not know the real reason for the cat to be tied, but because it was done by his guru, he said to the others that a cat had to be tied before the ceremony could start. This is how blind superstitions take birth.

Can you tell us something about occult knowledge?

Occult knowledge is the knowledge of the inner worlds, the inner planes which are linked to the physical world and to the material life. This knowledge or science is a million times more vast and potent than all the physical sciences put together. So you can imagine what a great science occultism is. And it has hardly been explored. The combinations that are to be found in occultism are greater than all the combinations and permutations man or machine can put together in the physical world. There is also here a greater variety than in the physical world. It is almost impossible for one person to know everything about occultism in a lifetime.

When you say inner planes, what do you mean by that, Bhaiji?

You see, you have a physical body, and enveloping it, permeating the physical body, is the astral or the vital body. This is the first inner plane. Behind the vital body is the mental body. The mental body is the second inner plane. I would not say there two are planes; rather, they are bodies which are in contact with their respective planes. There is a physical body, there is a mental body and there is a vital body. Just as you cut from a length of cloth enough material to make a suit out of it, so out of each plane, an individual takes a little of it and makes his mental personality, his vital personality and his physical personality. The vital personality consists of emotions, impulses, instincts, good and bad. When we speak of a person's aura, we mean by it his emotional, his vital personality. The mental personality of a person consists of intelligence, analysis, memory, logic and intuition – all these are aspects of the mind. In the mental plane there is an individual memory and a universal memory. In the mental plane thoughts flow in and out from every direction. Some people can catch them. This is the principle of telepathy. Similarly, the principle of clairaudience and clairvoyance belongs to the vital body.

So these phenomena exist?

Yes, they exist. Many people have experienced them. And if you can concentrate, you also can develop these capacities. If you go on concentrating on your hearing, and if you know how to extend your concentration, you can hear what people are saying far away. Similarly, with concentration you can learn to see far away. That is clairvoyance. Beyond the mental personality there are other planes which are not normally individualised. The mental individualisation is common, the vital individualisation is common. But beyond the mind are the Higher Mind, Illumined Mind, Intuitive Mind; these are all planes which have their own beings, gods, and powers – even forms, colours and symbols. It is like a film. If you change two, three or four frames in the film, you will see a different picture on the screen. Similarly, if you make a change in the inner planes, the outer event also changes in the external physical plane. Nothing happens on the physical plane unless the decision is taken and the thing is done in the inner planes.

Everything that is inwardly decided does not however materialise immediately in the physical plane. Whatever materialises in the physical plane has to be decided initially in the inner plane. But whatever is decided in the inner plane, all of it does not materialise in the physical plane. I will give you an example. One day the Mother and Sri Aurobindo were talking. The year, I think, was 1918. The Mother suddenly said, "India is free", and Sri Aurobindo said, "Yes." The Mother later said that in the occult world, India had become actually free, but on the material plane it took almost thirty years to become a reality. It might appear that circumstances made India free. But when asked if She had seen Pakistan, the Mother said, "No, this is a human distortion." Sometimes even the dates are decided, but generally they are not fixed. And because men were not open enough to receive the inner guidance, India was partitioned and thousands of people got killed and there was untold suffering. I will narrate another incident. Once, when the film, *The Wizard of Oz*, was shown in the Ashram, the Mother said that the director had occult perception. The colours of the inner planes that he had used were correct.

All the inner planes – inner worlds you may call them – have their own colours and forms. When your mind becomes quiet, you see figures, houses or any number of things. So these planes are far, far bigger than our universe. You have there a very large variety of forms. Intuition belongs to these inner planes.

We may divide occult science into four categories. First, there are the occult practices which take you closer to the Divine. We can put meditation under this category. We can call all the yagnas that invoke certain Gods, as occult practices; even prayer is a kind of an occult practice which deals with the inner higher worlds. All these are spiritual movements whose goal is spiritual. In the second category we can put the occult practices of the 'right side' – 'Dakshin Marg', as these are called – which can be for the good of mankind. These may include the yantras I was speaking to you about. In ancient India the initiates drew a diagram, invoked a certain power in it, and then put it in a house or a temple. And surprisingly, the presence of these diagrams attracted money and brought about prosperity. Even installing the image of Ganesh or any other deity is a form of occult practice. Many branches of astronomy, palmistry, psychology come under occult science. Many people have developed occult powers for helping mankind. The third category is called 'Vāmamārga'. These are occult powers of the 'left side'. Mantras are a kind of occult power and in the 'Vāmamārga' they can be used for harming others. The fourth category is the development of supraphysical powers in a person, the 'Astha Siddhi'. Modern science has now come to accept occult phenomena, but at the lower levels, the astral and mental levels. You must have read some of the books from Russia about ESP and related faculties. They come under occult knowledge. You find from such books that these faculties can be developed. One does not have to be born with developed faculties, just to have some capacity.

For developing occult capacity, there are three basic conditions. First, you should be selfless. The more selfless you are, the more fearless you become and this makes you a better instrument for practising occultism. Sometimes when your vital body goes out of your physical body, you feel almost like a dead person and you get frightened. When you go to the inner planes, you see at times figures that frighten you, and if you are full of fear, you cannot go very far in occult knowledge. So, the first thing is, you have to be selfless. Selflessness brings purity, selflessness leads to fearlessness. Then, you must have some occult capacity. But even if you do not have it, there is the way of surrender to God. By this, you develop occult knowledge. A guru can also give you occult capacity. He passes on certain vibrations and puts you in contact with them. Many advanced gurus have these occult powers and capacities.

Are these practices or faculties given by the guru? Are they like mantras? Is there an external way of teaching and learning, like taking lessons?

In occult knowledge, ninety-five percent of the knowledge is given internally. A guru unites a disciple's consciousness with his own and gives him the knowledge or the experience internally. I will give you an example. I learnt about occultism from the Mother; I learnt the maximum from Her. But one day the Mother told me that an occult priest had come and, since I was interested in occult knowledge, She felt I must go and meet him. She told me that as soon as he would see me he would know everything about me and would tell me all I would need to know. So I went. When he saw me, the first thing he said was, "The Mother has sent you." I agreed with him. Then I said, "Please tell me something by which I can collaborate in the help you want to give me." He said that he did not care for my collaboration. So I said, "Please tell me something by which I may not obstruct the help you want to give me." Again he told me he was not bothered about any obstruction I may cause. This was my first encounter with him. He invited me for lunch, but I did not understand its true meaning and I missed the lunch. The Mother wrote me a very strong letter asking me why I did not go. So the next time he invited me, I went. The food was very delicious. But I ate according to my normal appetite and then stopped. He then asked me to eat a little more. He was sitting next to me taking his food. I told him I was full, I had eaten enough already. Hardly had I finished saying this than I started feeling terribly hungry. And he made me eat three times more than my normal capacity, without any effort, without any ill effect on me. He told me it was the mind which was influencing the digestive system and the body. When I related this to the Mother, She laughed and laughed. I am telling you things which I experienced myself, not what has been recounted to me.

My friend and I went to the native place of the priest. We were staying at a guest house. Everyday at lunchtime the priest would first go to the temple and then come to our guest house and take us for lunch and bring us back. When he went to the temple, he went barefooted. I asked him one day why he did not take my sandals as it was very hot. He simply smiled. The next day when he came to call us, he asked me (but not my friend) to remove the sandals. So I removed my sandals and came out to walk with him. When we had walked half the distance in the hot sun, he asked me if I felt anything in my feet. I said no, and we walked with him to his house. He entered first and I walked in behind him. As soon as he entered the house, my feet started hurting. So you see it is quite possible to project your consciousness in another person and to cut off his connection with heat or cold. When you are given an object – a ring, locket, jewel, bangle or anything – its occult power would depend on the power of concentration of the person who gives it to you. The person concentrates the force from a particular plane into a stone or a flower.

So occult knowledge has many aspects. It can be used in a wrong way. For example, one can throw stones and they will materialise and fall from the ceiling of your house. This happened once in one of the Ashram buildings. The Mother concentrated and found that a person with occult power was dematerialising stones in one place, and then materialising them at another. She said that an occultist had found a good medium of action in a boy servant who was working in the house. The Mother removed that boy from the room and the stones stopped falling. So by the proper application of the occult knowledge one can counteract the mischievous or even harmful work of another person. If you are in a higher plane of consciousness, occult powers of the lower plane cannot harm you.

Money is power, occultism also, is a power. You know some people misuse money or political power; in the same way, people can misuse occult power. But just because some misuse occult powers it is no reason for others not to have them. You should make the right use of them with full knowledge of the process. How will your personality be complete without developing all your powers and faculties? Man is very imperfect in his present state. You can do unbelievable things with occult powers. You can plant a thought in another person without his knowing you have done it. He will think it is his own idea and will act accordingly. By occult knowledge you can combine your consciousness with another person's and thus act on the world. This is what Sri Aurobindo did during World War II, whenever He found it necessary to use these powers.

Occult knowledge gives you all kinds of powers to do all kinds of things. It can give you power to do good for mankind. It can provide an effective protection without which man is very weak and vulnerable. A man is not aware of his weakness, he is not conscious of his limitations. Occult knowledge can help remove the limitations to a great extent. In life there are bound to be certain limitations. But a person's limitations can be removed to such an extent that it cannot be imagined. The difference between an ordinary man and a man of occult knowledge can be as great as it is between a man and an animal.

Can occult powers be cultivated by oneself?

Yes, occult powers can be cultivated by oneself to some extent; but, with the help of a guru, it becomes more powerful. Even a mantra becomes more forceful. If you read a mantra and start repeating it, it is not always effective but when a guru gives you a mantra, it becomes effective. A guru here does not necessarily mean a spiritual guru, but a man who has made that mantra potent. Once, something valuable was lost. I was worried and was strolling about feeling very sad. One of my servants asked me why I was sad and I told him what was wrong. So he gave me a mantra and asked me to repeat it. I repeated the mantra and within three to four hours the thing was found. The result came because the man knew that mantra. He had made a siddhi of that mantra, and he could communicate it to others. If three men communicated the same mantra to three other persons, the result would not be the same in each case. It would be effective according to the capacity of the giver and the receiver. So it depends on how far you can develop occult knowledge and how successfully you can communicate with others. From the spiritual viewpoint both go together. On your side, you have to be selfless; the more selfless you are, the more receptive you become.

What does 'selfless' mean?

It means that *you* do not think or act; you are only an instrument through whom the higher forces are acting. As soon as you say you are acting, you are obstructing their path.

So that is ego, Bhaiji. How is it different from selfishness?

Ego, selfishness, unselfishness and selflessness, I will try to explain these terms. Instead of the word unselfishness, I use the word selflessness. You may do a work without any desire for monetary gains or any other regard for prestige, fame or name. This is unselfishness. But even in unselfishness, the idea that *you* are doing the work is there. In selflessness, you do not even have the notion that you are doing or speaking, it is a force that is speaking through you, is working in you, using you as an instrument. You see the force working in and around you and you feel you are just an instrument. In unselfishness, your ego is still there. But in selflessness there is an attitude of surrender to the highest consciousness and force. Without your having to give any direction to the force, the force itself directs you. In occultism the force uses your physical body, your mental body, your vital body, as well as your consciousness. You find things are happening through you but you are only a witness.

But selflessness does not mean anything negative; it is positive, isn't?

Very positive.

How does one have it?

There are two steps towards selflessness. There is, on the one side, desire – desire for wealth, desire to help people, desire for anything. So first, desire should be eliminated. Even the desire to help people, I would consider as selfishness. It is a kind of self-satisfaction because the Divine can help people much better than you can. In fact you can help people truly, only by becoming the Divine's instrument. The Divine in His compassion helps everybody. So even the desire to help, desires of all kinds, whether or not connected with the material life, come under this category. Only the desire to realise God does not, of course, fall in this category because its source and vibrations are different. We call it aspiration. So to attain selflessness, you must first become desireless.

The next step is to feel that even your material life can be made better, and your spiritual life can be fulfilled only when you rise higher than the mind into the Divine consciousness which grips you and uses you. Then you are selfless. You become conscious of the fact that you are leading a limited life, you are leading a cramped life, you are leading the life of a weak person, though others may think you are strong. If you are in unity with God, your field of action will expand, His compassion will manifest more, He will pour His knowledge and power into you and make you His instrument. This kind of clarity comes with purity of the heart, purity of the mind. It is very simple. If you want to go to place 'A', and if you know your way, you will go there faster. Similarly, if you have contact with the Divine consciousness, even in your material life, you will know the meaning of everything that happens at a particular moment, because every moment you are linked with the Divine consciousness. Selflessness without this purity is very difficult. Through Bhakti, clarity and purity come without much strenuous effort. Bhakti brings clarity. So selflessness requires two things: desirelessness and a clarity of consciousness that your life can find its fulfilment only in unity with the Lord. You should allow Him to act in you without obstruction, so that your life becomes a life of His action. And this realisation itself is selflessness.

Now Bhaiji, you said one word was selflessness and the other, fearlessness. I want you to explain the causes of fear in occult life.

You see, often the fear people have of occult life has several aspects. One is fear of death. When you go out of your physical body and move about in your astral body you keep a link with your physical body. This link is a very thin line of consciousness, a very thin thread known as the golden thread. And this could snap if one does not have the knowledge. If that happens then another being, say of the vital world, can possess your body. Also, when you are out of your body, and if at that time somebody shakes the body suddenly, the thin thread could snap and you could be a dead person. At that time another being could possess your body, because ninety-nine percent of your consciousness has gone out.

Another fear is the fear of the beings of other worlds – the vital world, for example – attacking your astral body. There, the beings are very powerful in the inner planes. When you meet these beings and if you are afraid, they become even more powerful. If you have no fear, if you are able to face them, they shrink. All that happens in these planes is very amazing.

So you have the fear of death, the fear of the beings from other planes, and the third fear is born of a kind of ignorance. You do not know whether this or that is right. What will happen to me? What will happen to others? It is a kind of fear, due to a lack of faith, combined with ignorance. It is fear which deters you from exploring new grounds, from treading new paths. This is the third kind of fear.

The fourth kind of fear is the fear caused by attachments. Man has become very much attached to people and things. You cannot have occult knowledge if you have attachments. You feel you will lose this, you will lose that and all the small things, that you cherish in your normal life, you are afraid of losing. When you are detached, you really do not lose them. But when you are attached the fear exists. But the first fear, the strongest fear, the basic fear, is the fear of death.

Bhaiji, can fearlessness be cultivated? if so, how?

Fearlessness can be cultivated. First, you must have faith in the guru that he actually gives you the protection. Second, you cultivate an inner faith by having no preferences and no desires. You say, I am not doing it for my personal gain but I want to serve God and He will certainly give me protection. Then, even if something does go wrong, what does it matter? It is always better to progress and die in the attempt than to remain cramped all your life and die anyhow. So on the one side, you have to remove your fear by practising fearlessness, by taking an attitude which looks boldly at life and, on the other side, by experiencing the protection of your guru and by surrendering to the Divine. When people go to war they know they are facing death. What can be done? Of course, people like Caesar and Napoleon feel they are invincible and no bullet can get through to them. The most powerful is a kind of faith in God, in His protection. As you practise, you gradually become fearless.

But why do you say 'a kind of faith', Bhaiji?

I say 'a kind of faith' because faith can be of many kinds. One kind of faith can initially be created by a mental argument with yourself. You try to convince yourself that this is this, and this is not that. Faith can also be born of real experience. From a certain point of view, it can be said that it is not faith because faith is always without experience. If you get faith after an experience then it is an experience and does not need faith. So something deep within you gives you faith. You cannot explain faith mentally. That is the real faith. People call it blind faith but faith is always blind. I have known of people who even after experience do not have faith. There are all kinds of people in this world. Many people are like that; I do not know if most are like that, but certainly there are some who lack faith, who always doubt.

Bhaiji, is occultism associated with witchcraft?

That is black magic – it is of the 'left side', as I told you, and that is bad, it is of the lowest level.

Why is occult knowledge of the higher level not equally well known? After all, it should be visible to all people.

You see people who have attained a higher level do not practise it just to display their capacity. They give help without letting people know and without showing it. Besides, it is specifically prohibited to display it in spiritual life.

Why is it not allowed?

That is the occult law. If you start showing your siddhis, the hostile forces take them away, and they have a right to do so, because you have disclosed your power for the sake of the ego.

Is it possible for anyone to develop these powers, or does one have to be initiated in this knowledge?

Anyone can develop these powers to a higher or lesser degree. But I feel occult knowledge will one day be a part of all regular education, maybe a hundred years hence. Usually, the sign of readiness is that you are not satisfied, that you are looking for something deeper, higher than the present level. And indirectly, that means that God is wanting you to progress. The more you are able to receive the higher consciousness, the easier it will be for the occult knowledge to dawn on you. You do not have to do it by your own effort. All you have to do is to receive the higher consciousness. When you develop it, you become only an instrument. Let me put it differently. You have the highest occult power when you are united with the Divine and let Him manifest in you. This is the highest, the most important, and the most effective occult power.

Do you have occult power?

My way of looking at these things is different. At one time I did want to understand, I did want to practise, I did want to know about occultism. But today my attitude is different. I want nothing but greater and greater unity with the Divine; and greater and greater unity also includes allowing Him to transform the lower personality, so that I may act in a wider and more effective manner. There was a stage in my life when I thought this was the best thing to do. Now I leave everything to the Divine.

You mean occult knowledge does not belong to that high a plane?

As I told you, everything from the physical plane upto the Divine plane comes under occult knowledge. On the physical plane you concentrate on some object, some flower or you give a mantra to somebody. Or you make a yantra, draw a diagram and concentrate on a particular power, and then give it to a person. These practices exist, not only in India, but even among the Chinese, the Jews, the Egyptians. Next come the mental practices, as I told you, clairvoyance, clairaudience, telepathy. With the psychic plane, you develop psychic powers. When you become united with the Divine, you are a part of the Divine. Then all these things happen automatically even without your wanting to do them. If you have to communicate with somebody the power goes and communicates for you. The Divine does everything. Now, if the Divine gives a mantra to another person through you, it is far more effective than if you had given it through your mental decision. So that is why we call it the highest occultism. Though this comes under the category of spirituality in action, just for understanding it today, I call it the highest occultism.

Bhaiji, in the last few days I have been asking you many questions; even if you start somewhere else, you somehow always come back to the same theme again and again. Can you tell me something about how you got interested in spirituality?

I would divide my inner search for the Divine into several parts. In the first stage I had many questions. How can I do my maximum to help mankind? What is the highest I can do? Why was the world created? A stage came when I got the answers to these questions. So these questions disappeared and new ones came up. But to all these questions and a thousand more in my life, always from within me I got the same answer; I never got two answers. It was amazing. There were thousands of questions, but always I received one master answer, that fitted in with every question. The answer to all questions lay in a greater and greater unity with the Divine and an accelerated evolution for man, leading from man to superman. This brought me the highest material and spiritual fulfilment. If this is done, then only will man come out of the rounds of death. No longer will the fear of death hold him. My philosophy of life is that if I can keep the Divine consciousness in me as integrally and as completely as possible, the best will always happen at all times. But the best cannot happen till the mind, body and everything else is transformed; also, till the collective life is transformed. For the time being, I believe this is His command to me – to make this effort. Tomorrow if He changes His command, I will change my action.

A Spiritualised Society

The subject today is: 'A Spiritualised Society'. How can one have a perfect society? The first thing to understand is, what is a society. It is a group of people; geographically, it could be people living in the same place; business-wise, it could be goldsmiths, silversmiths, traders and so on; it could be religion-wise, all the Christians, all the Muslims, all the Hindus, all of them forming a group; it could be family-wise, as in India, where traditionally we have descendants of Bhrigu, Bhargava. So a society has many aspects. People could group themselves in many ways; it could be by family, it could be geographical – village, town, district, nation; it could be by trade or it could be all the women doing something together for women. So there can be many groups of the community, many groups of the society. All these are interconnected and not exclusive. You can be a member of a geographical society and, at the same time, you are a member of your ethnic group, also a member of the students' group, and simultaneously, you belong to a particular religion and to a particular family. So when you talk of social obligations, there are many, not one.

There are two aspects to this: what we give to the society and what we take from it. What would you like to do for the society, give more or take more? You would no doubt like to give more to the society, to give your maximum. How to give your maximum? Unless you have, you cannot give. If you have spiritual knowledge, you give to others spiritual consciousness; if you have money, you give money; if you have the Divine in you, you give the Divine. You see, your value to God and society can be judged by what you give, not by what you take. The attitude of most people is normally to take; very few people have the attitude of giving, whether through polity, education, or whether it is money. If you give yourself to the Divine, then what happens? You become one with the Divine. If you give yourself to the society, then what happens?

All significant social groupings have a soul. Sri Aurobindo and the Mother often speak of a group soul, a nation soul. If you do not give yourself to the country, you do not participate in the nation soul. So, it has to be a double giving: giving to the Divine and giving to the society. They are not opposite aspects, they are one.

Now, how did the society develop? Before I take this up, I want to give you some background. Let us first take the family. A man and a woman marry and they start a family; they have children, then grandchildren, then great-grandchildren and the family becomes big. Some of the families in India have several lakh members, but they trace their origin to just one man and one woman. This is one aspect of the society's function.

There is another aspect, also. There was a 'kul', a clan, and there was a clan leader, a 'kulapati'. It started with the family but gradually it diversified into, let us say, a clan, a small clan. Now this clan expanded and became bigger and evolved into a village. A number of villages became a small kingdom. The idea of a nation is a very recent one. How many years has man been living on this earth? Hundreds of thousands of years and the nation idea is only a few hundred years old. Before that there were only small kingdoms. The nation idea has grown only in the last few hundred years, otherwise some king would conquer and establish a kingdom, not a nation. So, the nation idea is the maximum expansion so far, next to the United Nations, internationally. The United Nations has no government, it is a comity of nations, but the idea has started. So, the biggest geographical unit today is a nation and beyond that, is the United Nations. In India, some of the families may have one million, two million members, but they trace their origin to just one man and one woman.

Now let us take up belief-wise grouping – Christianity, Islam, Hinduism. We Hindus believe in rebirth. You may be born a Christian in this life, a Muslim in the next, a Hindu in the third. You cannot say this religion is the best and that is bad. It is only that your soul is having experience of different physical and psychological environments. So also it is with political beliefs. The old politics, what were they? If you were powerful enough you could take away anybody's land, anybody's property. The old education system was mainly directed – I am not talking here of India's educational system, which was integral – at the physical level, to train soldiers, to get commanders to make an army, to have conquerors. In ancient times, most of the education was directed towards attaining proficiency in the martial arts, achieving perfection in physical prowess.

Then came a change. The real change started from the French Revolution. Before that, a Caesar came and said, "You have five horses, give me four" or "I want forced labour for so many days." It was quite all right, nobody grumbled. People thought it the right of a conqueror. In India also, a prince of a small kingdom used to have forced labour and people thought it quite an honour to go and serve the prince, though they were starving. But that psychology has gone. It was after the French Revolution that a new idea, a new thinking of a different kind of freedom, that every man should get the fruit of his labour, was born. And that is the idea behind capitalism; that you must get the fruit of your labour, what you strive for, you must get and nobody should take it away from you by force.

So you have in capitalism, a grouping based on a certain belief. Then people became a little more conscious. They said if you are very intelligent, if you have a mind, you can make money out of it. You find a gold mine or you get divers to dive for pearls from the sea. But that is a common property. It is from a common property that you are getting it and if you exploit the society and leave money to your children, other people will exploit your children. This is not a wise thing to do. Even if you are more capable than others, you must give some fruit of your labour to others, then there is more equal distribution. And that is socialism.

So socialism is an improvement over capitalism in the consciousness of man. Its misapplication becomes bad. You see, we say, obey your parents, obey your elders. But if your father and mother give you a wrong order and you go on obeying them, then, somewhere there is misapplication. Similarly, capitalism got misapplied. The real idea behind capitalism is to give you nothing except the incentive to work hard, to earn; but if you became a Shylock, then socialism enters and the distribution becomes better.

Then came communism, which is an even better concept. Capitalism said take all that your labour brings you. Socialism said, no, don't take all, give something to others also. But communism went a step further and said you take only what you need and give according to your ability, give your maximum to mankind. But again, they made it political, so everything got spoiled. Instead of man deciding for himself, the government decided that everything should come to the government. Sri Aurobindo called it *State Capitalism*. He called communism, *State Capitalism*. He said everything goes to the State. In India the concept was different; it was spiritual communism – you may call it 'God Capitalism' – everything should be offered to God. You are a trustee; you cannot make a deal with Him. It is a psychological condition.

Sri Aurobindo has said that in the present evolution there have been bigger and bigger social groupings, from family to larger and larger families, and geographically to nation and ultimately, internationally, to the United Nations. What will be the society of the future? Let us take the whole perspective: communism has dreamt of an ideal society where there will be no government. What is the utility of a government, what is its role? Should we at all have a government or is it better not to have one? It is this question which we shall try to study through this paper on spiritualised society, the society of the future. Another thing is that the society of the future must know what is the goal of creation; why is the world created and what are the movements in line with it; it should also know the role of each community. What is the role of each nation in the world? What is the role of a vocational community? What is the role of women, of carpenters, of masons, what is the Dharma of each? (In India we use the word Dharma, which is not religion.) What is the role of an administrator, the role of a minister? Unless we become clear, there will be confusion in the world. So, we must know the Dharma of each community. Then comes your belief. What is the Dharma of a family? You say you are an Aryan. What is the Dharma of an Aryan? In this way, you must become clear.

Now let us take education. What is the role of education in life? Should we study for twenty years and then work for fifty years or should our whole life be an education? What is the best way for a man to grow? Can we create conditions whereby in our whole life we continue to receive education, in our whole life we are progressing?

What is the aim of industry? Should it be to make money? What is the aim of doctors? Should it be to make money or to cure patients and keep them healthy? The aim of industry should be to produce better and better products. But look at the situation today! I turn out ten thousand radios and announce that my radio is the best. You cannot get along without a radio; if you miss the news, you miss everything in life. When I first went to New York and while I was going in a cab, I saw an advertisement on a bus which read: If you have not read *The New York Times* today, you have missed the bus. I said to myself, what, if I have not read *The*

New York Times, I have missed the bus! It made me pause for a moment. These Americans advertise too much. In a bank I found a poster which said: Have a wish fulfilled. Save systematically. This kind of advertising affects even a man who has cut himself off from his moorings. So you can imagine what effect it can have on an ordinary man. There was one advertisement over the radio: So-and-so became rich and famous because she had so-and-so product in her house. All kinds of advertisements! Well, is this the kind of society you want or of a different kind? What should be the aim of production, should it be competitive or co-operative?

And here comes Sri Aurobindo's beautiful vision and it will take us ten thousand years to realise it. For ten thousand years He has mapped out the way for us. It is a spiritualised society that we would like to build. Line by line, we shall try to understand what Sri Aurobindo has written: *A spiritualised society would live like its spiritual individuals, not in the ego, but in the spirit, not as a collective ego but as a collective soul.*

Now what does this mean? Unless an individual becomes spiritual, the society cannot become spiritualised. What does a spiritualised man mean? It means that he is guided by the Divine and not by his mind. A man guided by his mind is a man; a man guided by his vital is like an animal, and a man guided by his physical – tamas – is like a stone; he is lazy and inert and just lies around the whole day. But a man guided by his spirit is, what the Gita speaks of, a 'triguṇātita', a person who has gone beyond mind, life and body, who is guided by his soul. When there are several people guided by their soul, it becomes a spiritual group. If there is only one man who is guided by his soul then it is like the ancient Indian Ashram with one realised soul and many people around him.

It is a spiritualised society which we are trying to build in our Ashram and at Auroville, where everybody will try to be guided by his soul and nobody will be another's servant. *A spiritualised society would live like a spiritual individual, not in the ego but in the spirit*..., is what Sri Aurobindo says. What does this mean? How can an individual live in the spirit and not in the ego? How can a society grow out of its collective ego and live in a collective spirit? What does a collective ego mean? I am an Indian, I am a Gujarati, I am a student of so-and-so college, my college is the best, nobody should fight with the students of my college, if the students of another college hit us, we will hit back. All kinds of things. So this is the collective ego.

There is an individual ego and a collective ego. A spiritualised society would live like its spiritualised individuals, not in the ego but in the spirit. So first let us understand how an individual lives in the spirit, then we will be able to understand how a society can live in the spirit, and by the time we finish these four pages, I think we will have had some understanding. How does an individual live in the spirit? (As to what is collective soul, we'll come to that later.) First, how does one live in the spirit and not in the ego? What is ego? Ego in Hindi means 'Ahaṁ' – 'Ahaṁkāra'. What is 'Ahaṁkāra'? What is 'Ahaṁbhava'?

Ego can be looked at from many angles. Ego is that point in our consciousness where the Divine has chosen to forget Himself. There can be many definitions; we will take a few. We have seen it from a higher angle, now we will look at it from the human angle. Ego is that attitude of our consciousness which looks at the world from its own centre: I am speaking, I am listening, I am being praised, I am being abused. So, ego is that attitude of our consciousness which looks at the world from its own centre and not from the Divine Centre. The second is the result of the first. You see, it does not matter to you if Madras sinks, it does not matter to you if Pondicherry sinks; *your* house should not sink. That is ego. It does not matter if somebody's child does not get education, but your child must get the best education; another man may be more capable, but you must get the promotion. You look at the world from your ego-sense. So, ego is this attitude of our consciousness.

We may think ego is the same as selfishness. This is not true. Selfishness is only a result. You can be very generous in your ego, not only selfish. But generosity is again another form of ego. Egolessness is a state where you feel the Divine is working in you, through you and in everybody. Nobody is a miser, nobody is generous, nobody is rich, nobody is poor. Everything belongs to the Divine. If you speak, it is He who is speaking through you; if you hear, it is He who is listening through you. The 'I-ness' disappears.

So, spiritual consciousness is that in which the sense of 'I-ness' disappears. You are just in tune with Him, automatically. When we are united with Him, the control of events is automatically there. When we are united with Him, whatever has to be spoken, gets spoken; whatever has to be done, gets done. We must bring this consciousness right down to the physical plane, otherwise the result will not be perfect. That is why in our Prayer today we said,*Grant that nothing may retard Thy Manifestation*. Lord, You must manifest Yourself in Your full glory and neither our mind, our vital nor our physical body should detract from Your Manifestation. It means that our body should also be made conscious. A spiritualised man is one who is conscious of the Divine working in everything, around everything, through everything, all the time, under the restrictions the Divine chooses to impose on Himself. It is our mind which restricts, our vital which restricts, our physical which restricts, but from the highest viewpoint, it is the restriction the Divine has imposed on Himself. He has decided to impose restrictions on Himself and that is why they are there. When you are boxing with a small child you do not give him a hard blow, you give him a soft, playful blow; you restrict your power. Similarly, the Divine for His 'Lila' also restricts His power. So, a spiritual individual is one who does not live in his ego, but in the spirit. The Gita speaks of 'triguṇātita'. Krishna tells Arjuna to become 'triguṇātita', that is, to be a man who is beyond life, mind and body, beyond the three gunas.

Gita also speaks of the 'sthitaprajñā', that means a man whose consciousness has become stationary in the higher consciousness. Now what does sthitaprajñā exactly mean? Arjuna asks Krishna how does a sthitaprajñā live, act, speak, how does he conduct himself? Similarly, how will a spiritual man live? Will he still manage his business or stop all industries and live like a sannyasi? When you become spiritualised, will you stop going to college, will you stop working, or will you continue to do work, but differently? That is the question. What will be the change in your attitude and spirit?

When the society is spiritualised, it will not work as a collective ego but as a collective soul. What is the difference between a collective ego and a collective soul? You see, just as an individual has a soul, the collectivity also has a soul. When Pandit Nehru left his body, the Mother gave a very significant message: *Nehru leaves his body but his soul is one with the Soul of India, that lives for Eternity*. It was a very revealing statement the Mother made, that a portion of the Soul of India had personified itself in Nehru and that is why he was all the time thinking of India, India and India. His soul was part of the Soul of India and India's Soul is part of the eternal Soul.

How is the collective national soul formed? How is the individual soul formed? We will take up this topic another day as a separate subject. Not only Sri Aurobindo but also our Tantras explain in a very scientific manner how individual and collective souls are formed. But what is important to know today is that every collective group has a collective soul. But a collectivity is not normally conscious of its soul. We should be consious of the Paramātma, the Divine soul, India's collective soul, our collective group soul – it may be of the Ashram, of Auroville, or a number of collective groups – and of our individual soul, all at the same time. But people are not conscious of the soul, collective or individual or of the Divine. The question arises: how can one become conscious of the collective soul? You have first to become conscious of the individual soul, then you have to become conscious of the collective soul. When you give yourself up completely to the Divine then you find everything. There is an Urdu poem which says: when the seed you put in the soil gives itself up and becomes one with the soil, it becomes a tree. If you want to flourish in the world, give yourself up to the Divine. Then, when a person sings, you feel as if it is you who are singing and you feel very happy. On the other hand, if you live in the ego, the ego in you will say, I wish I could sing so well. If you see a beautiful house the ego in you will say, I wish I could live in such a house. There is no limit to the craving of the ego. It wants the whole world to itself! There is nothing inherently wrong in this and if you want it, you can get it. But you can get it only psychologically and not physically. When you take a spiritual approach everything changes, other people think you are singing, but it is the Divine singing through you. When you see a big house belonging to another person, you feel equally happy because you feel you are enjoying it, though you may be living in a hut. It does not matter to you, because your consciousness is not limited by the ego.

I remember I was one day sitting with an Indian yogi in his house, a nice small house. He asked me to stay with him. I thought, where is the space? He told me, "What difference does it make? You stay here, the house is not mine though it may stand in my name. How much space do I need at night? About six feet to lie down. You also remain here." I liked his attitude. All these things come natural to you when you are spiritualised. To find your individual soul is not enough, you must also find the collective soul. You can find the collective soul only by identifying yourself with it. As you go deep within yourself to find your individual soul, so also you must do for the collective soul.

Beyond the mind, beyond the mental thoughts, beyond the vital desires, beyond all the material organisation of a nation, there is the soul of a nation. Let us take the soul of India. The soul of India has expressed itself in three basic concepts of India: First, 'Sarvaṁ khalvidaṁ brahma', everything is the Divine, everything is Brahman – that is one concept. The second, which is the result of the first, is, 'Vasudhaiva kutumbakam', the whole earth is one family. This is the second basic concept of India. The world should be organised like a family. If someone is less capable, he should be given more attention. Here, I would like to give you one advice: never miss an opportunity of doing good to others. Someday in your life you may regret for not having done good but you will never regret for having done good. Never miss an opportunity to do good to others. This is a great satisfaction and happiness you can get in life.

When we take up for study the subject of Human Unity, we will also examine, though briefly, the cultures of the world which find expression in the national anthem, in the political thinking, in the industrial organisation, in the educational system of various countries. To come back, what is the third concept of India? The first is, as I said, 'Sarvaṁ khalvidaṁ brahma', everything is the Divine, the universe is Brahman. The second is 'Vasudhaiva kutumbakam', the whole world is one family. And the third concept of India is the idea of evolution – involution and evolution. The evolution will go further, the ten Avatars will give rise to Kalki Avatar. You see, the idea of avatars can be interpreted as an evolution: the first to come was the fish, next came the tortoise, and so on. Man is not the last stage, there is a further stage. The next avatar which will be the Kalki Avatar, will be born of a Brahmin, according to the Hindu tradition. But the Brahmins in ancient India were not Brahmins by birth, they were 'gunakarma vishārada', they were Brahmins on account of the qualities of their minds and by their actions, and not just by virtue of being born in a Brahmin family. Man will evolve into the Supramental Being; a new gnostic society will be created. That is the work of the Kalki Avatar.

Sri Aurobindo's Work in the World

My intention in speaking to you today of the work of Sri Aurobindo in the world was really to discuss with you the programme of the future.

You know, in last year's message the Mother had said: *The World is preparing for a big change.* The full or rather deeper meaning of this message dawned on me, when I undertook this tour of various places. When I was at UNESCO, I was told that a young electrical engineer had been trying to meet me for three days. The engineer told me that when he first read an article on Auroville in the French magazine *Planet*, he could accept only ten percent of it and the rest he put aside. Then he read it again and again, and he came to the conclusion that it was the only solution for the problems of the world, the only thing worth doing in life, the only thing that could give him fulfilment. He now wants to come here. That is how the world is preparing for a big change.

People who are ready for such a life, who are thinking on the same lines and people who see the problems but have not yet found a solution, all these people are looking to Auroville for a solution.

They have come to a stage where they feel the limitations of the ordinary life and of the human mind. When I was discussing Auroville with the Secretary-General of the UNESCO Commission in one of the countries, he said, "Please give me one more set of Auroville literature. My daughter – I have only one daughter – has gone to live in a commune. She is not satisfied with our present way of life and I am not satisfied with the life in a commune. I really do not know what the solution is." When I met the youth leaders, they told me that the young people are not satisfied with the present society. This life of going to office everyday at ten and returning at five, has no meaning for them. They have become conscious that it is not only for earning money that they should be living . Until now, most of the older generation were quite happy to live to earn money, to earn their livelihood. But all this has changed now and it is a very good sign.

Wherever I went, I made it a point not only to meet the government representatives and the heads of big organisations, but to draw out the common man everywhere and to link up with his concerns. On planes, in trains, in buses, in restaurants, in lifts, or on the road, the topic of our discussion was always Auroville. And I found the common man quite awake to spiritual truths. It is interesting to find how the Mother's Grace always puts us in contact with people who are destined to meet us.

In Italy, in an embassy, a girl approached me and asked, "Can I do anything for you?" As I had an appointment, I gave her the Auroville album to glance through. When I came down after the meeting she was waiting for me. She was enthusiastic and said that she had two friends who were architects and would be very happy to meet me. I found later that her friends were absolutely in harmony with our ideal, because they were seeking an integral vision of architecture even though they had never heard about Auroville. Both of them got so interested that one of them is now trying to come here and the other will work for Auroville in his own country.

Similarly, when I was sitting in a restaurant in America a girl was intrigued by my Indian coat and came and sat down beside me. She asked me many questions and I asked her what she had studied. Most strikingly, she replied that at the university her subject had been 'Growth of Consciousness'. She got so interested that she came again to meet me. When I explained to her Sri Aurobindo's philosophy, that man was not the last step in evolution, she got up, her face beaming with joy, and exclaimed, "Thank God, man is not the last stage in creation!" She has volunteered to work in America for Auroville.

Again, when I was travelling in a train with an Englishman – he was an engineer – we began talking about Auroville. At the next halt a Dutch boy got into our compartment. The Englishman started explaining all about Auroville to the other boy and he spoke a great truth, even better than I could have done it myself, when he said, "They are building not *in* Auroville, but *from* Auroville."

I am reminded of another incident. A lady, a health officer in London, once went to a very small school for poor children and spoke to them about Auroville. After the talk one child got up and asked shyly whether the lady would accept a small contribution. She said, "Surely", and all the children contributed their pennies and thus offered two pounds. When this was given to me I said, "These two pounds are of more value than a million pounds because it is these young hearts who will build Auroville." And I have asked her to send me the name of the school and also the children's names so that I may send them a present from Auroville.

A few years ago when I was invited to visit America with all expenses paid and a secretary to travel with, the Mother refused permission. This time when I was not invited, the Mother, on Her own, decided to let me go. She must have known that the world was now preparing for a big change. Wherever I went I found that people of all nations want peace and harmony. They are dissatisfied with the world as it is, with the governments and the religions and to them Sri Aurobindo comes as a hope – as their only hope. But this also puts a great responsibility on us that we do not betray their trust.

The world is looking towards us to lead it out of the present chaos, and we must, at each moment, consciously mould our lives according to our ideals, so that those who come here see their hopes actually being realised and do not go away disappointed. The world is bound to change. We have the privilege of being the pioneers and if we do not at each moment live as true disciples of Sri Aurobindo and the Mother we would miss a great opportunity.

The change is a very big one. We should not look at our incapacities but at the Divine's Grace to bring it about. We are not going to do this, it is the Divine who is going to do it. And always the means are available for the work to be done, if at each moment we are conscious. If we are conscious of the Divine there is no problem in the world which cannot be solved.

Sri Aurobindo has made it clear in His writings that the spiritual age will be ushered in when some people will prepare themselves especially, I mean extraordinarily, for the manifestation of the Supramental and, at the same time, when the whole world feels a need for the change. Both these conditions have to come about. For us the effort now should be for a supramental change.

I met many politicians, industrialists, labour leaders, and the problems they discussed with me were many but the solution was absent. The great thing was that they had begun to realise there is no lasting solution. The Deputy Prime Minister of one country admitted to me very frankly, that whatever solutions they were thinking of were all temporary. They could find no permanent solution.

I was discussing with Mr. U. Thant [the late Secretary-General of U.N.] about Sri Aurobindo Birth Centenary Celebrations, and I impressed upon him that no political organisation could really solve the problems. Unless man's consciousness is changed, unless he evolves into a higher consciousness, there is no way out of the present impasse. People were wasting so much time, energy and money but were unable to find a solution. Mr. U. Thant told me that he and I were on the same wavelength. After the meeting, the director of his office came to me and said, "You will succeed. All the people come here with problems. You are the only one to come with a solution. So you are bound to succeed." He was also extremely helpful in our work.

In Russia, after my discussion about Auroville, one of their chief officers asked me the difference between communism and Sri Aurobindo's philosophy. The man spoke beautiful Hindi. I explained to him the difference and many other points besides, and also emphasised that after the supramental realisation there would be no need for governments. He took so much interest that he wanted all the books of Sri Aurobindo for the Oriental Institute of Moscow. He said that the Russians would celebrate Sri Aurobindo's Centenary throughout Russia.

When I was moving the Centenary Resolution at UNESCO, a Hungarian delegate on my right, whom I had been seeing for fifteen days without knowing we had a common interest in Sri Aurobindo, said, "I have been reading Sri Aurobindo's philosophy." An Indonesian delegate on my left leaned over and said, "I have already been to the Ashram." And the Swedish delegate came over and said, "I also have been reading Sri Aurobindo, and I would like to clarify some points with you." Then the Afghan delegate came and told me, "All our presses, all our facilities are at your disposal for the celebration of Sri Aurobindo's Centenary."

At the first meeting of the National Centenary Celebrations Committee, Smt. Indira Gandhi mentioned that Sri Aurobindo represented something new and we should not celebrate His centenary like any other, but we should try to realise His ideals. And she added that she saw in Auroville the possibility of presenting to the world a living embodiment of Sri Aurobindo's vision and that we should try to expedite its realisation. We should consider how best we can bring to the world Sri Aurobindo's message. I remember something very interesting said by Rockefeller. He said that every asset creates a liability. If you consider money as a trust given to you by God, it is a liability for you to use it for God's purpose. Similarly, if you have any spiritual development or mental vision, it also casts on you a responsibility to use it for mankind. We should view Sri Aurobindo's ideals in this light.

Sri Aurobindo Centenary Celebration requires a very well-organised plan for two reasons. Everyone is not at the same level of development, everyone is not looking in the same direction, everyone has his own ideas, his own beliefs, his own way of looking at things and yet Sri Aurobindo has a message for each-one. It must reach everyone at his own level and help him find his own fulfilment. One person may dream of a political change in the world, another, of an economic change, of a solution for unemployment, while a third may aspire for the highest literary possibility – Sri Aurobindo has a message for all of them. One may be a sweeper, another may be a king, but in Sri Aurobindo's vision they are both equal, yet each one is intended to do a different kind of work. Sri Aurobindo's message will help each one to receive his highest possibility, in his own way. I spent a lot of time abroad, studying the life, literature, culture of the people, so that Sri Aurobindo could reach everyone at his own level, through his own window.

The world is ready for Sri Aurobindo's message; but are we ready to carry it to them? I now come to the second aspect which I mentioned earlier about how a transformation can come, where each person can occupy his right place and every activity can take its right form. What is the role of money, the role of industry, the role of education, the true role and not what we imagine it to be? We have to completely change our view of life. The Mother has said that we must take a leap into the future. We have to break away from the past, otherwise, it would not be a leap. When I returned, I told the Mother, "Mother, the world is ready. The only thing needed is to organise groups work-wise, country-wise, so that the transformation can take place." She has given Her approval and so we are meeting today to see how we can implement the programme.

When I was abroad I was gratified to find how much respect people had for Indian spirituality, despite some misrepresentations. When you speak to them about Indian spirituality they feel that if they touch you they will become holy. And we shall fail, we shall fail totally in our duty to God, to our country and to ourselves, if we do not fulfil this great expectation of mankind. Those who are connected with the Ashram, have a great responsibility to develop a new consciousness in themselves and to manifest it for the good of mankind. What then will be our work in the world and how shall we proceed with it in an organised manner? Of this, we should be very clear.

During my visit to the various countries, I concentrated more on the capital cities and met with the delegates of nearly 110 member countries of UNESCO, and discussed with them their country's programmes. I also discussed with them their participation in the celebration of Sri Aurobindo's Centenary and work as a cohesive group for human unity. Everywhere the response was overwhelming – whether the man belonged to a Catholic country or to an Islamic country, it did not matter. Many of them went out of their way to help me. I did not know enough French. So in a shop a stranger came over and helped me to get what I wanted. Then he said, "We know you and we are going to vote for you at the UNESCO Conference." He was the Ambassador of Columbia. This is how everywhere Sri Aurobindo's message has caught the people's imagination.

An important dignitary came to Auroville and, after seeing everything, said with profound respect, "The whole project is God's project." Later, when I asked the Mother whether he understood what he was saying, the Mother replied, "No, it was his soul which spoke." Similarly, when UNESCO voted, it was really the Divine who voted. It was He who was making them accept the resolution consciously or unconsciously. It was not without reason that this resolution came to UNESCO. UNESCO has honoured itself by passing this resolution. And I see that the Divine's hand is behind everything.

To return to our topic, how are we going to celebrate? First, everybody who wants to participate, should try to make his life a sadhana. If you cannot meditate, do not worry. A very dear friend who visits Pondicherry often, once told me, "I am not fit for yoga. Till I feel I am fit for seriously doing yoga, I do not want to settle in Pondicherry." I asked, "What do you mean by saying seriously doing yoga? Are you going to realise the Divine by your effort, or is the Divine going to give you the realisation? It is not you who chose the Divine, but it is the Divine who chose you." The important thing to know is that as we are, with all our difficulties, we should work for the Divine. It is my experience that work puts you in contact with the supreme consciousness in such an integral manner that no meditation can do. This is because it forces a link to be created between the Divine and you. And the Divine has to work through you, if He does not want His work to be spoiled. If once you sincerely say to Him, "Use me as I am. All my life, all my mind, all I am, I offer to You", the Divine will use you for His work in the world, because then the ball is in His court and it is His responsibility, not yours.

It is not for Sri Aurobindo's good, but for our own good, that we are celebrating the Centenary. Our salvation lies in His message. We want to live for the manifestation of the ideals He has put before us. If we take this decision it would mean that we accept Sri Aurobindo as our Guru, and He will guide us. If once this acceptance nce is there, and if we have chosen the Divine, it means that the Divine has chosen us. Then what is the difficulty except our own stupidity? He will do the rest and lead us to the goal. He will not leave us half way. But we also must accept Him fully, and make our whole life His and not offer Him only a portion.

The only way to do Sri Aurobindo's Integral Yoga is to offer to Him all we are, all we have, all we do. There is no other way, but a complete and unreserved surrender. And if we are surrendered to the Divine, I repeat, we do not have to worry about anything, because immediately the responsibility falls on Him. So the first thing we have to do is to make our surrender total and integral.

Before leaving for Paris, I had to go to Delhi, but there was no ticket available. I phoned all my friends in the airlines but they said they could do nothing, as even the priority seats had been released due to a Chief Ministers' Conference. And I had to be in Delhi the very next day. So while going from the Society House to the Ashram I said to myself, "Can't Sri Aurobindo help me?" Believe me, when I reached my room there was a trunkcall waiting for me from a friend in Delhi who wanted me to come immediately to Delhi for some important discussion. I said, "I can't because there is no seat." He replied that he would immediately arrange for a ticket from Delhi. When I got a call from Madras asking whether I had phoned Delhi for a seat, I said, "No, they phoned me." And things happened in this manner throughout the trip, wherever I happened to be – in Europe, Russia or America. It is we who do not take the courage to stand up to work for the

Divine. The Divine Grace is not wanting.

I toured all the countries without prior appointments with officials, without any special introductions, with only a single circular sent by the Indian Government to the Embassies. But everywhere appointments were fixed for me, sometimes at just two minutes' notice. I would be sitting with a secretary of the government and I would tell him that I wanted to see the minister. He would say, "How can you? You are leaving the country in two hours and it takes days to fix an appointment." Still I would ask him to try, confident that the Mother's work would be done anyhow and if it was the minister's destiny to come in contact with the Mother he would call me immeditely. Just then the phone would ring asking me to be taken in to the minister immediately. That is how it happened at every place. No human planning can do this, no computer programming can do it. It is only the Grace that can do it.

All of us, for our own fulfilment, should offer our instrumentality, all our resources, all our capacities, all our contacts for the service of the Divine. This is the first step but this itself will give us a clear vision of our work and the path.

Let us now organise the work. Our attempt is to open a Central Secretariat here. I will be personally giving attention to this department. The help of Indian Embassies, UNESCO delegations, industrial houses all over the world will be available.

The change is bound to come. As Sri Krishna told Arjuna, "We are fighting a winning battle." We have now to organise groups who can look after legal affairs, correspondence, accounts, prepare material for recorded talks, slides, films – everything has to be made ready. And I would welcome the co-operation of each one of you. Whoever can give of their ideas, collaboration, time, in India or aborad, all are welcome.

This will be the beginning of the world-work of Sri Aurobindo. The Mother once told me, "So long as one person remains unchanged in the world, my work is not done." It is only the Divine Mother who can give us such an assurance. And we are Her children. Therefore, if we want to work for Sri Aurobindo, we must realise that nobody is unworthy in the world. People are acting under conditions of ignorance; they will act differently in conditions of Light. The thing to do is to see how we can create conditions where everyone can occupy his right place in light, truth and joy without the burden of the past always weighing heavily upon him. We must break the chains so that everyone can be free.

From today we should try to see the Divine everywhere and in everything. The other steps will follow. If we can make this beginning we shall see the Divine Force generating itself everywhere and taking up the entire responsibility of our work.

(*Some excerpts from talks given by Shri Navajata on his return to Pondicherry, after attending the UNESCO General Conference in October/November 1970. During his tour abroad he visited many countries to study the situation firsthand and to invite participation in Auroville from all countries.*)

A single occupation,

a single aim,

a single joy –

the Divine.

The Mother

Navajata Bhaiji – a Tribute

Shri Navajata's earlier name was Keshav Dev Poddar. He first visited the Ashram with his father in his childhood. Those were the days when the Mother used to come on the terrace every morning. One day She noticed a young boy in a silk kurta, standing on the pavement with a sadhak. The Mother obviously recognised his soul. Later in the day She enquired who the boy was. "Keshav Dev, son of Ram Narayan", She was told. And that was it. Keshav Dev's destiny was made.

His childhood dream was to see the whole world as one happy family. This aspiration made him leave his vast, flourishing business and surrender himself and his all to Sri Aurobindo and the Mother. The Mother blessed him with a new name – Navajata, "The New Born".

He was a rare combination of an idealist and a realist – a man of vision and a man of action. So many projects of the Ashram, the Society and Auroville were launched because the Mother had looked in that direction. What did it matter if there were no funds, no persons to work, no space nor proper equipment. The Mother wished and that was enough for Navajata. The thing had to be done and in a befitting manner. "My faithful" – this is how the Mother called him.

Sri Aurobindo Society is the Mother's creation. But the person the Mother chose to execute Her vision, to act as Her instrument, was Navajata. He was the first General Secretary and Treasurer of the Society under the Presidentship of the Mother. When the Mother left Her body in 1973, She continued to be the Permanent President and Navajata became the first Chairman of the Society, carrying often singlehanded the entire burden of work.

Navajata's mission was to interpret the spiritual vision of Sri Aurobindo and the Mother and his life was a love's labour for its realisation. His simple and lucid explanation of Sri Auroindo's Integral Yoga made spirituality practical and effective in the various activities of our daily lives.

His loving and generous nature, his magnetic and radiating personality, made him easily accessible to all. Wherever he could find the slightest potential in persons for serving the Mother, he pro-

Shri Navajata — 1980

tected them against all odds. Their pain was his pain; their problems, his problems.

For us all he was simply 'Bhaiji', a messenger of the Mother's Love and Grace.

(A homage from those whom he helped to find refuge in Sri Aurobindo and the Mother)

[illegible] — 1950

[illegible] proclaims his [illegible]

[illegible] Humility [illegible] messenger of the Mother [illegible]

[illegible] Mother.